Elizabethan and Jacobean Drama

LIVERPOOL ENGLISH TEXTS AND STUDIES

GENERAL EDITOR: KENNETH MUIR

Titles in this Series

The Poems of William Habington
EDITED BY KENNETH ALLOTT

Rollo, Duke of Normandy *or* The Bloody Brother
EDITED BY JOHN D. JUMP

The Poems of Joseph Hall
Bishop of Exeter and Norwich
EDITED BY ARNOLD DAVENPORT

Poems by Nicholas Breton
EDITED BY JEAN ROBERTSON

John Keats: A Reassessment
EDITED BY KENNETH MUIR

The Poems of Henry Constable
EDITED BY JOAN GRUNDY

The Poems of John Marston
EDITED BY ARNOLD DAVENPORT

Life and Letters of Sir Thomas Wyatt
BY KENNETH MUIR

Samuel Daniel: A Critical and Biographical Study
BY JOAN REES

Collected Poems of Sir Thomas Wyatt
EDITED BY KENNETH MUIR
AND PATRICIA THOMSON

The Poetry of Sir Philip Sydney: An Interpretation
BY J. G. NICHOLS

Yeats and Anglo-Irish Literature
CRITICAL ESSAYS BY PETER URE
EDITED BY C. J. RAWSON

Elizabethan and Jacobean Drama
CRITICAL ESSAYS BY PETER URE
EDITED BY J. C. MAXWELL

Elizabethan and Jacobean Drama

Critical Essays by Peter Ure

EDITED BY J. C. MAXWELL

Reader in English Literature
University of Oxford

LIVERPOOL UNIVERSITY PRESS

1974

Published by
LIVERPOOL UNIVERSITY PRESS
123 Grove Street, Liverpool L7 7AF

Copyright © 1974 Liverpool University Press

Printed in Great Britain by
William Clowes & Sons, Limited
London, Beccles and Colchester

ISBN 0 85323 142 7

First published 1974

Preface

This volume falls into three sections: three essays on Shakespeare, eight on other Elizabethan and Jacobean dramatists, and three not exclusively—in one case, not at all—on the drama. Within each section, the order is chronological, but the first three essays are all relatively late, reflecting the shift of Peter Ure's interests increasingly towards Shakespeare. But he never ceased to see Shakespeare in the context of his contemporaries; two essays of the 1960s return to authors he had first written on ten years earlier, and it is fitting that the very last piece of writing by him to be published on this subject is his contribution to the *New Companion to Shakespeare Studies* (Cambridge, 1971) on 'Shakespeare and the drama of his time'.

I have silently corrected errors in quotations and references, and have inserted the place and date of books where one or both was absent from the original publication of the essay. I have sometimes made the references to an author uniform, where Ure had used different editions at different times, or where a better edition has since been published.* I have added footnotes only for corrections, or supplementary information, of a more complicated kind.† These editorial footnotes are indicated by *, †, etc.

Apart from this, all but one of the reprinted essays appear in their original form. The exception is 'The poetry of Sir Walter Ralegh'. This was published in 1960, but there also survives a typescript of the paper as first delivered at a Summer School in 1957. The published version shows signs of revision, and purposeful compression, but there are also some omissions which seem to have been dictated rather by considerations of space. Where the two versions run together, I have always preferred the 1960 version, but I have introduced one passage from the

---

* Occasionally, I have dropped a reference to an edition if the passage can be easily located without it.

† Two editions that are particularly often cited I list here, to avoid constant repetition in footnotes:

The Tragedies of George Chapman, ed. T. M. Parrott (London, 1910).

Ben Jonson, ed. C. H. Herford and Percy and Evelyn Simpson (Oxford, 1925–52).

1957 typescript. I am grateful to Mr John Buxton for his advice in this matter.

The one unpublished paper is that on *Macbeth*. It is preserved in an extremely neat manuscript (untitled), which has every appearance of being a final fair copy. There is also a typescript adapting some of the contents for use as a lecture. This contains nothing of importance that is not in the manuscript, and it is not in any sense a revised version, though it must be later, since four pages of the already paginated manuscript have been repaginated for use as pp. 2–5 of the separately paginated typescript. The only thing I have taken from it is the information on p. 62, n. *.

Those who read the three Shakespeare essays consecutively will see how the *Macbeth* essay develops, and applies to that play, ideas already outlined in the two earlier essays. It is evident that Ure had in mind a book-length study on the subject.

Peter Ure published a good deal else on the authors treated in this volume. He edited two plays: *Richard II* (1956) and Ford's *Perkin Warbeck* (1969). On Shakespeare, in addition to shorter notes, he wrote on *The Problem Plays* in the British Council 'Writers and their Works' series (1961), and also the essay in the *New Companion* mentioned above. The most important article not here reprinted on one of the authors represented is 'Chapman's "Tragedy of Bussy d'Ambois": Problems of the Revised Quarto' (*MLR*, xlviii, 1953), which seemed rather too specialist for a collection of this kind. He also contributed two chapters to *The Age of Shakespeare* (1955), volume ii of the Pelican Guide to English Literature, on 'Two Elizabethan poets: Daniel and Ralegh', and on 'Chapman as translator and tragic playwright'.

J. C. M.

Contents

Plates

I

Shakespeare and the Inward Self of the Tragic Hero

It is for me a very great honour to succeed Professor John Butt in the Joseph Cowen Chair of English. All those who worked with Professor Butt in the College and University are vividly aware of the great gifts which he brought to our life here; but perhaps one who was a member of the Department of English for all but one of the thirteen years which he spent at King's College can speak with special feeling about what he gave us. He found time while at Newcastle to make to English scholarship contributions of major importance, and yet he had inexhaustible energy left for sharing his wisdom with his students and colleagues. Above all, Professor Butt communicated to us some of his own inquiring zest, of his daily enjoyment of the riches of the life of learning, riches which he seems to have always in his mind's eye. Some of us find it hard to keep always fresh and burnished that image of the life of learning which it is our great privilege in a university to live, but he helped us to do so, and for that reason, as for so many others, I for one am deeply grateful to him. For me to attempt to follow in his footsteps is indeed a rash and strange undertaking, and it is rather in the same hubristic temper that I have chosen to speak about our greatest writer, one in whom everyone, and not just Professors of English, may be presumed to have a jealous and educated interest.

I

In ordinary speech we apply a variety of metaphors or locutions to the object which we seem to be least equipped to provide a scientific account of—I mean, the human being. Many of these locutions suggest that a single individual is habitually imagined as being composed of two parts or elements. We speak of the

First published by the University of Durham, 1961.

inward and of the outward man; we say, occasionally, that a candidate in an examination has not 'done himself justice'; we ask, 'What is so-and-so *really* like?' It is very difficult to get away from the notion that deep down inside every individual there is a 'real self', what Othello called his 'perfect soul', which will 'manifest him rightly', if not to the law or to the human observer then to the god to whom the psalmist prayed: 'O Lord, thou hast searched me and known me ... My frame was not hidden from thee when I was made in secret, and curiously wrought in the lowest parts of the earth.'

For the student of the human character as it is presented in drama and the novel, these ways of speaking ought to be of significance. The psalmist was referring not to the creator of a fictional character but to the god of Israel when he said: 'Thine eyes did see mine unperfect substance, and in thy book were all my members written, which day by day were fashioned, when as yet there was none of them.' But he might well have been speaking of the dramatist or novelist at his work of creation. It is a characteristic of the authors of those literary kinds, drama and novel, at least in all but their simplest forms, that they are concerned with the inward self and the outward man as a *continuum*; with action and the motives for action; with what happens to the personality as a result of its commitment to a course of action which the self may have hesitated long about before choosing— or may have chosen, as we say, 'without thinking'. And so on— for the matter offers itself to be stated and elaborated in a thousand ways. In fiction there is a constant traffic between inner and outer, and the promise that is fulfilled by the great creator of character is that he will give us a God-like view of the individual, one that is very rarely vouchsafed to us in ordinary life and never with the certainty that we have all the evidence at our disposal, a certainty which the drama or novel can afford us: 'Thou searchest out my path and my lying down, and art acquainted with all my ways. For there is not a word in my tongue, but lo, O Lord, thou knowest it altogether.' Such is, or can be, the promise which the creator of a fictional character makes to his reader.

Where the material is so rich, and where the ways of putting it are so abundant, the problem is to choose some useful limitation. Almost any way of speaking which acknowledges inner and outer, the 'real self' which the reader or the audience alone is privileged to see, and the outward man which the other characters in his drama see, will take us some way towards the description of a character in fiction. For a work of art about people has this strange and unique characteristic: that, inside it, life goes on as usual, with people asking 'What is so-and-so really like?', and catching at an answer or mistaking it clean; while outside it sits the godlike reader who is given, in secrecy and intimacy, the answer to their question. But in my search for a limitation within which to speak about some of Shakespeare's personages, I shall choose two metaphors which seem promising, although I shall not confine myself to them as strictly as perhaps I ought to.

We speak of a man's devoting himself to a task or occupation. This phrase implies the existence of a self on the one hand, of a task or occupation on the other, and the setting up of some mode of connection or intercourse between the two. We speak also of a man's performing his part in life, his allotted role, whether chosen by him, or bestowed upon him by fate or another person. We would not wish normally to define this part or role very strictly; it need not be a job, or an office, or a profession. It can, for example, be any means or mode of operation by which the man fulfils himself, as we put it, well or ill, to the satisfaction of desire or imagination, or to their frustration, including a relationship with another person, the role of lover, enemy, father, or friend. In the perspective of history, John Shakespeare's part in life was to be the father of William Shakespeare, as Calpurnia's was to be Caesar's wife, and there is no reason why a story should be less selective than history. Yet story has the advantage over history in being much more interested in what the individual feels about the part he is called upon to play. Again in this locution we have the two elements—the individual self, the part or role performed, and the third element, the continual traffic between them constantly transforming the substance of both. I shall conflate these two metaphors—the man devoting himself to an occupation, the individual playing his part—into a loose framework of reference for what I want to say about Shakespeare's tragic heroes.

A theme in the tragedies is the hero's devotion of himself to a role in society, to the burden of an office such as kingship, or of a relationship such as fatherhood, or of an occupation such as soldiering. It is the character's awareness of himself as playing one or other of those parts, playing them rightly or wrongly, joyfully or in pain, that helps to make him come alive in our imaginations. Henry V is never more moving or more actual than when on the eve of Agincourt he stops being a king and sees himself as a man bearing the burden of kingship. Richard III is monstrous partly because he can conceive no other role for himself except playing himself. This means that he can play any part—faithful brother, courtly wooer, loyal subject—without, as we say, putting his heart into it, without dedicating to the part even the smallest portion of the essential self. In the soliloquies we see him standing apart from his parts contemplating with mischievous cynicism how good he is at them. He is punished for this in the end according to the sound Baconian principle that those who have 'all their time sacrificed to themselves become in the end sacrifices themselves' to fortune. The punishment fits the crime, for, although most of his time Richard thoroughly enjoys being himself, he ends spreadeagled on a wheel of fire, his own ego:

> What do I fear? Myself? There's none else by.
> Richard loves Richard; that is, I am I.[1]

The theme here noted in the history plays is continued in the great tragedies. Hamlet has had his natural princely and filial role stolen from him by Claudius the usurper and by his feeling that his mother has divorced herself from him by a marriage crime. Because of this he himself rejects Ophelia, unable to cast himself any longer for the lover's part. He is left miserably envying the First Player because pale and weeping he can act out with such lifelike force the purely fictive role of Aeneas lamenting the destruction of Troy:

> What would he do,
> Had he the motive and the cue for passion
> That I have?[2]

But the only role which life, speaking through the lips of a dead man, seems to offer to Hamlet is that of revenger. To whatever

---

1. *Richard III*, v.iii.182–3. The text of all quotations from Shakespeare in this essay is that of *The Complete Works* (ed. Peter Alexander, London, 1951).
2. *Hamlet*, II.ii.553–5.

it may be ascribed—incompetence of soul, or fear, or scruple—his failure to assume this role forms the substance of his play. Indeed, what some might think to be the brilliant immoralism of Hamlet, both as a person and as a play, derives from the protagonist's managing in the end to commit revenge, which is a crime, without ever committing himself to revenge, which would have enrolled him as a criminal. How is this man to be punished for what he has done?—we can imagine them asking, all the professional punishers and holy guardians of morality, led by King Claudius and old King Hamlet in person. Hamlet is the hero of all those with whom the police have not yet caught up.

Macbeth, led on by the hope of being a king, becomes instead a murderer and a tyrant; what keeps the audience imaginatively with him and ensures his dramatic existence are the enormous and terrible efforts, accompanied by many lapses into despair and horror of himself, with which he manfully assumes those burdens. In the end he is crushed by them, his selfhood is altered and diminished, and the full-blooded, ambitious man becomes inwardly tired and null, so that his outer acts, harsh and dry, mirror his inner desperation. If we wish to compare what happens to the 'real selves' of Hamlet and Macbeth, we shall probably conclude that Hamlet's real self does not change, that it remains as it always was, uncommitted—happy because not committed to a crime, unhappy because never fulfilled in a role which satisfied love or imagination; whereas Macbeth's real self is radically transformed by his commitment to his roles. The traffic between inner and outer in that play is specially strong and free-flowing, and it is organized with extraordinarily subtle insight into the relation of the character of the hero to the moral truth that we become the creatures of our deeds.

But in order to indicate something more of what is meant when we talk about change of character in a play, as well as to discern the nature of the tragic process in special cases, I shall now take four examples of the tragic hero, Richard II, Othello, King Lear, and Coriolanus, and discuss them in turn.

II

Everyone remembers the last moments of Webster's Duchess of Malfi, how she asserts her name and title to the end, maintaining her identity against those who wish to drive her out of herself or to make her accept death's generalization and dissolution of the individual: 'I am Duchess of Malfi still.' Her resistance has all the qualities of triumph of the imagination, creating the self anew by affirming the name by which it is known and the part that it plays. *Richard II*, the nearest to tragedy of any of the history plays, is one where this tragic process is carried a stage further to the point where despair and anonymity ensue. It is a play much concerned with the taking away of Richard's name. A peculiar horror attends upon this process in the protagonist's mind, because he thinks of his place and name as divinely bestowed, something which once given by God cannot be taken away by any act of man. Richard identifies himself with his royalty, considered not as power or ability to rule or something sanctioned by human election or approval, but as his sacred name. His slow, agony-filled separation from this is a process whereby the self is deprived of its only means of imaginative expression. The sacred name is the source at once of his comfort and of his despair—of his comfort when all power to substantiate his right seems lost:

> *Aumerle.* Comfort, my liege; remember who you are.
> *Richard.* I had forgot myself; am I not King?
>   Awake, thou coward majesty! thou sleepest.
>   Is not the King's name twenty thousand names?
>   Arm, arm, my name! (III.ii.82–86)

—of his despair, when he seems to have committed an act of apostasy towards his own title and has left himself nothing to live by, as in the deposition scene:

>   I have no name, no title—
> No, not that name was given me at the font—
> But 'tis usurp'd. Alack the heavy day,
> That I have worn so many winters out,
> And know not now what name to call myself!
>   (IV.i.255–9)

After this act of abdication, Richard is left face to face with himself unkinged and untitled, but because he had identified the title with himself there is no longer anything there for him to see. This is rendered when he sends for the looking-glass and, after gazing at its lying message, smashes it, a destruction of the face which emblematizes the destruction of the self:

> Mark, silent king, the moral of this sport—
> How soon my sorrow hath destroy'd my face.
>
> (IV.i.290–1)

When Richard is in prison at the end of the play, his sense of his own existence has perished. No longer a king, he seems to himself something less than a man—a beggar, part of the mechanism of a clock, a horse ridden by Bolingbroke, but most profoundly:

> I am unking'd by Bolingbroke,
> And straight am *nothing*.
>
> (V.v.37–38)

In giving away his rightful name, the object of his self-devotion, he has given away all human titles and means of living. The special character of his suffering is underlined by much emphasis on names and titles elsewhere in the play. For example, as Richard loses his name, Bolingbroke regains his own name, that of Duke of Lancaster, which at the start of the action Richard had deprived him of; Bolingbroke comes back to England in arms seeking, as he puts it, his name, which during his exile has been literally torn from the windows of his palace. So as Richard falls from king to man to namelessness, Bolingbroke rises from namelessness to 'Lancaster' to the greatest name of all: 'Long live Henry, fourth of that name!'

Richard II, then, is a play depicting a man's inward self ceasing to continue to be, coming to a full stop. When Richard's royal occupation is gone, he has nothing left by which to live. But it is not Richard but a greater than he, Othello, who speaks of his occupation, the 'royal occupation'[3] of making wars:

> Farewell the plumed troops, and the big wars
> That makes ambition virtue! . . .
> . . . O ye mortal engines whose rude throats
> Th' immortal Jove's dread clamours counterfeit,
> Farewell! Othello's occupation's gone.
>
> (III.iii.353–4, 359–61)

---

3. But this phrase is Antony's: *Antony and Cleopatra*, IV.iv.17.

It is speeches such as this that have caused some critics of the play to take the view that Othello's is not a case of the ordinary self-regard of the tragic hero, the conventional necessity of tragedy that the protagonist should present himself in the centre of his life's stage, but of an abnormal and excessive form of it; and that it leads to his sentimentalizing himself in a way that clearly indicates Shakespeare's intention of presenting him as a brutal and egotistical self-deceiver. Although it is plainly relevant to my subject, I shall not enter into this controversy here, but content myself with saying that Othello has an extraordinary sense of his own life, though not of his own worth. 'He is, as it were,' says Wilson Knight, 'conscious of all he stands for: from the first to the last he loves his own romantic history.'[4] There proceeds from Othello a sense of an exceptional pressure of being. He is a man who lives his life and performs even the most ordinary tasks with an extraordinary fullness, with the complete and beautiful energy at which W. B. Yeats rejoiced when he saw it coming out of 'the personality, the soul's image'. 'Keep up your bright swords, for the dew will rust them.' In its context, it is a line of almost extravagant beauty. The index of the full-flowing energy with which Othello lives is what Wilson Knight calls his 'silver rhetoric of a kind unique to Shakespeare'.[5] His words before they come to the point of utterance have been passed through some creative, inner alembic which turns them all to precious metal. Because of this transmutation, and despite Othello's own declaration that he is rude in his speech, we are tempted to think of him as the possessor of a poetic faculty. Dramatic verse, it has been said, is a device for representing or 'miming' the psyche, for rendering states of and changes in feeling with the utmost precision, and this is what its poeticality is for. But because of Othello's lyrical speech we feel that the character is to some degree composing about his feelings, as a lyric poet does, seeking the most expressive and beautiful way of rendering them. And this care for beauty and for expressiveness seems in Othello's case to imply his belief that his life is indeed matter for poetry, for that fullest rendering which only truly rounded and duly ornamented speech can bestow.

Dr Helen Gardner is surely right when she affirms that not

4. *The Wheel of Fire* (London, 1949 ed.), p. 107.
5. Ibid., p. 103.

self-regard but self-dedication is the truest description of the quality of life that this poetry constrains us to admire. 'He has always acted for a cause', she says.[6] He is, Wilson Knight thinks, 'dedicate' to the values of love and glorious war and romance. But he is dedicated to them with all the single-minded energy that the belief in their value, to which his speech constantly witnesses, deserves. He plays to the full pitch his roles of lover and soldier, which are linked in his mind. 'O my fair warrior', he calls Desdemona:

> O my soul's joy!
> If after every tempest come such calms,
> May the winds blow till they have waken'd death,
> And let the labouring bark climb hills of seas
> Olympus-high and duck again as low
> As hell's from heaven. If it were now to die,
> 'Twere now to be most happy; for I fear
> My soul hath her content so absolute
> That not another comfort like to this
> Succeeds in unknown fate. (II.i.182–91)

That is Othello the lover; and this is Othello the soldier, with more *gravitas* but as much force:

> The tyrant custom, most grave senators,
> Hath made the flinty and steel couch of war
> My thrice-driven bed of down. I do agnize
> A natural and prompt alacrity
> I find in hardness; and do undertake
> These present wars against the Ottomites.
>   (I.iii.229–34)[7]

In both speeches we glimpse what is an important property of Othello's personal imagination—how it is filled with extreme and final states and with steep antitheses, hell and heaven, love and chaos, the steel couch and the bed of down, each intensifying the other.

Othello, then, turns all the currents of his being into his love for his fair warrior, the role which perfectly fulfils his imagination. Then Iago thwarts these currents, making it impossible for Othello to dedicate his whole nature to love and war. What

6. 'The noble Moor' (*Proceedings of the British Academy*, xli, 1955, 194).
7. I here adopt the readings of the New Shakespeare text.

happens? Nothing surely is more striking after the first phase of the temptation scene with Iago than the immediacy and uncompromising completeness with which Othello rushes in his imagination to the extreme form which the new situation might take. The very worst possibilities are instantly present to him in his mind's eye and he foresees nothing less than the utter rejection of Desdemona. He has only begun faintly to mistrust her, yet already he can *imagine himself* loathing her:

> If I do prove her haggard,
> Though that her jesses were my dear heart-strings,
> I'd whistle her off and let her down the wind
> To prey at fortune. Haply, for I am black
> And have not those soft parts of conversation
> That chamberers have, or for I am declin'd
> Into the vale of years—yet that's not much—
> She's gone; I am abus'd; and my relief
> Must be to loathe her. (III.iii.264–72)

And with this goes an imaginative realization of the role of cuckold. He does not yet believe himself in any sense to *be* a cuckold, but already the horrible burden has acquired a living history and aetiology, fully presented in these phrases of resolved disrelish:

> O curse of marriage,
> That we can call these delicate creatures ours,
> And not their appetites! I had rather be a toad,
> And live upon the vapour of a dungeon,
> Than keep a corner in the thing I love
> For others' uses. Yet 'tis the plague of great ones;
> Prerogativ'd are they less than the base;
> 'Tis destiny unshunnable, like death:
> Even then this forked plague is fated to us
> When we do quicken. (III.iii.272–81)

These are what Dr Leavis calls the 'misgivings of angry egotism';[8] a juster term for them would be Henry James's: Othello has the imagination of disaster.

After this soliloquy Othello hardly looks back but proceeds with awful speed to the place that his imagination marks down

---

8. 'Diabolic Intellect and the Noble Hero', *The Common Pursuit* (London, 1952), p. 146.

for him. He has as Mr Maxwell says, 'reorganized his world . . .
on falsehood'.[9] Before the first 'proof' is offered to him, he says
farewell to his occupation, whistles his role of lover and soldier
down the wind; after he has heard Iago's lies about the dream
and the handkerchief, he begins to live another role with all the
force of his personality and all its steep antitheses:

> All my fond love thus do I blow to heaven.
> 'Tis gone.
> Arise, black vengeance, from the hollow hell!*
> Yield up, O love, thy crown and hearted throne
> To tyrannous hate! (III.iii.449-52)

'Your mind perhaps may change', Iago offers slyly, with his usual
trick of awakening Othello's extremism by hinting at the possibility of compromise:

> Never, Iago. Like to the Pontic sea,
> Whose icy current and compulsive course
> Ne'er feels retiring ebb, but keeps due on
> To the Propontic and the Hellespont;
> Even so my bloody thoughts with violent pace,
> Shall ne'er look back, ne'er ebb to humble love,
> Till that a capable and wide revenge
> Swallow them up. (III.iii.457-64)

Spasmodic gestures of brutality, horrid irony, even momentary
paralysis of all his faculties are the indices of the confused pain
with which Othello plays his new part, but he plays it to the hilt,
without further stay or doubt, and, in the murder scene, with the
expressive and lyrical utterance which we noted in the unfallen
Othello. Othello is the only character who makes up a poem
about his victim when he is on the point of destroying her.

This is the tragedy of a man who dedicates himself absolutely
to his part, of one who is always in the state which Hamlet found
it so hard to achieve, where what his imagination seizes upon
must be lived out in action. Although Othello's actions change

---

* By an oversight, Ure printed 'the hollow cell', where Alexander, whose text
he professes to follow, has 'the hollow hell' (F). Whether he intended rather to
read 'thy hollow cell' (Q) cannot now be determined.

---

9. 'Shakespeare: the middle plays', *The Age of Shakespeare* (ed. B. Ford, Harmonds-
worth, 1955), p. 226.

horribly for the worse, it is much more difficult to say that his inward self changes. The same life-processes of absolute devotion to the 'cause' seem to operate when he kills Desdemona as when he loves her. Although the one role is played out in joy, the other in suffering, even the role of murderer is performed with that energy, *gravitas*, and beauty which indicate that for Othello the murder, as later his own self-slaughter, is matter for that fullest rendering which witnesses to his belief in its rightness and value, and which we have been tempted to call poetry, or, at least, lyric. This is not a man whose faith in himself or his own existence has been destroyed, as Richard II's was. His noble mind is at times almost paralysed, but it is not o'erthrown. No longer able to live to himself as Desdemona's lover he lives as her judge. What the audience, perhaps, can hardly be persuaded to overlook is their intimate knowledge of his dreadful misjudgement of her, misjudgement of a kind of which (it might be said) Hamlet was in his secret heart afraid. Emilia's cry 'O gull, O dolt, as ignorant as dirt' is at least a part of what we feel, nor is it possible to attend to his final speech, so rammed with the life of the 'Othello music', with quite that patience which Dr Gardner and Professor Dover Wilson severally afford it. After all, while it is being spoken there lies Desdemona 'murder'd in her bed'.*

I do not think that to point this out is to do what Dr Gardner says we must not do—agree to find some psychological weakness in the hero that will protect us from tragic experience by substituting for its pleasures the easier gratifications of moral and intellectual superiority to the sufferer.[1] For, if we say that Othello's habit of playing his life at full pitch to the music of his silver rhetoric is that weakness—as it is certainly, as it turns out, what destroys Desdemona—we are in a quandary. For that is his strength, too, the capacity that sets him apart from others as a man of heroic energy and fullness of imaginative life, the properties that make his bitter tale worth the telling. Is not this what makes for the sharpness of tragedy—the glory and the fault locked together in a war-embrace?

* Ure elaborates on this in a review of the New Shakespeare *Othello*, in *Durham University Journal*, NS, xviii, 1956–7, 130–1.

1. See 'The Noble Moor', p. 198.

III

When Othello's occupation is gone, he instantly finds as it were another and more terrible one. When Richard II's 'name' is taken away, he moves continually, by contrast, towards the annulment and not toward the restoration of the self. The process which comes to a halt in *Richard II* and which completes a circle in *Othello*, is one that is carried further than in either of these plays in *King Lear*.

The basic difference between *Othello* and *Lear*, from the point of view taken here, is as follows: Othello changes his occupation, from a lover and a soldier becoming an 'honourable murderer', without changing his character, his way of interpreting his parts in life; Lear clings to his occupation, but reinterprets his manner of labouring in it. It is this reinterpretation that enables us to say that Lear's whole self alters—that his character radically changes—while Othello's does not.

Lear's role is that of father and king, or abdicating king, two functions intertwined. His demand that his daughters should declare how much they love him and the way he takes their answers is a stark moral emblem of the self-regarding soul. Love is something to be paid over for the gratification of the ego, something which, if given to him as a father, he will reward with a kingly prize. Although Lear gives away his kingdom in this first scene, he does not abdicate from what has been for him the reality of kingship—outward respect and unquestioning obedience, even when his judgement is quite blinded by anger and the remoteness from actuality induced by a habit of self-centred majesty. His fatherhood is of the kind that issues only in acts of reward or punishment, of a hypertrophied and almost parodic form which indicates the grossness with which self-pleasing age infects his being: the good daughters shall be given half a kingdom each, the one who has displeased him shall be madly punished:

> For, by the sacred radiance of the sun,
> The mysteries of Hecat and the night;
> By all the operation of the orbs
> From whom we do exist and cease to be;
> Here I disclaim all my paternal care,
> Propinquity and property of blood,

> And as a stranger to my heart and me
> Hold thee from this for ever. (I.i.108–15)

There is plenty of evidence in the ensuing scenes that these conceptions of kingship and fatherhood, namely that they are offices which require that love, respect, obedience should flow in a constant stream towards *him* on pain of punishment of the offenders if they do not, are deeply rooted in Lear. The desire to punish and his powerlessness to do so are the burden of his thoughts; their intensity arises from his sense of how keen ought to be the penalties exacted from daughters so highly rewarded as his have been by their 'kind old father'. Even in the final mad scene his feelings obey this pattern as he attempts to put Regan and Goneril on trial before the fool and the beggar, in a dreadful parody of the forms of royal justice:

Arraign her first; 'tis Goneril. I here take my oath before this honourable assembly she kick'd the poor King her father. (III.vi.46–48)

At the same time Lear's consciousness in these central scenes becomes miraculously accessible to other impulses besides punishment and self-pity, awakening to pity for others and to self-accusation. For he now arraigns himself because he has neglected his office. The new feelings do not yet supersede or much diminish the old ones, but in the weltering ruin of his mind the contrary impulses struggle together, prevented only by the necessary coherences of dramatic language from bursting out into simultaneous expression. Thus in the last scene but one before his prolonged disappearance from the stage we find the old, hard shell of crazy, penal rage:

> this tempest in my mind
> Doth from my senses take all feeling else,
> Save what beats there. Filial ingratitude!
> Is it not as this mouth should tear this hand
> For lifting food to 't? But I will punish home.
> (III.iv.12–16)

But a moment later comes the sudden, penetrating freshness of his fatherly concern for the shivering, storm-soaked Fool:

> In boy; go first.—You houseless poverty—
> Nay, get thee in. I'll pray, and then I'll sleep.

And then follows the prayer which, Bradley said, made one worship Shakespeare.[2] It mediates an interpretation of the royal occupation as opposite as can be to the old, punishing, prize-giving function which Lear still sets so much store by:

> Poor naked wretches, wheresoe'er you are,
> That bide the pelting of this pitiless storm,
> How shall your houseless heads and unfed sides,
> Your loop'd and window'd raggedness, defend you
> From seasons such as these? O, I have ta'en
> Too little care of this! Take physic, pomp;
> Expose thyself to feel what wretches feel,
> That thou mayst shake the superflux to them,
> And show the heavens more just. (III.iv.28–36)

The curious, only partly naturalistic, development of the story frees Lear from the burden of action and permits him in this and other ways to explore and ponder every aspect of his role, from the implications of the fact that the king is but a man to the backslidings of greatness whose particular examples are the bloody-handed beadle, the usuring judge, and the scurvy politician. These things, to borrow Keats's phrase, Lear 'burns through'. Although Shakespeare does not say so, it can be said (on the grounds that this is the way drama seems to work) that this process results in the new Lear of the last scenes with Cordelia.

In these scenes Lear has his second change of playing his double role of abdicating king and royal father. If the first scenes contain a false abdication, the last shows a true one when Lear finally abjures greatness in the speech beginning 'Come, let's away to prison'.

> We two alone will sing like birds i' th' cage;
> When thou dost ask me blessing, I'll kneel down
> And ask of thee forgiveness; so we'll live,
> And pray, and sing, and tell old tales, and laugh
> At gilded butterflies, and hear poor rogues
> Talk of court news; and we'll talk with them too—
> Who loses and who wins; who's in, who's out—
> And take upon 's the mystery of things,
> As if we were God's spies; and we'll wear out

2. *Shakespearean Tragedy* (London, 1904), p. 287.

In a wall'd prison packs and sects of great ones
That ebb and flow by th' moon. (v.iii.9–19)

He does not give everything away and find that he has become 'nothing', as Richard II did; he has passed into a life of loving communion with his daughter. This is the most positive achievement of an imagination enlarged and altered by its vision of the great world wearing out to naught. His giving of love here is as absolute as his demanding of it had been before; what was a self-gratifying appetite in fatherhood has become a selfless generosity. The stress on the punishment of others has been transformed into penitent submission. The 'touching simplicity'[3] of language, Lear's new habit of speech in these scenes, is the index of his new inward state and unlike Othello's recovery of his old music, which indicates Othello's unchanged self. The play which begins with the enthroned Lear cursing Cordelia ends with him holding her dead in his arms, his whole being in attendance upon her in utter absorption and self-forgetfulness. Since punishment has become submission and love is given instead of asked, Lear's self within the role of fatherhood has completely changed its position and mode of operation. In *Othello* the art with which the hero plays each successive role seems only to emphasize the lack of fundamental change; in *Lear* the reinterpretation of the one continuing role is the measure of the alteration in the inward man.

Richard II, Othello, and Lear are all characters who are made expressive of their changing or unchanging selves through their imaginative devotion to their occupations. The efforts of thought and passion they make in rendering these parts help to give us a sense of life being lived out before us by showing us the intercourse that goes on between the individual self and the task before it. But we ought to remind ourselves now of the case of Richard III, which I mentioned at the beginning. His answer to Lear's famous question 'Who is it that can tell me who I am?' is 'I am myself alone', 'I am I', and therefore every part he plays is merely a trick, from which in the soliloquies he promptly reverts to the brotherless Richard playing 'himself alone' to the audience in the theatre outside the play. Another contrast, of somewhat the same kind, to Othello and Lear is Coriolanus, a

3. The phrase is used with reference to Gloucester by L. C. Knights, *Some Shakespearean Themes* (London, 1959), p. 108.

much more profound study than Richard III of the man who is himself alone, or tries to be.

IV

The contrast between the expressive sincerity which Richard III devotes to being himself and the way in which all his other roles tend towards parody or insincere excess is one means we have for judging the depths and intensity of his self-love. But Coriolanus does not confide in the audience. We do not see him take the decision to be himself alone, nor does he comment from the vantage point of the solitary 'I' upon the triumphs and man-oeuvres of the disguised self. At first his chief role is the soldier's, performed fiercely and terribly but effortlessly. He is not shown thinking about this function or bracing himself to his task, as Othello and Lear are shown bearing their burdens. With his 'grim looks and / The thunder-like percussion of his sounds' he is as near as a human being can get to being simply a weapon of war, a gun or a catapult. His deeds of valour break from him like natural phenomena; he strikes a besieged city 'like a planet':

> His sword, death's stamp,
> Where it did mark, it took; from face to foot
> He was a thing of blood, whose every motion
> Was tim'd with dying cries. (II.ii.105–8)

But he has nothing to say about himself, and we do not feel that he is satisfying or expressing himself through his task as we feel that Othello pours his life and imagination into his occupation. Furthermore, when he is praised by other men for his courage, he resents it; to accept praise is to accept another man's state-ment about his inward self—that it is courageous, for example; and this, Coriolanus, guarding the privacy of his so far unknown and unexpressed self, cannot willingly do. His reaction to blame is similar, and it is an irony of the play that in it most of the characters spend most of their time discussing a hero who can-not bear to be talked about. As the play proceeds, it becomes more and more easy to infer that the root of this intolerance is not an excessive modesty about himself but an excessive pride. He refuses to play any part which demands that he give some-thing of himself in sincere response to others' claims and wishes. He absents himself from the Senate when he is formally cited for his bravery and receives his title of honour with churlish taciturnity. 'Hearing his nothings monstered', as he puts it, is a deep offence to him. He diminishes those who would praise him by calling their praise flattery, and the inference is that no one is good enough to praise *him*. When he is asked to sue for the consulship by standing in the market-place to beg the people's voices, he protects himself from what he regards as a degradation by performing the task with brutal irony. All this is what Coriolanus calls 'playing the man I am' (III.ii.15–16). Where Richard III quite cynically assumes various disguises to effect his ends, as Volumnia suggests Coriolanus should on this occasion, Coriolanus' idea of himself is so absolute that he cannot put on even the appearance of betraying it by acts of humility or social communion done before other men. This makes him, in his queerly compelling way, a more admirable character than Richard and his behaviour at this point more sympathetic than Volumnia's own.

Coriolanus does, however, in the end betray this idea of himself. Returning in the fifth act as commander of the Volscian army, his eye 'red as 'twould burn Rome', he tries to become simply a Volscian weapon of revenge, and refuses all recognition and communion to his Roman friends who come to him for mercy. This is his old function of a mindless instrument of war and a self unresponsive to others' wishes. When finally Volumnia and his family appear, he clings desperately to this notion of self-dependence, of being himself alone:

> My wife comes foremost, then the honour'd mould
> Wherein this trunk was fram'd, and in her hand
> The grandchild to her blood. But out, affection!
> All bond and privilege of nature, break!
> Let it be virtuous to be obstinate.
> . . . My mother bows,
> As if Olympus to a molehill should
> In supplication nod; and my young boy
> Hath an aspect of intercession which
> Great nature cries 'Deny not.' Let the Volsces
> Plough Rome and harrow Italy; I'll never
> Be such a gosling to obey instinct, but stand
> As if a man were author of himself
> And knew no other kin. (v.iii.22 ff.)

He does remain proof against the 'colder reasons' which Volumnia advances in her plea, and it is surely significant that he does not yield until she gives up and turns her back on him:

> Come, let us go.
> This fellow had a Volscian to his mother;
> His wife is in Corioli, and his child
> Like him by chance. (v.iii.177–80)

Coriolanus' surrender after this indicates that all his life he had had a false or incomplete idea of himself. The pride, the secrecy, the refusal to participate, which were the signs of his nature, spelled only self-sufficiency and independence of soul until he is put to the test of having his mother's favour withdrawn from him; but when this test is applied, we see that there is at the deepest level within him a self and soul which is bound to his mother, forcing him to recognize her as the ultimate source of the approval without which he cannot live. Beneath the proud, warlike automaton who gives nothing away there remains the boy who, Plutarch says, 'being left an orphan by his father was brought up by his mother a widow . . .' After Rome is spared, to the disgust of the Volscians, nothing is more ironically pathetic than the spectacle of Coriolanus attempting for the first time to play the part of a peacemaker, ally, and moderate man. Of course he fails, for Coriolanus' self does not change and re-form like that of King Lear, nor does it continually refashion his life according to an unchanging imaginative need as does Othello's; it is simply uncovered in a moment of dramatic revelation— beneath the appearance of independence the reality of dependence.

If we wish then to make a summary statement about what happens to the inward selves of these four characters it would be this: Richard II's inward self is annulled, Othello's remains unchanged, Lear's is radically transformed, and the real nature of Coriolanus' self is revealed beneath its appearance. We can perhaps go further than this and say something equally summary about the different tragic designs. *Richard II* is a tragedy which ends in abolition; existence comes sadly and suddenly to a stop as in the medieval stories; the man has fallen from the wheel of life. *Othello* yields the most painful image of all. The hero dies with all his powers about him, in the full panoply of his lyric strength; a most cunning pattern of excelling nature, he is brought down in his leap, like the lion by the hunter's rifle. *King Lear* uses the notions of repentance and self-transformation which we associate especially with religious ritual; the line continues round the corner of, or melts away, the barrier of human intractability. That man can change before he dies is the great myth of metamorphosis fostered by an occasional miracle, by poets of the romantic movement, by the sacred dramas of many cults, and even by some forms of political action. We rightly call it an optimistic myth; tragedy which draws upon it is felt to point beyond the present pain to some happier resolution in a different place. *Coriolanus* is a tragedy written by an observer, by a man grown old with watching; what he sees is a fact that accords most with our modernity: that man within is ruled by powers that he does not know, stumbling with hideous incompetence in the darkness of his own soul. These four tragedies, in this view, combine to make one of the mighty Shakespearian *arpeggii*; if all else perished, it would be possible to reconstruct from them a substantial portion of the whole mind of Europe.

But I cannot leave the subject on an occasion such as this without trying to draw a less ambitious moral. Shakespeare's plays are great images, of supreme artistic strength and brilliance, amongst the most complex and wonderful artefacts in the history of the world; but their substance is the human character. The commonplace that the human person is the centre of his art and his insight into it the supreme endowment of his mysterious personality needs to be reaffirmed from time to time, for it is on this and on the complementary achievements of other great writers that the student of literature may wish, as I do, to rest his ultimate claim for his subject. Amongst his wondrous works the god of Israel numbered the stars and the whale, but he also asked his servant Job: 'Who hath put wisdom in the inward parts?' or 'who hath given understanding to the mind?' Literature is a kingdom of marvellous structures, but there are many other kingdoms containing objects as wonderful; what distinguishes literature, and the related disciplines of linguistic and historical study without which it cannot flourish, is that it is informed throughout with the human voice and with human relations, the

voice and experience of the great literary artist, of a man speaking to men. On these grounds it will yield the primacy to none;
wherefore, with St Paul, 'we faint not; but though our outward man is decaying, yet our inward man is renewed day by
day'.

2

Character and role from
Richard III to *Hamlet*

A man, it is commonly said, devotes himself to a task, or undertakes a duty, or fulfils himself (or fails to) in a role. The two
elements, and the relationship between them, are sometimes
determined and prescribed, as, for example, the priest who
performs a ritual or the fireman who rescues the old woman
from the burning tenement. Priest or fireman have submitted
themselves; they are not expected to reinterpret or decide
afresh what is to be done. Literature has not on the whole greatly
relished such absence of the liberty of interpreting, although
perhaps it celebrates more than it used to those who feel themselves to be, in Stephen Crane's phrase, intruders in the land of
fine deeds. Even Conrad, who wrote those words for Podmore in
The Nigger of the Narcissus, the saying of Podmore's life—'Galley!
. . . my business! . . . As long as she swims I will cook!'—often
cheapened the mystery of heroism by the florid comments which
the novelist owed to his art.

Shakespeare's heroes are leaders of men; to move easily in an
air of fine deeds seems to them their birthright. The unvarying
eloquence, the high assumption that a rainstorm of words will
perpetually refresh an occasion and sensibly benefit the inexpressive multitude springs from the tradition in which he
worked; it is responsible for those wastes of ingenious verbalizing
which disfigure much Elizabethan writing and for that contempt
for the unlanguaged which sometimes disfigures even Shakespeare himself. But chiefly it is used by him for the sake of that
liberty of interpreting which the performance of a ritual or a
'business', in Podmore's sense, normally precludes. A method of
the plays is to stress the two elements: to depict the hero's de-

First published in *Stratford upon Avon Studies*, vol. v, *Hamlet* (ed. J. R. Brown and
B. Harris, London, 1963), pp. 9–28.

votion of himself to a role in society, to the burden of an office such as kingship, a relationship such as fatherhood, a 'royal occupation' such as soldiering, and to depict as well the elo-quence with which he confronts them. It is often because we are made aware of the gap, not the consonance, between man and the office that the situation becomes profound and exciting, and permits rich inferences about what the hero's in-ward self is like. It is the character faced with his role, forced to decide about it, the quality of his response, that Shakespeare shows us, not just his performance in the role. Does he act it out with joy or pain, rightly or wrongly? Is it something which gratifies his imaginative needs, his need for love or glory or power, or is it something which starves and appals? Shake-speare's great characters come alive and appeal to us in their mistakings as well as in their imaginative fulfilments of them-selves. He often allows history or tradition to define the nature of the role that is offered, the more sharply to bring out the spectacle of the individual fitting himself (or failing to fit him-self) to it. Presumably most persons in the Globe audience in 1599 shared Polonius's knowledge that Brutus killed Julius Caesar in the Capitol; but it seems doubtful if they came to watch him do it in the spirit of those who attend a ritual, even if the lofty scene was, as we are nowadays told, acted over in front of a cosmogonically significant structure that proclaimed orthodoxies about order and disorder from every painted star and marbled pilaster.

What they saw, indeed, was a Brutus in a state of agonized depression finally bringing himself to fulfil the role which everyone around him had cast him for and was busy prescribing as his peculiar duty. Cassius has heard, he says,

> Where many of the best respect in Rome—
> Except immortal Caesar—speaking of Brutus,
> And groaning underneath this age's yoke,
> Have wish'd that noble Brutus had his eyes.
>
> (I.ii.59–62)

'Brutus, thou sleep'st,' says the urgent voice, 'awake, and see thyself . . . Speak, strike, redress!' But Brutus must get his con-ception of the task laid upon him into a posture satisfying to his imagination and to his idea of himself before he can strike, although it is in part his tragedy that this idea of himself is to some extent a reflection from Cassius's politic mirror. He warms up as this gradually happens. When he has persuaded himself that Caesar must be killed (and his awkward, private reasoning is quite different from the spleenful envy that Cassius had offered as reason enough), we see him wrenching and redefining the role to make it match his own conception of what is due to him. His voice takes on the urgent note of reinterpretation, of the man who has at length found a way to make his task satisfying to his imagination, as when he persuades the conspirators not to swear:

> Swear priests and cowards and men cautelous,
> Old feeble carrions and such suffering souls
> That welcome wrongs; unto bad causes swear
> Such creatures as men doubt; but do not stain
> The even virtue of our enterprise,
> Nor th' insuppressive mettle of our spirits,
> To think that or our cause or our performance
> Did need an oath. (II.i.129–36)

He had disliked the role of conspirator, naming it 'a monstrous visage'; it does not fit the self which he loves. They shall not swear, in order to make it the less a conspiracy, not a conspiracy at all, some nameless, finer enterprise. The murder, too, must not be a murder—redefine it, instead, as a sacrifice or a purgation ('We shall be called purgers and not murderers'). Another term which he uses is 'actors'—'with untired spirits and formal constancy'. Elsewhere in the play Caesar, too, acts up to his idea of himself ('I am constant as the northern star . . .'); and Shakespeare is equally careful to make us understand the effort that this costs him: there is the scene where he twice changes his mind about going forth on the Ides of March; there are many places where he wilfully and consciously assumes the 'Caesar' voice as an actor assumes his formal constancy. Brutus and Caesar are both so intent on adjusting the situation to their imaginative needs, to the figures which they wish to cut before themselves and the world, that they overlook its practical perils; Cassius and Antony do not seem to have the same needs as they, and in death alone is Brutus released from the distorting pressures of the single-minded. The same release is afforded to Dryden's Mark Antony from similar pressures. Brutus might well have said, with that later Antony:

> For death, for aught I know,
> Is but to think no more.

It is his reinterpretation of the fixed role that accounts for much of the liveliness of Brutus. We may look in other plays for a variety of relationships between character and role; possibly what is called 'characterization' in Shakespeare accounts for our sense (once much emphasized by the commentators) of the extraordinary vitality of the personages, and the intimacy of their appeal resides somewhere in the interplay between character and role. The fact that the role—fallen king, famous regicide, revenger—is often defined by history or tradition need not make the hero's approach to it any less effectual in drawing out, by the sternness of the test it imposes, the unreachability or rigour of its prescription, all that is unique in the character and all that defines his individuality and separates it from anyone else's. This is why it is dismaying to find a recent commentator, who so well understands this conception of the role of Shakespeare, writing of it as though the role in *Hamlet* overrides what used to be called Hamlet's character:

As for Hamlet's character, the experience [of *Hamlet*] is related less to that than to what overrides it and renders it irrelevant. In this play, as in many other tragedies, the experience of the protagonist is not the deployment of a determinate character, but the assumption, and then the enactment, of a determinate *rôle*. Rôle predominates over character, because once it is assumed by an actor, it will be much the same whatever his nature may be. It overrides that nature: the play is its acting out.[1]

Here it seems fair to extend the analogy between an actor and a character in a play, and to say that a character in a Shakespeare play sometimes resembles an actor because he has to choose or refuse a part, learn it, rehearse it, try to understand it, and finally perform it (or perhaps refuse to perform it) well or ill or with one of the many gradations in between. That is his experience; it is surely one that allows plenty of liberty for the expression of qualities that individuate him as a man and as an actor.

1. J. Holloway, *The Story of the Night* (London, 1961), p. 26.

Perhaps some such process is meant to be included in the phrase 'assumption and enactment', used by Holloway; but this meaning is not much supported by the reading itself of *Hamlet* which he gives us. It would be a great mistake to try to reinstate 'determinate character' in its old place of honour in Shakespearian criticism; but must 'determinate role' be substituted? It is not, perhaps, too wild an injustice to Holloway's subtle and powerful book to say of it that, like Brutus in the play, it requires all the murders to appear like sacrifices, and all the characters to tend to the condition of ritualists. But Brutus had overlooked (as Antony did not) the possibility that a ritual and a sacrifice, however sincerely and fervently performed, can be made to resemble, for the unpersuaded, a common murder after all. 'Ordinary wishes and sympathies', Holloway writes, concerning the closing scenes of four great tragedies,

> such as make up the normal fabric of life (or are commonly supposed to do so) are suspended, while the characters engage in the self-conscious completing of a recognisable kind of event, with such a validity of its own as sets it beyond considerations of pleasure or pain. Here is the note of ritual, of ceremony . . . [2]

But what we observe in *Antony* or *Macbeth* are characters who nerve themselves to complete their roles. The ritual is always faltering on the edge of 'ordinary wishes or sympathies':

> No more but e'en a woman, and commanded
> By such poor passion as the maid that milks.

The emblematic chalice is held by a hand that trembles somewhat, and this directs our attention to the man or woman that holds it; we can even think—and Shakespeare's theatrical metaphors often invite us to—about the actor whose name is written down on the programme and of how he is doing. In Shakespeare, mastering the role at all levels, both inside and outside the play, is a process which is constantly being re-enacted and never ceases so long as the character is still alive and the audience is still present. This peculiar quality distinguishes his theatre from most other kinds of ranking classical drama. He does not raise his personages on stilts of Alexandrine rhyme or cover the tawdry human face with a mask. The difference is one that has often

---

2. *The Story of the Night*, p. 147.

aroused amongst cultivated people such as Thomas Rymer the suspicion that some kind of undignified trick is being played upon them, that the priest has departed from the sacred text and is making up the words as he goes along. Hamlet and Lear, Yeats supposed, 'do not break up their lines to weep'; but this is just what Shakespeare directs them to do.

This idea of nerving oneself to a role, of rehearsing, of improvising, is one which bears strongly on *Hamlet*. There are plays earlier than *Hamlet* which might, from this point of view, be regarded as being amongst its predecessors. Of these, *Richard III* and *Richard II* mediate opposite extremes amongst the varieties of interplay between individual and role.

It is partly because Richard III proposes so many roles for himself and because his story gives him the freedom to do so that it is permissible to make inferences about his individuality. Richard assumes by turns the parts of the loving brother, the passionate wooer, the pious make-peace, the protector-uncle, the heir reluctantly called to the throne. He assumes them with an alacrity and lack of scruple or preparation which shows that they are only means to the end of his own advancement; he sees them as devices and not as burdens which demand any portion of his essential self, as mere happy prologues to the omen coming on. His imperturbability is that of the clown, so content and efficient in making fools of others that he is impervious to their curses. The element of parody in all these performances, just below the borderline of detection by the gulls (although he can afford to go very far indeed in the presence of the exceptionally stupid Lord Mayor and his company), signals to the audience the extent to which they are obliquely related to the real thing— the brother who is truly affectionate, the prince who is genuinely pious—and at the same time expresses Richard's happy confidence, his mastery as an artificer, his understanding of how men are deceived by shows and professions. The parodic rendering is accentuated as his confidence increases. This is Richard's character, the skill and fulfilment of his life. He is defined through this activity. The particular way in which he does it, not simply as a clever hypocrite or an evil Machevil, but as one whose joy is to go outside his being, to give splendid performances of expected and traditional roles, deceiving by means of their recognizability the credulous and conventional, indicates his contempt for the moral and emotional needs which created the roles in the first place and so made them available either to be played sincerely or—if one is like Richard—to be exploited with all his calculating energy.

All this is done, we must infer, so that he may attain supreme power. But he says little or nothing about this ultimate objective, and this is significant. It is not for him to brood over riding in triumph through Persepolis, or to approach the golden rigol with the numinous circumspection shown by Prince Hal. His pleasure, like Iago's, is in the action of the moment. When he does become king, he is, in a sense, trapped, and not only by his enemies gathering outside. He can no longer engage in his characteristic pleasurable activity, and play the part of king with his usual merrily critical detachment, when he *is* the king. The heavily traditional role now has to be really lived, the self and the role must coalesce, and in this kind of living Richard is incompetent. Driven into the centre, towards which he has so long been working, he must build upon the centre; but the self on which he must build, now that he is driven into it by fear and by being deprived of his power to sway men by his peculiar skills as a player of parts, turns out to be an inexpressive chaos:

> Richard loves Richard; that is, I am I.
> Is there a murderer here? No—yes, I am.
> Then fly. What, from myself? Great reason why—
> Lest I revenge. What, myself upon myself!
> Alack, I love myself. Wherefore? For any good
> That I myself have done unto myself?
> O, no! Alas, I rather hate myself
> For hateful deeds committed by myself! (v.iii.183–90)

From this nothing can be fetched except a rigid, despairing bravado. The centre has become a bear pit's centre, or a boar hunt's. Richard is a character who enjoys playing parts so long as their effectiveness as tricks keeps his audience (within the play) in a daze; out of his pleasure at these continually successful feats he comments to the audience (outside the play) and invites them to admire his skill, and even plays another part for the benefit of that audience alone: the Vice Iago figure so well expounded by Bernard Spivack,[3] the merry hunchbacked

3. See *Shakespeare and the Allegory of Evil* (New York, 1958).

villain, the dreadfully wicked prince. So always he keeps his inward self concealed, until he mounts the supposedly longed-for throne. This role alone turns back upon him and demands, because it is by the design of the play the last and most important, that he show his inward being: 'Now that you are king, *be* king.' But Richard cannot in reality *be* anything, or cannot in reality submit himself to an audience, he can only astonish it, and keep his counsel.

Richard III, then, is a ready taker-on of roles of a circumscribed and shallowly theatrical kind, the kind that merely deceive, and do not communicate with the mimic's self. Through this, and through the counter-truth that he fails in another kind of role—one which compels such communication—the characterological, and no doubt the moral, point about him is made. His successor, Richard II, more nearly resembles Brutus because we see him adjusting the part for which others cast him to inner imaginative needs before he can play it with any confidence or satisfaction.

In the deposition scene (IV.i), for example, Richard has had his part set down for him by Bolingbroke and Northumberland, and by the whole current of events and design of the play. In Act III he has been stripped of all power and transformed, it seems, into the usurper's puppet, a condition which he wearily and sardonically acknowledges to Northumberland:

> What must the King do now? Must he submit?
> The King shall do it. Must he be depos'd?
> The King shall be contented. Must he lose
> The name of king? A God's name, let it go.

> Most mighty prince, my Lord Northumberland,
> What says King Bolingbroke? Will his Majesty
> Give Richard leave to live till Richard die?
> You make a leg, and Bolingbroke says ay.
>
> (III.iii.143–6; 172–5)

The emphasis on *king* and *must* stresses Richard's awareness, even at this stage, of the desperate and paradoxical impropriety of what is happening. He is next expected to perform a public act of abdication; Bolingbroke requires this of him for political purposes, or 'the commons will not, then, be satisfied'; he must surrender his right in the 'common view' so that men may deem that he is 'worthily depos'd'. It is to be a carefully staged professional spectacle; the text for it will be the articles of the signed deed of abdication, which Northumberland tries to insist upon Richard's reading aloud. This is Richard's ordained role. But Richard, while he accepts the role—as he cannot choose not to do—radically reinterprets it in ways which bring before the audience's consciousness, if not Bolingbroke's, its inner dynastic significance and its personal, tragic meaning, the tragedy of the king who is forced to deliver up the sacred Name commingled in his anointed person. The entire episode as conceived by Bolingbroke and his party is by Richard wrenched awry in order to fulfil Richard's imaginative needs and to express the exact and individual character of his suffering. The structure of the scene supports him. It begins in a public and external way with the noisy quarrel in parliament, deepens with the Bishop of Carlisle's appeal to dynastic allegiance and national guilt, and culminates in Richard's Passion. A Passion is the most public and significant kind of performance on the most exalted scaffold; at the same time it embodies the completest actualization of the self, its supreme expressiveness. In Richard's the mishandled crown becomes an image of grief, the act of abdication his own apostasy, the bystanders not witnesses in the court of parliament but participators in a mysterious crime. When Northumberland tries to divert the current of Richard's reinterpretation and force him back to the prearranged text, Richard passionately maintains his hold on his own reading of the scene:

> *Richard.* . . . What more remains?
> *Northumberland.* No more; but that you read
>   These accusations, and these grievous crimes
>   Committed by your person and your followers
>   Against the state and profit of this land;
>   That, by confessing them, the souls of men
>   May deem that you are worthily depos'd.
> *Richard.* Must I do so? And must I ravel out
>   My weav'd-up follies? Gentle Northumberland,
>   If thy offences were upon record,
>   Would it not shame thee in so fair a troop
>   To read a lecture of them? If thou wouldst,
>   There shouldst thou find one heinous article,

Containing the deposing of a king
And cracking the strong warrant of an oath,
Mark'd with a blot, damn'd in the book of heaven.
Nay, all of you that stand and look upon me
Whilst that my wretchedness doth bait myself,
Though some of you, with Pilate, wash your hands,
Showing an outward pity—yet you Pilates
Have here deliver'd me to my sour cross,
And water cannot wash away your sin.
Northumberland. My lord, dispatch; read o'er these articles.
Richard. Mine eyes are full of tears; I cannot see.
And yet salt water blinds them not so much
But they can see a sort of traitors here.
Nay, if I turn mine eyes upon myself,
I find myself a traitor with the rest;
For I have given here my soul's consent
T'undeck the pompous body of a king;
Made glory base, and sovereignty a slave,
Proud majesty a subject, state a peasant.
Northumberland. My lord—
Richard. No lord of thine, thou haught insulting man,
Nor no man's lord; I have no name, no title—
No, not that name was given me at the font—
But 'tis usurp'd. Alack the heavy day,
That I have worn so many winters out,
And know not now what name to call myself! (IV.i.222–59)

Richard II is therefore at the opposite extreme from Richard
III. He pours his whole self, all his capacity for imaginative understanding of the moment, into his role, which becomes in this
sense entirely his own, prescribed for him though it is. In so
doing he exhausts the self. In yielding up the crown he yields up
his identity, symbolically destroying himself when he smashes
his image in the looking-glass. In the prison scene he has become, because no longer a king, something less than a man to
himself—the Jack in Bolingbroke's timepiece, his beast of
burden, *nothing*:

by and by,
Think that I am unking'd by Bolingbroke
And straight am nothing. (V.v.36–38)

Throughout the play he has so identified himself with his sacred
name of king, has employed it so much as a centre of imagina-

tive strength which overrode everything and maintained its significance even when all its armies and followers melt away from him, that his abandonment of it draws upon and expends the last resources of his life. Losing that name, he becomes literally a nameless thing. Meanwhile the name has gone elsewhere—to 'Lancaster', and to 'Henry, fourth of that name'.

In this play, the varied imaginative communion which the protagonist enjoys with his kingly name is, as the crises of the story disclose, at the root of his being, which is annulled when he is forced to resign it. Richard's personal interpretations give us the taste of his individuality; there is plenty in the play to show us how limited, and how disregardful of grim actuality, his interpretations are, and yet how they are related to some historically important practicalities bearing on the sacred name, which later are to prove bitter to Bolingbroke and his son. Richard III, by contrast, with his habit of withdrawing himself from his roles, finds that the role can in the final crisis demand something in himself which it is not in his power to bestow; his detachment conceals not Stoic constancy or apathy, but corrupted self-love which can afford no outgoings. In both characters it is plain that the inward man has miscalculated his relation to his assignment, taking it for too much or for too little: an outgoing that leads to wasteful annulment in the hostile air, an ingoing that mines inward upon inexpressive and uncreative confusion. But if both characters are in this sense morally exemplary, Richard II, unlike Richard III, is amongst the first of Shakespeare's major tragic characters. The nature of his tragedy suggests that Shakespearian tragic heroes will tend towards the condition of Passion, not of ritual. The two are not the same; there is no passion in which the self does not suffer. Men have assigned the one function to gods and the godlike, the other to their servitors. Of the young soldier who felt himself to be an intruder in the land of fine deeds, Stephen Crane wrote:

It seemed to him supernaturally strange that he had allowed his mind to manoeuvre his body into such a situation. He understood that it might be called dramatically great.[4]

Perhaps it is in this area that Hamlet's tragedy arises. How is he to adjust to what Othello called his 'cause'?

4. 'A mystery of heroism', *Stephen Crane* (ed. R. W. Stallman, London 1954), pp. 384–5.

In *Hamlet*, John Holloway says, 'we have a recognisable kind of situation, a man engaged in a known career':

What is central is the recognisable rôle which has been assumed, the situation (familiar in a general way in the very idea of the revenge play and the malcontent) which is progressing phase by phase before our eyes.[5]

Hamlet does not delay; he deliberately dedicates himself in i.v to the role of avenger; the rest of the play is the story of how he discharges it. His soliloquies stress not procrastination but preoccupation with the role:

It is now possible . . . to see the stress on delay in the soliloquies as being not so much for the sake of stressing delay itself, as of showing how the protagonist is preoccupied with his role, in order to stress that it *is* a rôle: a recognizable 'part', undertaken by him with what might almost be termed a preordained course and end . . . Hamlet's life is one to be lived under the imposition of a great task, an imperious demand from outside. The speeches show him for a man taken up with the demands made upon him by the fact.[6]

This is a Hamlet who seems to require a minimum of adjustment, even less than Brutus, who at least endured a sleepless night accommodating his Genius to his mortal instruments. But Holloway's last sentence is amenable to expansion and qualification. And the predecessors of Hamlet—if we may number Brutus and the two Richards among them—suggest that if Shakespeare was perceptive of the recognition which is accorded to role by audience and *dramatis persona* he was at the same time deeply concerned with agreement and disagreement between character and role, with what happens to the individual when the traditional function makes its demands upon him, or he upon it. There is a wavering frontier where the individual is in communion with his role, reshaping it or being shaped by it. This element of indistinctness is particularly marked in *Hamlet* and it is impossible to feel that Holloway's account does full justice to it. If *The Spanish Tragedy* is any guide, immediate recognizability indeed is one of the things which are deliberately not built into the revenger's role by its tradition: as soon as he has cut down

5. *The Story of the Night*, p. 28.   6. Ibid., pp. 28–29.

the dead body of his son, Hieronimo immediately acknowledges the duty of revenge:

> At tamen absistam properato cedere letho,
> Ne mortem vindicta tuam tum nulla sequatur;[7]

but his first conception of it is of legal justice, and it is a long time before circumstances and his own ponderings lead him to reject the *vindicta mihi* principle and become the revenger that we all know. The first audiences of *Hamlet* had a right to expect some fairly wide variations; a characteristic of the revenger in the hands of Marston, Webster, Middleton, or Tourneur is precisely its fluid and evolutionary deployment, and the expectations attaching to the role might be considered to be much less well defined and more relative than those attaching to, for example, the tyrant or the Machevil. The obstinate sense, also that there is something in Hamlet's temperament which, when he is confronted with his task, demands that he, like Brutus, must adjust it to a posture satisfying to his imagination, to his idea of himself and of the world, makes it very difficult to ask from the play the answers to two obvious questions: *What* is the nature of the ordained role? and *when* does he assume it? For Holloway the answer to the first is apparently supplied by the putative type figure of the revenger/malcontent, and to the second by what Hamlet does in I.v. But when there is a constant intercourse going on between character and role, the one modifying the other—and it is this that would seem to be the story of the play—the Hamlet and the role of I.v may later on each become something so different, as a result of their intercourse, that we can no longer say that the same relation—one of 'assumption'—obtains between them. It is perhaps not begging the question to say that *what* and *when* keep on needing to be answered right through the play to the end. But it is just this that requires some demonstration.

Hamlet begins the play in a state of severe and suicidal depression, of 'unmanly grief' compounded with shock and fear. The Ghost's commands to him are complex, not only 'Revenge his foul and most unnatural murder', but the reminder that the old king was

> Cut off even in the blossoms of my sin . . .
> If thou hast nature in thee bear it not,

7. *The Spanish Tragedy* (ed. Philip Edwards, London, 1959), II.v.79–80.

and also

> Let not the royal bed of Denmark be
> A couch for luxury and damned incest.

It is probably safe to assume that this means 'Kill Claudius', too, because the incest will cease with his death. Finally, 'Taint not thy mind, nor let thy soul contrive / Against thy mother aught . . .'. Hamlet immediately assumes the role, ready to 'sweep' to his revenge:

> And thy commandment all alone shall live
> Within the book and volume of my brain
>
> (I.V.102–3)

and writes down in his tablets a memorandum in code, an apophthegm which means 'Claudius!'; and, as Holloway says, the swearing ceremony at the end of the scene constitutes 'a deliberate self-dedication, made as conspicuous as possible, to the rôle of a revenger'.[8] Its discovery has given him a cause. The eagerness with which he embraces it is the response of the undirected, suicidal Hamlet of the first soliloquy welcoming the imposition of a recognizable pattern upon his life.

However, the role has to be lived through as well as formally acceded to, and it is now that its development and variations begin. The next piece of information we have about Hamlet is his farewell to Ophelia as reported by her in II.ii. The eager excitement of the soliloquy after the Ghost's appearance, when Hamlet looked forward to clearing the decks for action, has disappeared. The experience of casting off the role of lover so that the exclusive role of revenger may be assumed turns out to be extremely painful, doubly 'piteous'. For Hamlet does from the first seem to interpret the one role as though it excluded any other, and perhaps the Ghost would have approved, though he does not enjoin this. Then we have the sad, deprived Hamlet of the 'except my life' speech, the 'heavy disposition' of the speech to Rosencrantz and Guildenstern (II.ii.304 ff.). Divesting himself of all 'pressures past' turns out to be a heavy task which reduces him to a simulacrum of his first condition; the process of stripping for the role gains no comfort from the role itself. It is not

8. *The Story of the Night*, p. 27.

easy to accept the view that Hamlet's radical discontent and
apparent loss of direction here is merely the malcontentism of
the revenger (which in any case became part of the tradition
largely through Shakespeare's invention of it for this occasion),
because the mood is so clear an echo of the one that prevailed in
the first soliloquy, before Hamlet became a revenger at all.
What seems uppermost is the personal sense of deprivation, of
vacuity; it is as though Hamlet had never taken on the role at
all, as though all were to be done again; the process of stripping
himself of everything but the exclusive commitment has gone
so far that the prospect of *any* commitment seems to have
disappeared. This is pointed up in the scene with the players
(ii.ii), where Hamlet envies the capacity of the First Player to
fling himself into the role assigned to him. There could hardly
be a clearer demonstration than this scene of the difference, as it
seems to Hamlet, between himself and the man who 'forces his
soul' into a part, who pours his skill and imagination into his
chosen role. The soliloquy ('O what a rogue and peasant
slave . . .'), besides asserting his consciousness of what he must
do, also asserts, unless we ignore the plain meaning of Hamlet's
statements, an equally exacting awareness that he ought to have
done it already:

> I
> A dull and muddy-mettled rascal, peak
> Like John-a-dreams, unpregnant of my cause.

The 'cause' has not yet quickened him; his imagination will not
waken. There seems to be a difference between formally undertaking a role, before one quite realizes what it is and as a relief
from undirectedness, and actually performing it.

Hamlet offers one explanation for the condition in the next
soliloquy, which it is hard not to see, in part at least, as a resigned
and puzzled comment on the gap between undertaking and performance. In the scene with Ophelia that follows (iii.i), the gap
begins to close. The rejection of Ophelia, of the lover's role,
which evolves from the 'piteous' to the brutal, and the threat to
Claudius ('all but one, shall live') have a community, not an
antithesis, of feeling; this community of emotional tone between
the stripping off of the one role and the assumption of the other

argues that the character is fast approaching the condition of murderous integrity and single-mindedness in which the deed of revenge can properly be done. The play scene only confirms this; after the play, Hamlet now really is a revenger, according to his own definition of the function in a previous soliloquy, ready to make mad the guilty and appal the free. This is what it is really like to be a revenger, he thinks, and he savours it ('now could I drink hot blood'). This is sincere acting, his imagination has been caught. It is Shakespeare—this seems the only way of putting it—or Shakespeare's conception of the chances that rule mortal life, that intervenes, and not only because there were two more acts to get through but also out of tenderness for his hero and for the sake of the end, justifying the means, of making him a more interesting and far-exploring character.

For matters are so arranged that when Hamlet, full revenger, encounters Claudius he is at prayer. The instructions given to Hamlet by the Ghost are fairly explicit on the point

> Thus was I . . .
> Cut off even in the blossoms of my sin,
> Unhous'led, disappointed, unanel'd;
> No reck'ning made. . . .

It would plainly be wide of the Ghost's mark and the revenger's function to kill Claudius at this moment; Hamlet's reasoning, fully consonant with the revenger's role in its most complete aspect, cannot be gainsaid. It is neither his fault nor his excuse that at the one time when he is fulfilled in the revenger's role his interpretation of that role, 'correct' as it is, demands that he should *not* execute the revenge rather than that he should.

The murder of Polonius (III.iv) is in part the groundwork for further plot-making. As the only explicit act of destruction carried out by the embodied revenger, it is protected against necessarily sealing a full commitment to the part by the way in which it is performed. It therefore resembles the manner in which Hamlet is prevented, or protected, from sealing revenge by finding Claudius at his prayers and not drunk, asleep or in some other condition that would more equitably have corresponded to the old king's. For Hamlet kills Polonius in a blaze of thoughtless fury, his mind empty and unknowing, certainly not with the full lunge of the revenger, his bloody intention enforcing his sword's point against the chosen victim:

> *Hamlet.* How now! a rat?
>   Dead, for a ducat, dead!
> *Polonius.* O, I am slain!
> *Queen.* O me, what hast thou done?
> *Hamlet.* Nay, I know not:
>   Is it the King? (III.iv.23–26)

It is only later that Hamlet says, 'I took thee for thy better', an observation that refers not to his state of mind when he attacked the unseen figure behind the arras, but to the thought that came into his mind when he heard the Queen's exclamation of horror. There are other things in the scene that ensues that make it difficult to say whether Hamlet is still as adjusted to his role as revenger as he was in the prayer scene. The Ghost had said

> Let not the royal bed of Denmark be
> A couch for luxury and damned incest,

and this is the burden of Hamlet's charge to his mother ('go not to my uncle's bed'). But, as we have seen, it is not easy to assume that the Ghost was saying 'amongst your other duties as revenger is that of putting a stop to the incest' instead of 'kill Claudius, and a good reason for killing him is that it will end the profanation of the royal bed'. Hamlet had brooded on the incest in the first soliloquy; it is part of him before ever he assumes the revenger's duty. The reappearing ghost, with his talk of 'almost blunted purpose', does not much help to resolve the ambiguity, if ambiguity there is; only if we could feel sure that it is an important and as it were separate clause in the 'dread command' ('At least put an end to the incest') could we read what Hamlet now says to his mother as a sharpening of vengeful purpose.

More than half aware of what is in store for him, he submits to being sent to England and as he goes meditates once more on his role in the Fortinbras soliloquy. It is close in spirit to the two other major soliloquies that preceded it ('O what a rogue' and 'To be or not to be . . .') and goes far towards cancelling out those moments when Hamlet is revenger incarnate. It mediates his sharp awareness that he is under a dread command; but surely by now this awareness constitutes more than just a sign or an acknowledgement; his awareness is that of a man who is more susceptible to being aware than is common, who habitually 'thinks', in the sense in which Dryden's Mark Antony applies the word. The scope and quality of the soliloquies at least would be superfluous and inartistic if Shakespeare were not making a point about Hamlet's individuality: that he is continually looking *at* his role, measuring himself against it, and that it is this more often than the name of action that the role persistently calls forth in him and that he brings to it. Once again he explicitly accuses him of being unpregnant in his cause, he does not know why:

> How stand I, then,
> That have a father kill'd, a mother stain'd,
> Excitements of my reason and my blood,
> And let all sleep? (iv.iv.56–59)

There seems no reason not to believe Hamlet here. Hamlet searches for a posture in which to grasp his role, and this indicates how he approaches it. The 'how' is itself a sign of Hamlet's constant tendency to move into the shifting borderline between 'assumption' and performance, even though he has once already in his experience crossed the borderline into Revenge itself. When Richard II or Brutus settle into their interpretations, we can recognize the fact immediately by their eager demeanour, by their confident and passionate utterance, by their mastery of opposing currents in the scene. We cannot accord this recognition to Hamlet soliloquizing apart from the currents of action that run on, like Fortinbras's troops, without him. Hamlet nourishes his imagination on enactment, but much more rarely releases it into the stream of action itself; he differs in this respect from the earlier heroes and unmistakably from Othello, who must immediately live out what his imagination seizes upon, and whose deeds such as the murder of Desdemona, are shaped by his own creative reading of them; he transcends murder, as Brutus does, or so he thinks. There is direct communication between his unforced 'soul' and his cause. Hamlet is not like this. Even after he has in one impulse assumed his role, in another experienced or enacted it, neither event seems finally to commit him to it. He can withdraw back into the condition where the deed yet to be done, signalling its message of obligation, constantly reminds him that it can only do so *because* it has not yet been done.

Is Hamlet then committed after his return from the sea voyage? Does he come back marble-constant, settled in his assignment? The count against Claudius has of course lengthened and defined itself:

> Does it not, think thee, stand me now upon—
> He that hath kill'd my king and whor'd my mother;
> Popp'd in between th' election and my hopes;
> Thrown out his angle for my proper life,
> And with such coz'nage—is't not perfect conscience
> To quit him with this arm? And is't not to be damn'd
> To let this canker of our nature come
> In further evil? (v.ii.63–70)

The 'dread command' of the Ghost (nowhere mentioned directly in this part of the play) is here included in and transcended by what amounts to a bill of indictment. The audience, too, have seen Claudius more openly at his evil work for several preceding scenes; he has become something that must be stopped. Hamlet accepts the role of justiciar, but there is a great deal in this part of the play that seems designedly to contrast with what has gone before. Whatever Claudius is finally punished for, he is not punished only because he 'kill'd my king and whor'd my mother', and his plots are seen in broad daylight and are no longer filtered primarily through Hamlet and the Ghost. Hamlet no longer conceives of his own emotional temperature of the moment which made him feel that it could not be done at all unless he was in the mood for it. He does not need to sound himself and discover that his thoughts are sufficiently 'bloody', as he does in the soliloquy after the play scene. On the contrary, in his account to Horatio of his adventures at sea he describes a kind of action where something is done without the doer's having to work himself up to it:

> Being thus benetted round with villainies—
> Ere I could make a prologue to my brains,
> They had begun the play. (v.ii.29–31)

For this, Hamlet has a metaphysical explanation, the guidance of Providence:

Our indiscretion sometimes serves us well,
When our deep plots do pall; and that should learn us
There's a divinity that shapes our ends,
Rough-hew them how we will. (v.ii.8–11)

And when, later in the scene, Horatio warns him how little time
he has left before Claudius' messenger arrives with the news
from England, he is confident and yet passive ('the interim is
mine'):

There is a special providence in the fall of a sparrow. If it be now, 'tis
not to come; if it be not to come, it will be now; if it be not now, yet it
will come—the readiness is all. (v.ii.212–14)

'Readiness' is something very different from that worked-up-
for-the-occasion state of feeling which characterized Hamlet
when he was the full revenger of iii.ii–iv. His dominant note
throughout the whole of the last act supports this. Submission to
Providence seems to take precedence over dedication to Revenge.
In that broader perspective—Revenge incapsulated, as it were,
within a larger movement—the punishment of a king now
doubly, trebly advanced in evil is something that will be achieved by Providence with Hamlet as its instrument; all that he
need do when the time comes is to let his brains begin the play.
   If we say that this represents a Hamlet absolutely, meta-
physically committed to the revenger's role, we must also say
that he was committed to it before in Act iii after the play scene
and during the prayer scene. But the two commitments are not
of the same kind. The measure of the difference between them
is that between 'bloody thoughts', with all their accompanying
tempest-driven perturbations, and 'readiness', with its note of
submissive calm intermingled with natural dread ('thou
wouldst not think how ill all's here about my heart'). Here
change of character, the development of Hamlet's individuality,
is signalized by the different approaches, or varieties of commitment, to the role. On the one hand there is the approach that
consists of still nerving himself to the task long after he has
formally assumed the responsibility for it and then the discharge
of it in a burst of passion which at the same time carefully
conforms to the pattern of the 'dread command' laid down by
the Ghost. On the other hand, Hamlet, 'benetted round with
villainies', submits to the course of events in the confidence that

Providence will order them. In those final events the process, which Hamlet is not accomplished in, of forcing his soul to his own conceit, is absent. Indeed, 'readiness' implies that Hamlet no longer *needs* to work himself up and pour his imagination and passion into the deed because he no longer labours alone under the imposition of a command that had seemed to him in the beginning to demand an absolute dedication and concentration of his whole self, the stripping off of all his other roles, the abandonment of 'all saws of books, all forms, all pressures past'. These changes are responsible for the feeling at the end of the play that Hamlet does not commit himself to the revenger's role in the ways he once did when he assumed it in i.v and when he enacted it in the prayer scene, that it is Providence—the way the story turns out—which, in making itself responsible for the story, commits Hamlet, who freely accepts. (As in *Measure for Measure*, it is hard to tell whether Shakespeare is saying that Providence is a kind of storyteller or a storyteller is a kind of Providence.) If Hamlet does not commit himself but is committed, however freely he submits, it can be said that he is less the revenger, that he is able to achieve the act of revenge without ever really becoming a revenger, that the larger perspective frees his inward self from the role: because all does not now depend upon him and because the end can be accomplished without his being 'in the mood' for it, the identification of the self with the revenger, the coalescence of the two, is no longer enjoined upon him. The role is no longer seen as something which has to be created by being quickened with his inward self, his passion and imagination, as Brutus or Richard II create their roles; it is formed by Providence, not by the character, and is presented to Hamlet in the shape of a concatenation of events which play into his hand, just as they did on the voyage to England. Providence, or the storyteller, has to this extent abolished the role.

In sum, Brutus and Richard II resemble Hamlet in that what they are constrained to do is reshaped by them in accordance, so far as is possible, with their needs and values, their ideas of themselves and of the world. Hamlet's world is in the beginning unshaped to a greater extent by the first blow of the constraining duty, but the resemblance holds; if he has a harder struggle than they, he also has a further reach, a second chance. He does not exhaust himself in the one interpretation as Richard II exhausts himself in remoulding his deposition into a Passion; he is saved, as Brutus is not, from committing the final deed so soon as he has first nerved himself to it. From this limited point of view, these characters can be seen as preparations for Hamlet, just as the final condition of Richard III (the inward self unable to find any way of adjusting itself to the role) seems at times, if we are to believe the soliloquies, to be a condition that threatens Hamlet. Richard III stands at the beginning of the line, incompetent. If the nature of Hamlet's 'second change' is taken into account, Hamlet, however, perhaps in the end escapes from the line altogether, glimpsing a freedom which is beyond role. An independence of this kind, it may be suspected, makes for something which dramatic storytelling is hardly capable of bearing— the rest *is* silence. This is one reason why *Hamlet,* simply as a play, is less successful than *Othello.*

3
Macbeth

Who then shall blame
His pester'd senses to recoil and start,
When all that is within him does condemn
Itself, for being there ?   *Macbeth*, v.ii.22–25*

In the three previous tragedies the protagonists are faced with situations which are not, essentially, their own creation. Hamlet and Othello both seem to themselves to have dread commands imposed upon them, the one to avenge his murdered father, the other to punish his faithless wife; even Lear, although his conduct provides a kind of excuse, is placed at the mercy and ordering of others. All of them have to wrench their behaviour and force their souls into reinterpreting roles which they did not initiate. But Macbeth has to nerve himself to perform a task which he invented for himself in the first place; the seed, it appears, grew in his own mind and not anyone else's. Shakespeare shows us both the genesis and the fulfilment of what begins as a stretch, almost a sudden physical shudder, and then grows. Macbeth has an extra load to lift—everything must begin with him and must be shaped and created by him. The play is the most exhausting and violent of them all, and much of this exhaustion springs from the feeling that Macbeth has to create everything step by step as he goes along out of what is at first a mere chaos of revolt, obscure promises, and lost names. There is a kind of analogy between Macbeth's struggles and the struggles of the artist, the Michelangelesque hewing out of the perfected shape resident in the marble block, or Yeats's struggles with tenth-rate scrawls as he works toward the complete realization of the hidden image. Perhaps this is one reason why we

Not previously published.

---

* Some marginal page references show that Ure in this essay was using Kenneth Muir's Arden edition. Hence I have occasionally altered his quotations to agree with this text.

feel Macbeth is, in H. S. Wilson's words, 'a poetic person'.[1] Macbeth is poetical not only because of the poetry of his utterance, and not only because of 'his power to grasp fully and concretely what is happening to himself',[2] but also because he voluntarily puts his hand to the work of creating his own role and situation and seems constantly to be making claims, though of a blasphemous kind, to reorder Nature and Nature's germens into his own patterns. There are parts of the play in which Macbeth can be seen as evilly parodying the artist's entitlement to a creative function analogous to that of the Creator himself, just as Milton's Satan is a dark antithesis of the Almighty, establishing an infernal kingdom and begetting hideous angels.

The Witches rhyme powerfully upon his name in the first scene: it is the climax of their chant—'There to meet with Macbeth'. But Macbeth begins the play by acquiring an additional name, 'Thane of Cawdor', and it is this circumstance, perhaps more than anything else, which starts Macbeth off imagining himself as a murderer—that long exercise of the imagination in which he tries to see himself in the role of murderer and tries to work himself up to it. The smallness and apparent insignificance of this germ contrasts with the lengthy and explicit imposition of his task upon Hamlet by the Ghost, with Iago's 'evidence', or with the total reversal of circumstance that forces Lear into unaccustomed self-examination and imaginative re-creation of himself. Macbeth, beginning with this tiny speck, is observed accreting everything else around it. Duncan's rewarding Macbeth with this title is indeed the only event in the second scene of the play in the sense of being the only thing that that scene contributes to the forward movement of the plot. The scene itself is a curious combination of orderly calm and deliberation with wild, baroque disorder and gesture, like waves breaking at the foot of a monument. The antithesis of foul and fair, of discomfort swelling from comfort, which runs through the language and metaphor, is thus supported by the larger design of the scene. This, at any rate, is the impression that the scene gives on the stage; Duncan is confined to the spot, listening, mostly silent, yet central and in control as the news breaks

1. *On the Design of Shakespearian Tragedy* (Toronto, 1957), p. 69.
2. V. Y. Kantak, in *Shakespeare Survey 16* (Cambridge, 1964), p. 44.

upon him; the first speech of the bleeding Captain culminates
in the first presentation of Macbeth as the man of blood who

> Like Valour's minion, carv'd out his passage,
> Till he fac'd the slave;
> Which ne'er shook hands, nor bade farewell to him,
> Till he unseam'd him from the nave to th' chops
> And fix'd his head upon our battlements. (i.ii.19–23)

Before the next wave of verbal and pictorial violence can be
hurled against Duncan, the Captain collapses, and Ross, after a
pause of intensifying suspense, carries it to a greater height than
the first had reached. In the manner of speech of both Ross and
the Captain there is a kind of dramatic, attention-calling excess
and excitement which seems consciously to build up to the
'happy', victorious ending. The violence of the waves is not
entirely real; they are waves in a story, in a Senecan messenger's
speech. They express, like baroque art, a contrived disorder, and
I do not therefore feel that we need take too seriously the image
of Macbeth as the man of blood which is presented in them.
Unseaming enemies from the nave to the chops is a violence
which belongs to the descriptive facility of the messenger rather
than very closely to Macbeth himself, and there is not really very
much in this scene which leads us to qualify the epithets of
'noble' and 'brave' (somewhat neutral ones in the circumstances—it was the least they could say) which are applied to him
in it. But the scene does of course present blood and disorder,
even if it is firmly controlled and set in a frame. The act of order
which emerges from it at the end, Duncan's

> No more that Thane of Cawdor shall deceive
> Our bosom interest.—Go pronounce his present death,
> And with his former title greet Macbeth. (i.ii.65–68)

concludes the episode, seals up the revolt as something over and
done with; Macbeth, on behalf of Duncan's order, has suppressed
the revolt, and Macbeth gets his reward, and that is the end of it.

Yet, with an irony which the imagery of this scene has already
sufficiently introduced to us, from this comfortable return to
normality swells the whole subsequent storm. When the
Witches greet Macbeth with the equivocal titles, his 'start' and
'fear', on which Banquo comments, may be—and usually are—

taken as an indication that *something* has been germinating in Macbeth's mind, and yet we cannot be really certain that Shakespeare intends us to understand this: it is perhaps a bit naïve of Banquo to suppose (as he seems to) that Macbeth ought to receive the incredible invocation with a beam of satisfaction— would not the most virtuous of men be somewhat taken aback, sense a threat or an evil joke, at being greeted in a fashion which 'stands not within the prospect of belief', at having his destiny sketched out in a way which seems so wildly unlike probability? The doubt at any rate, if at all valid, merely underlines Shakespeare's intention of showing us the 'something' in its most microscopic, its barely identifiable, germinal state and emphasizing how much the vision of himself as a murderer and a king, which he is shortly to start building up, is Macbeth's own imposition upon himself. Shakespeare shows us the building process from the very beginning when we only suspect, and cannot be certain, like Macbeth himself, that there is something there to be seen. For it is when the Witches keep one part of their word of promise to his ear that Macbeth really begins to face the possibility of nerving himself to his role, to labour with the unspeakable possibility. The new title of Thane of Cawdor comes up again, proudly borne in, as it were, by Ross and Angus, and Macbeth's response is unequivocal: he wants to be able to *hope*. The title now bears on its underside the hidden promise of the 'greatest' (for the name of Cawdor is growing in a sinister way since it left Duncan's hands in the previous scene), and such are the circumstances that Macbeth perhaps might be excused for coupling it with a yet greater title, were it not that Shakespeare has very strikingly contrasted Banquo's responses with Macbeth's and put into Banquo's mouth a direct warning to Macbeth that the two names must be kept separate (i.iii.120–6). Again we are returned to Macbeth's nature, to the fertile ground there. And then finally we have the first soliloquy, the first painful symptom of germination. His heart thumps, his skin crawls; the new name, so proudly and orderly handled by others, as it presses upon him ('I am Thane of Cawdor') confuses his sense of his own identity, and leaves him momentarily nameless and robbed of action, wholly intent upon something that exists only in his imagination. This soliloquy is as near as Shakespeare could get, within the limits imposed by the extreme articulacy

of his form, to portraying the first surge of an idea in the moment
of its birth. Beside it Brutus' soliloquy (*Julius Caesar*, II.i.61–69),
with which it naturally invites comparison, seems like a commentary upon it, rather than an actualization of even faintly
comparable power. It is the birth of Macbeth's vision of himself
as a murderer that we are watching; it is physically disorganizing,
'against the use of nature', 'horrible', because of its own essential horror or because it is being resisted; it is formless because
it has not yet been properly born or because Macbeth cannot
bear to look at it properly. In each case the second alternative
points at a determinate, basic fact that Shakespeare wants us to
know about Macbeth: that he is not a man to whom such a
vision can be other than revolting, fit for instant rejection. Yet
the internal events leading up to it have been revealed in such
carefully calculated glimpses that we know that some element
in Macbeth is alone responsible for what another element in
him struggles to suppress. It seems the most desperately private
moment anywhere in the plays, if we except the last soliloquy
of Richard III; Macbeth, like Richard, is in communion with
nothing but the struggling elements within himself, whereas
Lear's or Othello's or even Hamlet's soliloquies tend to become
invocations to outside powers (including the audience) or somewhat objectified versions of themselves. This is perhaps because
we are taken further back into Macbeth's history than we are into
that of any of the other characters, and this is because the
role is created by the protagonist's own nature in a more fundamental sense than is the case with Hamlet and Othello or even
with Lear. Such a condition cannot last long, and Macbeth falls
away from it into a kind of Stoic apathy—'Perhaps I don't need
to do anything to make it happen';

> . . . chance may crown me,
> Without my stir.

And his next remark is, in the context, an almost pointless
aphorism:

> Come what come may,
> Time and the hour runs through the roughest day.

Certainly nothing has been decided; Macbeth must of course
dissemble his 'rapt' condition (I.iii.150–1); the speech to Banquo

may be a feeler towards a sinister alliance, but Banquo (unless he has here momentarily become a relic of Holinshed's Banquo) doesn't recognize it as such.

As a potential murderer, in the next scenes Macbeth struggles to behave in what he considers an appropriate way, one suited to an idea of the role. This is an effort of the imagination, which endeavours to overlay conscience, which in Macbeth is itself imaginative. He composes passages about the role as though to verbalize the vision of himself as murderer were a means of countering that other impulse (and all the powerful reasons as well) which say that he ought not to undertake the role at all. We have the first of these passages just after Duncan has bestowed another of his fatal titles:

> The Prince of Cumberland!—That is a step
> On which I must fall down, or else o'erleap,
> For in my way it lies. Stars, hide your fires!
> Let not light see my black and deep desires;
> The eye wink at the hand; yet let that be
> Which the eye fears, when it is done, to see.
>
> (I.iv.48–52)

This language of rhyming invocation is not Macbeth's usual style; these monosyllables move with an uneasy formality which half-suggests the stage villain shrouding his face melodramatically in his cloak. It is a gesture, the striking of an attitude, whose unreality is immediately emphasized by Lady Macbeth's intimate account of a much more complex Macbeth (I.v.15–30) who needs *her* inspiriting before he can genuinely feel himself in the role of murderer to which in this speech he is only pretending. Lady Macbeth's own invocation is quite different and carries instant conviction as having all her will and imagination poured into it. Her prayer to the demonic spirits signalizes her passionate wish to become an instrument wholly adapted to getting the murder done, for her nature to be transformed and become as cruel as the deed; there is to be complete consonance between performer and performance, an integrity so absolute as to make her the human equivalent of the murthering ministers themselves, who are evil by metaphysical device. Her prayer, as the play goes on to reveal, is not wholly answered; but it shows that she, unlike Macbeth, commits herself completely to the task,

allowing the nature of the deed itself to determine her own
nature; the role shall be her master, infusing her with its own
life and driving out her own. Lady Macbeth does not attempt
to excuse or justify the deed, or indeed to look at it at all; she
simply allows its evil, which is clearly realized by her, to take
charge. This is, as it were, the degree of commitment to which
Lady Macbeth would like to pledge her husband as she looks
forward to pouring her spirits into his ear and chastising him
with the valour of her tongue. To effect it, she must remove the
impediments which she has described in the soliloquy about
his character, the essential human kindness, the 'fear' (perhaps
more rightly to be called 'scruple'—we must allow for her
point of view), the ambition that won't be logical, all that essentially normal mixture of good and bad which earlier had allowed
Macbeth to rest in

> If Chance will have me King, why, Chance may crown me,
> Without my stir.

And when Macbeth enters, for what in the play is his first meeting with her, we see that he is as uncommitted as ever, that he
has scarcely moved a step by the end of the scene from his
position at the end of the first scene with the Witches when he
says to Banquo, as he now says to his wife, no more but 'We
will speak further'. In spite of her entirely specific references to
'this night's great business', he is remarkably reticent; but that
he makes no gesture of repudiation also suggests that he sees in
Lady Macbeth a figure of the Chance that may crown him
'without his stir': 'Leave all the rest (apart from behaving with
the smiling countenance of a host) to me', she says; Macbeth
has from the first felt that if he could just *let it happen* without
having to commit himself to doing it, that would be a tolerable
way.

There is not much evidence that Macbeth can play even the
minor part of smiling host that Lady Macbeth has set down for
him. She takes it on herself in i.vi, and Duncan remarks upon
his absence with surprise. What is most surprising about the
soliloquy in the next scene is the way in which it 'jumps the life
to come', that is to say disregards the possibility of retribution
and punishment for sin in another world. In facing the act of
murder Macbeth considers its consequences, that it is hard to

'get away with murder', but the traditionally supreme sanctions are dismissed right at the beginning:

> if th'assassination
> Could trammel up the consequence, and catch
> With his surcease success; that but this blow
> Might be the be-all and the end-all—here,
> But here, upon this bank and shoal of time,
> We'd jump the life to come. (i.vii.2–7)

The remark is strangely impersonal, as though it were the fruit
of Macbeth's observation of what really motivates men: they
are afraid to commit murder because it sets a bad example of
which they themselves may in time become the victims. The
thought of the deed itself no longer inspires the physical horror
which it once aroused. It is rejected because it breaks a social
bond which keeps the individual safe from others. Then Macbeth thinks of his obligations as kinsman, subject, and host—
another series of social bonds, which argue to the same end. Then
he turns from himself to think of Duncan and his virtues. The
great image with which the passage ends is not an image of
supernatural *vengeance* but of all humanity weeping with *pity* for
Duncan. The soliloquy rises through prudential considerations
to an overwhelming expression of Macbeth's social and moral
sensibility. The idea of murder occupies his whole mind, is
received there, and can be defined; and this shows how hugely
the original minuscule seed of i.iii has grown. The idea of himself
as murderer is no longer something 'fantastical', but real
enough to be rejected, so that the soliloquy serves the double
purpose of showing how his imagination has shaped what was
once shapeless and how he cannot commit himself to what he
now sees does really exist in his mind as an 'intent'. Macbeth
from now on is someone conscious of a task, even though he
rejects it; he is in communication with his role as a living thing
in his imagination. It is the paradoxical effect of this soliloquy,
which so cogently expresses Macbeth's reasons against murder,
to make us feel that he is nearer to enactment of it than he has
ever been before. He is seeing murder, after all, as an act within
the context of the life he participates in, the life of society, with
its moral and kingly bonds, its logic of the bad example, and its
human grief, and not as something unidentifiably shocking and

nameless. It has changed from a 'horrid image' to 'th' assassina-
tion'. If this is now the condition of Macbeth's sensibility, it is
less surprising that his wife, in the ensuing passages, is able to
commit him. He does not try to bring into his communion with
her the broader aspects of his moral sensibility or 'nature'
(although, if her soliloquy in i.v.16–25 is any evidence, she may be
said to know about them and to calculate accordingly), but his
refusal draws upon the area, his life and position in society, upon
which his soliloquy was centred:

> We will proceed no further in this business:
> He hath honour'd me of late; and I have bought
> Golden opinions from all sorts of people . . .
>
> (i.vii.31–33)

In a sense, this makes it easier for her, for all she has to do is to
replace Macbeth's image of himself as host, kinsman, and subject
with another human image—the 'man' who dares, who takes
what he wants, and is the more the 'man' because he does so.
When Macbeth says,

> I dare do all that may become a man;
> Who dares do more is none,

it is man defined as he defined himself in the soliloquy that he is
offering. But as she overwhelms him with her will and disposes
of the practical objections, it is *her* definition of 'man' that he
finally takes with complete acceptance when he cries:

> Bring forth men-children only!
> For thy undaunted mettle should compose
> Nothing but males. (i.vii.73–75)

The step from one definition to the other is not so very great
(most societies, indeed, seem to be able to recognize both without notable difficulty, especially if they are, like Macbeth's,
militarily inclined). By means of this trick Macbeth is committed
to seeing himself in terms appropriate to the enactment of
murder. His last words in the scene have that hollow and slightly
melodramatic ring which characterized 'Stars, hide your fires!'
—they consciously override with a Senecan declamatory effect
the more complex poetry of the Macbeth who conceived the
'Pity' image, of the Macbeth whom the audience knows can

be described, in language which objects to this new, stiff bravado, as 'too full of the milk of human kindness / To catch the nearest way...':

> Away, and mock the time with fairest show:
> False face must hide what the false heart doth know.
> (I.vii.82–83)

In the murder scenes Shakespeare specially exploits these varieties of speech.

Now that he has come to it, the Macbeth of the soliloquy about the dagger is the Macbeth to whom murder is a horrid image, born out of some atavistic place within himself in a context of lost identity and supernatural soliciting. It is obvious that this Macbeth, the one who sees ghosts and whose hair stirs with horror, has not been overridden by the 'man' in either of its senses. Yet it is against this Macbeth that Lady Macbeth's man screws up his courage, and the language of the speech passes insensibly into another mode. Macbeth works himself up into the mood of 'I will be as wicked as I ought to be' in words that are designed to have something of the inspiriting function of an alarm to battle, the cry before the charge.

> Now o'er the one half-world
> Nature seems dead, and wicked dreams abuse
> The curtain'd sleep: Witchcraft celebrates
> Pale Hecate's off'rings; and wither'd Murther,
> Alarum'd by his sentinel, the wolf,
> Whose howl's his watch, thus with his stealthy pace,
> With Tarquin's ravishing strides, towards his design
> Moves like a ghost.—Thou sure and firm-set earth,
> Hear not my steps, which way they walk, for fear
> Thy very stones prate of my where-about,
> And take the present horror from the time,
> Which now suits with it.—Whiles I threat, he lives:
> Words to the heat of deeds too cold breath gives.
> (II.i.49–61)

This is the Macbeth who deliberately composes about himself, with, as he recognizes, 'words' consciously ordered, as though he were a kind of poet. The scene is carefully set and objectified and curiously distanced: the abstract 'Murther' is amplified in controlled parenthesis with his attendant wolf, who is, in a quite elaborate conceit, a sentinel whose watchword is his regular howl; and Murther is further illuminated with the rare, classical, poeticizing image of Tarquin, an image amplifying the idea of might, breathless silence, and striding evil. He invokes the earth, as formerly he had invoked the stars, and concludes his poem with an objective vision of himself in which he is assimilated to the figure of Murther playing his part in a scene which must uphold him by being appropriately set. Yet the poem is not entirely satisfactory to Macbeth, does not quite tip him over the edge, and he covers the moment by leaving the stage with another of those stretched, resounding declamations:

> Hear it not, Duncan; for it is a knell
> That summons thee to Heaven, or to Hell.
>   (II.i.63–64)

It seems that this passage is Macbeth's method for making the task bearable to himself; he can just reach it, sufficiently narrow the gap between assumption and enactment of the role, adequately prick the sides of his intent, by using this spur and raising himself on these stilts of art. But it is a very precarious achievement recognized as such even in the moment of its attainment, while its artificiality, its conscious and deliberate formality and single vision, can be seen merely to put in abeyance, without abolishing, the Macbeth who is more complex, and much harder to satisfy.

This is the Macbeth we see after the murder, his artificially stimulated 'strength' unbended (II.ii.44) and his 'constancy' (II.ii.67) fled. The deed has become again a 'horrid image', but much worse than before because it is now completely projected and actualized; Macbeth's imagination of rejection works hard upon all its circumstances, which are raised in his mind to symbols of retributive alienation from the ordinary life of man, praying, or sleeping, or washing his hands. As he faces his deed in retrospect, there is a specially vivid intercommunion between his inward self and the part he has played, but it is not really different in kind, only in degree, from what obtained before, when he was contemplating the deed in prospect with the 'nature' of the true Macbeth, not the Macbeth who deliberately assimilated himself to Murther in order to get the deed done. That posing and attitudinizing Macbeth, a development of Lady

Macbeth's 'man', falls away at a touch and leaves the Macbeth who, like Hamlet or Brutus continually 'thinks' before and after.

The murder of Duncan, of course, condemns Macbeth in realms that range beyond his characterological pattern. What to him is a horrid image is elsewhere a subversion of the natural order, which in time reasserts itself and brings his punishment. This awe-inspiring process is greater than Macbeth, but it is a process rather than a person, even though it expresses itself first through storms and maddened horses and finally through such equally functional personages as Malcolm and Macduff. It is vital to the total effect and memorability of the play and has been properly emphasized by the commentators. But Macbeth himself still strives to live as something more hopeful and vital than a condemned man awaiting the end; although everything he now is dwells, in the audience's knowledge, beneath that dark shadow, and colours our apprehension of him, he concentrates a special kind of attention by unfolding, in further story, the relationship between his inward self and his deeds.

The murder of Banquo, although the story of the episode in all its details is quite a different one, seems to show the same pattern of character in Macbeth as the murder of Duncan. The soliloquy (III.i.47–71) counterparts the 'If it were done . . .' soliloquy. Macbeth weighs the deed responsively, considering the relation between himself and his victim; just as his thoughts were once concentrated on murder in relation to his social position as host and kinsman, so now they link it with his kingly position, particularly as the begetter of a royal line. Rejected, as it was formerly, or accepted, as it is here, murder is something that can be thought about in relation to the self as a course of conduct which may disadvantage or advance him, ensure his safety among men, or rob him of men's golden opinions. Both soliloquies are the words of a man who wants to keep what he has got: his safety (common to both), respect, royal position, an idea of himself as an integrity, a creature whose acts are meaningful, not self-cancelling. They give contrary answers to the same question: will murder achieve such ends? And yet both have a quality much less constricted than this description implies, which is peculiarly Macbeth's: it expresses itself in his free-hearted recognition of his victims' virtues and in the way in which each speech rises to a glimpse of religious myth ('heaven's cherubim', 'mine eternal jewel / Given to the common enemy of man'). Because it entertains the thought of murder as a possible means to an end, Lady Macbeth, as we have seen, had not found it too difficult to replace the more fully human image of the self with her version of what it means to be a man. There is a similar transition here in the Banquo episode when Macbeth puts it to the Murderers: are they merely men, as the catalogue has it, or are they the kind of 'man' Macbeth wants, the kind that will strike secretly at their enemies? Yet Macbeth, as his conversation with Lady Macbeth (iii.ii) makes clear, is still the haunted victim, whose frame is shaken by terrible dreams and whose mind is full of scorpions; the definition of safety passes insensibly from being safe on his throne to being saved from horrid images. And again he covers this up by a formalization of imagined murder, composing with conscious art a passage about the murder of Banquo which has many resemblances in feeling and style to his 'poem' about the murder of Duncan:

> Then be thou jocund. Ere the bat hath flown
> His cloister'd flight; ere to black Hecate's summons
> The shard-born beetle, with his drowsy hums,
> Hath rung Night's yawning peal, there shall be done
> A deed of dreadful note . . .
>   Come, seeling Night,
> Scarf up the tender eye of pitiful Day,
> And, with thy bloody and invisible hand,
> Cancel, and tear to pieces, that great bond
> Which keeps me pale!—Light thickens; and the crow
> Makes wing to th' rooky wood;
> Good things of Day begin to droop and drowse,
> Whiles Night's black agents to their preys do rouse.
> Thou marvell'st at my words: but hold thee still;
> Things bad begun make strong themselves by ill.
>   (iii.ii.40–44, 46–55)

This is primarily an invocation to Night to aid the accomplishment of the murder, as he had previously conjured Earth to be silent during the murder of Duncan. But the invocation serves him by objectifying the moment and giving him control over his restless mind. Calling forth a dark enchanter's power, it sets the scene for an act which will, he hopes, assure his safety, and create an illusion that he stands at the centre and controls his fate. By formally signalizing his dedication to the murder of Banquo, it is meant less to chill our blood than to show us Macbeth freezing his doubt-ridden soul into an attitude of mastery, a fixed shape of gloomy terror that will dominate the event and make it run his way.

His experiences after Banquo's murder force Macbeth back into his old condition of stultified horror. The order 'whole as the marble, founded as the rock' that he has tried to create he continues to uphold in the banquet, struggling against the 'saucy doubts and fears' which the news of Fleance's escape have aroused. The banquet itself and Macbeth's toasts to Banquo are not the bravado of the villain, or even merely excitements of the spectators' sense of irony, so much as declarations that he can master events by imposing upon them a semblance or order with himself unchallengeably at the centre. But the ghost's appearance breaks through this from the world of the horrid image; it is as though Macbeth's instinctive rejection of murder has created ever more elaborate forms—the shuddering bewilderment of the first soliloquy developing through the nightmare visions before and after Duncan's murder into the completely uncontrollable phantasm of the murdered Banquo. All these seem to come from some deep place in Macbeth's own personality, the part that is at war both with the Macbeth who can rationally and morally consider murder as a means to an end and the Macbeth who endeavours to master both the inner and outer worlds with the strained and exalted language of his invocatory poems. Banquo's ghost is the most desperate of these creations of his heat-oppressed brain, and Lady Macbeth recognizes its provenance and kinship:

> This is the very painting of your fear:
> This is the air-drawn dagger, which, you said,
> Led you to Duncan. (iii.iv.61–63)

He is convinced that it has objective reality, and it confuses his sense of his own identity and of the nature of the world in which he lives. It is the moment where the drama of Macbeth's inner life actually takes the form of two *personae*: the haunted man and that which haunts him, so that we feel ourselves looking at a kind of allegorical embodiment of his relationship with his deeds. Banquo is not only the ghost of a murdered man, but a figure of 'fantastical' Murther itself:

> Thy bones are marrowless, thy blood is cold;
> Thou hast no speculation in those eyes,
> Which thou dost glare with. (III.iv.93–95)

The 'horrid image' of the first soliloquy, the 'wither'd Murther', the 'horrid deed', 'the terrible feat', and the 'deed of dreadful note', the 'dark hour' have all risen up to appal Macbeth with an actualization of what he has so often named and used and thought about. His chosen role, the crime to which he gave birth, the special act which brands him, is now complete before him.

Macbeth breaks away from this repeated pattern of character in an excess of despairing vigour. Shakespeare closes up like a fan all that complex intercourse between character and deed, each shaping the other, which has presented Macbeth's life to us. This, it seems, happens quite suddenly in the play, and it is as easy to ascribe it to an authorial intervention as it is difficult to identify its cause in what is shown to us of the motives of the character. It is true that Macbeth's isolation has increased (in his refusal to share the secret of Banquo's murder with Lady Macbeth) and that he has partially at any rate learnt what he was not at all practised at previously, to make his face a vizard to his heart. These are signs of the hardening of his nature, but he certainly fails each time he tries to act a brazen part; after Duncan's murder, Malcolm, Donalbain, and, of course, Banquo are not really deceived, and Macbeth's failure to sustain his poise after Banquo's murder is his worst and most public. The Macbeth who is so continually on the rack up to the ending of III.iv cannot be said to have grown as cruel as his deeds, although he darkens them deliberately with the persuasive trappings of Hecate, Night, Murther—trappings which may be described as deliberate attempts to make his inward self of the same nature as the deed that's done but which so completely fail to sustain him when he really sees the deed for what it is. If the new brutality and directness of Macbeth's resolution after III.iv do not appear arbitrary or in any way diminish the play, it is because the spectators have already had the two murders directly brought home to them in their full horror: it is mediated to them, paradoxically enough, by Macbeth's own horror, which we share, but also by the direct evidence of Duncan's graciousness, Banquo's virtues (and the witnessed annihilation of them), the storms and portents of outraged nature, and the general sense of a movement of recoil amongst the gathering forces of restoration and retribution. Acts which so cogently persuade us of their evil character lead easily to the inference that the man who can do them must quickly come to the point of no return and become a creature like his deeds. He does so; but we are not shown the antecedents of his transformation. The murderer of Banquo, who is fundamentally the same sort of person as the murderer of Duncan, becomes the murderer of Lady Macduff without our really being forced to ask what has altered the pattern of his character, why the long adjustment to the deed and the horrid imagination breaking through after it are no longer there. A practical motive for his abridgement of the whole process can be sought for—the need to check the gathering revolt at once; or we can say that it is born out of sheer despair, a wild lashing-out at Fate. But these are inferences, too, and only refer us back to the larger inference, that the nature of the criminal *must* be hardened and narrowed into despair by unrepented crime. Macbeth suddenly discovers this hard nature and drives on with it. But he could—the potentiality is there up to III.iv in his remorse, his heavy disliking of his task, the continual rebirth of the horrid image—just as easily, had Shakespeare's story permitted it, have turned to repentance—more easily, since it is the remorse and horror in his character that continually makes the toughness which he assumes give way before it. It is the *fact* that he has murdered rather than the *way* in which he has murdered which shuts off any escape route from him. This may be a very sound assumption about the nature of things, as it is certainly a true rendering of the rule that appears to apply in Macbeth's Scotland and Macbeth's cosmos, and it is plainly a good sort of deterrent against those intending murder from whatever motive. But it does not exactly offer the terms for explaining, in the light of what we already know about Macbeth's character, how he can suddenly alter that character and devise a new, more brutal—one could almost say 'uncharacteristic'—approach to murder.

In future, then, Macbeth will 'think' no more:

Strange things I have in head, that will to hand,
Which must be acted, ere they may be scann'd.
                                    (III.iv.138–9)

The gap between 'head' and 'hand' is to be ferociously narrowed; *scanned* has the double sense of examined 'by myself' as
well as discovered 'by others'. Macbeth goes to the Witches in
order to 'know, / By the worst means, the worst', in order to
direct his course the more unswervingly, and his sense of how
much this is the 'worst' means is mediated by his willingness to
bring about ultimate destruction in order to have his path clear
(IV.i.50–61). Yet he faces this, out of his frantic desire for the
simultaneity of his thought with his doing, which is intensified
by the news of Macduff's escape:

Time, thou anticipat'st my dread exploits:
The flighty purpose never is o'ertook,
Unless the deed go with it. From this moment,
The very firstlings of my heart shall be
The firstlings of my hand. And even now,
To crown my thoughts with acts, be it thought and done.
                                    (IV.i.144–9)

This conjunction of head/hand, heart/hand, thought/act leaves
no space for the old Macbeth, whose characteristic vitality,
interest, and appeal derived precisely from the complex and
changeable inner life of head and heart called forth by his pros-
pects and retrospects of the work of his hand. By eliminating all
that area of Macbeth's activity Shakespeare has shown us not so
much a change of character (for we never actually see the process
of change—the area is not gradually but sharply shut off) as the
result of such a change. A different Macbeth is revealed, and the
interest and pathos that it has depends heavily upon the fact of
our knowing that he was not always like this. Macbeth's character is like a portion of a spectrum in which the two colours are
quite sharply distinguished from one another but are none the
less harmoniously related in the sense that they form an aesthe-
tically satisfying spectacle—but perhaps a *morally* less satisfying
one.

How much of the life of the play resides in Macbeth's imaginative actualization of his own deeds is pretty clearly demonstrated
by what may be called the Macduff episode (IV.ii,iii). The

destruction of Macduff's family is the most pointless and horrible of Macbeth's crimes; but since Macbeth's feelings are not engaged in it (that, indeed, *is* the point, and what he has come to), it lacks a dimension which the murders of Duncan and Banquo possess. Even Bradley seems to have felt it to be unnecessary, except as having 'a technical value in helping to give the last stage of the action the form of a conflict between Macbeth and Macduff',[3] but defended it on the grounds that it, and the scene of Macduff's grief, permits us to escape from 'the oppression of huge sins and sufferings into the presence of the wholesome affections of unambitious hearts'.[4] If this is so, the scenes, including the episode between Malcolm and Macduff, represent the order and values which Macbeth has violated, and which are now gathering head against him. Thus the primary element in the scenes, even though Macbeth is in the plot their cause, is something which flows against rather than from Macbeth, and has little relevance to the definition of his character in the sense in which it has been discussed in this chapter.

Macbeth's actions in the last phase of the play are shallow and short-breathed. They are harshly limited in being mostly reactions against the threats from outside ('They have tied me to a stake'), and at the other end are ridden on the short, rotten rein of the Witches' prophecies. Both the defiance and the confidence fail to rise out of the personality from any depths in the man; they are animal-like; reflex actions to situations and stimuli whose originating agents lie outside Macbeth's control. That he can discover nothing in himself which will respond at any deeper level is shown by the passive, exhausted way in which he takes the news of Lady Macbeth's death. For to set against the confidence (which is sometimes near to hysteria) we have Macbeth's exhausted commentary on the failure of his whole enterprise and the meaningless play-acting of life. Like Richard III he sees life as a succession of parts to which no real self is dedicated, which do not communicate with anything in the mimic, for the mimic is a shadow without substance, ridiculously shortened by time. This other mood of Macbeth has no relation in the man himself—only that which the audience may infer—with the defiant Macbeth; the two states do not interpenetrate. Their separation shows what has happened to

3. *Shakespearean Tragedy* (London, 1904), p. 391.   4. Ibid., p. 392.

the complete man, the man whose pattern of experience gave at least evidence that the conflicting elements in him arose from a personality that was still a full circle, not two broken halves. Macbeth's last state is no worse—and no better—than this. It is the common experience: the need to keep on, the sense of the failure and pointlessness of it all. Macbeth cannot integrate the two even enough to bring him to the point of suicide (there perhaps Lady Macbeth has the advantage of him). Is this 'Hell', as some think?* Surely not, if we expect Hell to be something more out of the common, more preternaturally defined. Macbeth's huge crimes, which rouse all Nature against him, are in ironic contrast to the ordinariness of his final state; that woods should march and prophecies be ironically confirmed seems an immense labour for the destruction of so unterrifying a thing. That master shape, that colossus brooding over a nightmare world—Macbeth even in his most determined imaginations never achieved so large a stature; he ends by merely hitting out, a child tragically armed with weapons that can destroy a country. The monster of evil that Macduff and Malcolm need to see, and that some of the commentators require also, is in the end simply not there; Macbeth never quite succeeded in imagining him.

EDITOR'S NOTE

The following paragraph was written in pencil on the verso of the last sheet of the manuscript. It cannot be incorporated into the essay, but it would be a pity to lose it.

This perhaps is his tragedy—not the tragedy of the hardened heart so much as the tragedy of the poet whose poetry fails, who doesn't succeed in creating the order that he wanted to, whose poetic compositions are taken out of his hands and rewritten by another and more commonplace order, which says that if you commit murder it will do you no good—the god of the copybook headings versus the *poète maudit*.

---

* Another version of this essay shows that Ure was thinking particularly of Virgil K. Whitaker, *The Mirror up to Nature* (San Marino, 1965), which he reviewed in *MLR*, lxi, 1966, 668–70.

4

On some differences between Senecan and Elizabethan tragedy

The influence of Seneca on Elizabethan drama which has received so much critical attention since Cunliffe's volume of 1893 is after all only one aspect of the contact between *romanitas* and the drama of the English Renaissance. Although Cunliffe's thesis in *The Influence of Seneca upon Elizabethan Tragedy* has dominated our accounts of the beginnings of Elizabethan drama—that period of twenty-five rather mysterious years between *Gorboduc* and *The Spanish Tragedy*—its day is now apparently past. The conclusions which were so confidently accepted by Mr Eliot in his fascinating essay on *Seneca in Elizabethan Translation* (1927) have not stood up to the critical reexamination given them in recent years. The anti-Senecan critics have asked with great insistence and effect, not: What was the influence of Seneca and of classical forms generally on early Elizabethan tragedy?— but: How much continuity is to be found between the early Elizabethan tragedies and the medieval 'native' tradition, more specifically that tradition as represented by the medieval and late sixteenth-century verse tragedy and the moral plays? These critics have found a good deal which seems to support the view that many of the characteristic features of the so-called 'classical' tragedy are a perfectly normal, if surprising, development of the medieval traditions. The verbal parallels drawn by the editors of *Gorboduc* or of *The Spanish Tragedy* between the English plays and the Senecan tragedies were never very convincing; but the Senecan critics have been challenged also about their attribution to Senecan influence of the chorus, five-act structure, the *nuntius*, the ghost, 'sensationalism', and blank

First published in *Durham University Journal*, NS, X 1948–9, 17–23.

verse formation. We can now see more clearly, because of their work, the real relationship which exists between, say, *Gorboduc* and *The Mirror for Magistrates* or *Apius and Virginia* or *Cambyses*.[1]

The case for the Senecan influence on the technical superficies of the early 'classical' tragedy has been shaken. Other comparisons, too, of a broader nature, can be drawn between Seneca the tragic dramatist and the Elizabethan writers. These seem both to make it less likely that what Senecan influence there was could be in any sense profound or far-reaching, and also to throw light on the more general topic of the influence of *romanitas* on Elizabethan tragedy. One generalization about Elizabethan drama which would perhaps be near the truth could be formulated in these terms: Elizabethan drama is great because it draws its life-blood from a culture which is in a state of unity with itself. During Shakespeare's working lifetime, or at most during the years 1585 to 1615, it is a form of art which appears to have been accessible to almost every rank in the rather rigidly maintained social hierarchy. That social hierarchy, although subjected to all sorts of disintegrating pressures, is, generally and for a brief moment in history, agreed upon as a suitable solution to the theological and social problem; therefore, it can equably and with the agreement of most, be re-

1. Cunliffe's original work was confirmed by his *Early English Classical Tragedies* (Oxford, 1912). It is accepted by the standard histories. Although Dr Boas in his edition of Kyd (Oxford, 1901) pointed out the influence of Virgil and so of medieval classicism on *The Spanish Tragedy*, he also adduced some not very convincing parallels between Kyd's play and the Senecan tragedies, none of which proves that the inspiration of Seneca was primary to the author of *The Spanish Tragedy*. Watt and Cunliffe adduce other parallels between Seneca and *Gorboduc* in their edition of the latter play. Professor Howard Baker has returned to Boas's early observation about the influence of Virgil on the prologue to *The Spanish Tragedy*, and reexamined the whole Senecan problem in his *Introduction to Tragedy* (Baton Rouge, 1939), a work written under the influence of Willard Farnham's *The Medieval Heritage of Elizabethan Tragedy* (1930). It is this latter work which most successfully demonstrates the continuity of the tragic idea from Lydgate to *The Mirror for Magistrates*. Baker was surely right to omit *The Misfortunes of Arthur* (1588), if he regards it—as does, for example, M. W. MacCallum in his *Shakespeare's Roman Plays* (London, 1910)—as merely the first work of the academic Senecans which culminates in the 'French' Senecan plays of Fulke Greville, Alexander and their group (on whom see Kastner and Charlton's introduction to their edition of *The Works of Sir William Alexander*, Manchester, 1921). It is a tribute to Baker's prescience that his remarks about the Terentian rather than the Senecan provenance of five-act structure should have been confirmed later by T. W. Baldwin's monumental *Shakspere's Five Act Structure* (Urbana, 1947).

flected in the drama. This drama, in fact, is itself the aesthetic expression of the common culture. Consequently, the dramatists, who for the moment become the representatives of the people in this widest sense, have an eagle eye for the manifestation of the disintegrating processes which threaten—and do in fact finally overwhelm—the cultural unity. The rediscovery of satire, which one might almost term the rediscovery of Theophrastus and Juvenal, put a weapon into the hands of the dramatists with which they sought to pierce and destroy the schismatics, religious, political, or artistic, who tried to distract the Elizabethan culture from its absorption in the common theme. Jonson attacks and ridicules these marginal enemies who, starting to work their way inwards, finally succeed in laying the train that exploded in the Civil War, which itself was preceded by a decade or more of increasingly grave social and religious disintegration. Jonson attacks, it is to be noted, not only the Puritan schismatics who refused to gaze into the glass of moral and social union held up by the last of the Tudors and by James, by their ministers, their theologians, and their poets, but also all those elements in Renaissance society whose indifference and self-absorption seemed to him equally dangerous to order and sanity. In *The Poetaster* (1601) Jonson figures Renaissance society under an allegory of Augustan Rome, and his characters bear the name and to a certain extent the historical personalities of Augustus himself, of Virgil, Horace, and the rest. In the person of Ovid he attacks a social phenomenon of his own day which seemed to him as dangerous a disintegrating force as revolutionary Puritanism—the amorous and dissolute nobleman, whom he sees as an extravagant parasite on the beauty and order of the hierarchical system, and through him the self-absorbed and blasphemous cultivation of aesthetic sensuousness, the literary cliques and coteries which damaged the unity of popular culture.[2] That whole social ethic is condemned in Jonsonian accents in the speech of Augustus:

> . . . their knowledge is meere ignorance;
> Their farre-fetcht dignitie of soul, a phansy,
> And all their square pretext of grauitie
> A meere vaineglorie: hence, away with them.
> (IV.vi.70–73)

2. See O. J. Campbell's *Comicall Satyre* (San Marino, 1938) for this interpretation.

Jonson is merely the most conscious amongst the various dramatists of the need for cultural unity, because he was the most
able to recognize that such things as different kinds of cultures
existed. It is that unity which seems to make most plain the
difference between the art expected by a coterie, however
elegant and self-depreciatory, as no doubt the Neronian coteries
were, and the kind expected by a society which sees itself as
central without being exclusive, and coherent without being
fanatical. It is, in short, the difference between Senecan tragedy
and Elizabethan drama, or at least a method of approach to the
definition of that difference.

Yet here at once we come up against a paradox which is caused
by one of the central problems with which the English—and the
Elizabethan—artist was necessarily faced. The forms of the
Elizabethan drama were native—or, at the least, medieval—
forms heavily modified by Renaissance classicism. The Renaissance, of course, made many aesthetic discoveries of its own, but
its greatest discovery remains, however greatly recent reorienta-
tions may have modified our view of this matter, a rediscovery—
the rediscovery of classicism. Seneca was just one murex fished
up out of the blue of classicism. He writes his tragedies about
mythological personages: the mythological theme was to him a
necessity in the same way that similar mythological themes
became a necessity to the Renaissance dramatists and poets.
But though Medea and Hercules may rave till they choke, their
world is not only a world which has banished the polytheism of
the popular religion; it is also a world which seems to deny what
I understand to be one of the characteristic compromises of
Stoicism itself—the recognition, in Drachmann's words, that 'a
psychological fact of such enormous dimensions as ancient
polytheism must have something answering to it in the objective world'.[3] But the gods, the hells, the mythological heroes of
Seneca are merely verbal material, rhetorical cannon-fodder;
they perish for want of being symbols, of partaking of the true
nature of myth. By making Cerberus explicit in the *Hercules
Furens*—and without being under the necessity of solving the
technical problems raised by the appearance of a three-headed
dog on a stage that didn't exist—Seneca, accidentally no doubt,
made him ridiculous. And just because of their failure to be

3. A. B. Drachmann, *Atheism in Pagan Antiquity* (London, 1922), p. 113.

related to the symbols of a religious system, all Seneca's characters partake to a greater or lesser extent of this ridiculousness.

But the Renaissance, which we may describe as obliged to
make very good use of the classical mythology because of the
absence of a mythology of its own, was only obliged to do so
because it badly wanted to see in the classical myths the symbolic quality, that 'correspondence with an objective world', of
which Drachmann speaks, of which Senecan tragedy gives little
evidence.[4] Here then, Seneca himself fails the Elizabethan
dramatists. But *romanitas*, or classicism considered in its general
aspect, did not fail them. And there are moments when an Elizabethan writer like Chapman or like Jonson is able to make fruitful and poetic use of the mythological as distinct from the moral
image within the context of the drama—moments when their
mythology, unlike Seneca's, serves more than an aesthetic and
verbal purpose.

How far *romanitas* in this sense has been modified in the course
of its transition through medieval classicism and the Renaissance
cultures is of immense importance, though the precise ways in
which the modification took place is not perhaps the immediate
issue here. The manner in which the Renaissance reinforced and
extended the interpretation of the classical heroic myths,
especially in its encyclopedias and handbooks and its meta-
physics and *moralia*, constitutes the building up of a whole
structure of thought, which is really something both old and
new, like a fresh tapestry woven with the old thread. It is within
that new structure, which has since perished again, that the
Elizabethan dramatic hero, as conceived by writers like Chapman and Jonson, who are most aware of the force and virtues of
the recreated *romanitas*, move and have their being. It would
appear that the result is a conception of the heroic figure modified by the contact with *romanitas* and taking forms which superficially resemble the Senecan heroic forms, but which in fact
are the Senecan forms endowed with a new significance, scarcely
present in Seneca himself.

It is known that there was a school of political thought in the
early seventeenth century which drew a parallel between the
political conditions of the early *imperium* and those of Jacobean
England and deduced therefrom a political moral, which may be

4. On this see J. Seznec, *La Survivance des dieux antiques* (London, 1940).

subsumed as the 'necessity of classical republicanism'.[5] By the time this belief appeared, it had been realized that the Tudor settlement was not, after all, a final solution along dynastic lines of the political problem, as some had hoped. But other morals and other deductions might be drawn from the fresh appreciation of the *romanitas* which this strain of political philosophy exemplifies. There is for example the nexus of ideas woven round the heroized man, the divinized ruler, and the human god, which, complicated enough in their original forms under the Hellenistic or Roman Imperial cultures, have nevertheless been transmitted, and leave a sufficiently vigorous impress on the work of Jonson or Chapman. Aristotle in the *Nicomachean Ethics*, and no doubt many others elsewhere, had suggested that, in the patterning of the hierarchy of nature linking man, beast, and god, it might be possible for the rational part of the central link in the hierarchy—man—to approach towards the divine. This idea found a development or a parallel in the religious worship given to the deified man like Hercules, who attained to his divinity by the exercise of heroic virtues on earth. From the worship of Hercules and the Herculean type evolved perhaps the worship of the deified emperor, embodying in his person both heroic virtue and imperial authority, a combination of religious and politico-moral ideas.[6] Nock comments upon the impact of the idea of the deified ruler on the literature of the Augustan period:

There were wide possibilities in worship. There were even wider possibilities for the language of literature and art. In these the comparison or identification of persons honoured with particular deities was old and natural, for the deities supplied the traditional types of beauty and power and benevolence. It was sometimes held that the ruler was a god come down on earth; so Horace suggested that Augustus may be Mercury. The other poets of the time are full of phrases which seem to us exaggerated and artificial.[7]

5. See Zera S. Fink, *The Classical Republicans* (Evanston, 1945), especially chap. 1.

6. See the account of this development given by Charles N. Cochrane in his *Christianity and Classical Culture* (Oxford, 1940). In the pseudo-Senecan *Octavia*, it may be added, these ideas appear: Seneca urges Nero to imitate Augustus' clemency since Augustus has gained the stars and is worshipped in the temples as a god because of his exercise of that virtue. Nero replies that he will indeed follow the example of *divus Augustus*, who did not hesitate to proscribe his enemies, and adds: 'Me, too, shall the stars await, if with relentless sword I first destroy whate'er is hostile to me' (*Octavia*, 472–532, 530–1 quoted, Loeb translation).

7. A. D. Nock, *Cambridge Ancient History* (Cambridge, 1934), vol. x, p. 487.

So, in our literature of the Elizabethan period we encounter what seems to be very similar artifice and exaggeration: the extension during the first part of the seventeenth century of the Tudor doctrine about kingly rights in the direction of divine right,[8] is expressed in a terminology strongly reminiscent of that applied to the rather different idea of the divinized ruler in the Augustan period. In many of Jonson's masques, King James, before whom they were mostly performed, is thought of as holding a central position, sanctioned by the universal order and in some sort representative of that order. In *The Masque of Oberon* (1611), for example, the monarch is viewed in a divine and metaphysical context, which seems to be a distinct reflection of a classically conceived relationship between god, divine man, and man. One of the masquers speaks as follows:

> Before his presence, you must fall, or flie.
> He is the matter of vertue, and plac'd high.
> His meditations, to his height, are euen:
> And all their issue is a kin to heauen.
> He is a god, o're kings; yet stoupes he then
> Neerest a man, when he doth gouerne men;
> To teach them by the sweetnesse of his sway . . .
> 'Tis he, that stayes the time from turning old,
> And keepes the age vp in a head of gold.
> That in his owne true circle, still doth runne;
> And holds his course, as certayne as the sunne.
> He makes it euer day, and euer spring,
> Where he doth shine, and quickens euery thing
> Like a new nature: so, that true to call
> Him, by his title, is to say, Hee's all.[9]

This is hardly a portrait which would be recognizable to us as that of James I; but it is a recognizable description of a fertility hero, or of a *divus Augustus* under the guise of the god Phoebus. It also lends meaning to an interesting Jonsonian paradox: for the Jonson who ten years before had attacked the cultured

8. See J. N. Figgis, *Theory of the Divine Right of Kings* (Cambridge, 1896).

9. *Ben Jonson* (Oxford 1941), vol. vii, p. 353. In this connection it may be noted that Jonson had earlier shown a very detailed knowledge of the doctrine of emperor-worship—at least as it affected Tiberius' policy—in his *Sejanus*, where Tiberius is shown cunningly rejecting the suggestion that a temple should be erected to him in Spain. So runs the account in Tacitus. Jonson's knowledge of *romanitas* is exceptionally fruitful: see, for example, his use of the Roman marriage ceremony in *Hymenaei*, as explained by D. J. Gordon in *Journal of the Warburg and Courtauld Institutes*, viii, 1945.

schismatics, is now himself obliged to act as a mouthpiece of one of the disintegrating forces which threatened the cultural unity—namely, the gross expansion of the claims of the monarchy.

If the classicized treatment of the monarch's position can be related to the problem of the modification of *romanitas*, the idea of the heroized man can be more nearly related to Seneca himself. Chapman's treatment of the idea casts some light on the way his conception of the heroic destiny alters. That Chapman was inspired by neo-Stoic ideas, particularly by what he found of the Stoic teaching in the *Encheiridion* and *Discourses* of Epictetus, is a familiar fact.[1] Chapman's part in the neo-Stoic revival is, however, a complex one, very different from the rather facile attempt to assimilate Stoic with Christian teaching that we find, for example, in the work of a translator of Seneca and jack-of-all-trades like Thomas Lodge. Chapman studies at great length the two antithetical types of hero—the 'Senecal man', who is modelled essentially on Stoic teaching, although he may be modified by Christian and by neo-Platonic intrusions, and the passionate man, the Herculean type, who, as Battenhouse has shown, is in the case of Bussy d'Ambois the 'Alcides' of Ficino's interpretation of the heroic myth.[2] The idea appears in others of Chapman's characters besides, though in a form whose gradual modification lends it its special interest: 'Fortune to him was Juno to Alcides', says Savoy of Chapman's Byron, and develops in a lengthy speech what seems to be an idea to the Roman conception of the heroic man, the combination between ἀρετή and τύχη, virtue and fortune, which Cochrane calls 'a theory of human nature more or less explicit in classicism'.

1. See F. L. Schoell, *Etudes sur l'humanisme continental* (Paris, 1926), which supersedes the work of Ferguson, *MLR*, xiii, 1918, and xv, 1920; two articles by M. Higgins on the Senecal man in Chapman, *RES*, xxi, 1945, and xxiii, 1947; and other works there cited.

2. See Roy Battenhouse, 'Chapman and the nature of man', *ELH: A Journal of English Literary History*, xii, 1945. This striking article seems to me to pay insufficient attention to a possible development and modification of Chapman's ideas and of the tragic hero in Chapman in the course of his long and productive career. What is needed is a study of the *development* of Chapman's thought. How different, for example, is *Ovid's Banquet of Sense* from Byron's dying speech. I regret that I have been unable to see R. H. Perkinson's 'Nature and the tragic hero in Chapman's Bussy plays', *MLQ*, iii, 1942.

Chapman's portrayal of the Herculean man in *The Tragedy of Bussy d'Ambois* is affected by the idea that there are certain men who, by virtue of their deeds on earth, become divinized after life. This is the thought that lies behind Bussy's dying speeches, in a scene where we are shown a Passion, like that of Hercules, and also a Herculean apotheosis. Chapman is in this scene giving us a version of the final scene of the *Hercules Oetaeus*—a version only very slightly modified by his own predilections and by a desire to reconcile the figure of the heroized man with Christian teaching about the need for repentance and the after-life.[3] Bussy's spirit is 'made a star', purged by the destruction of the body, like that of Hercules; but Bussy has previously made something very like a confession of his own unworthiness. This foreshadows the particular way in which Chapman in later plays tried to revitalize the Senecan hero. The dying Cato in *Caesar and Pompey* combines the idea of a heroic apotheosis with a series of arguments designed to show that the nature of the soul necessarily implies a fulfilment of itself in heaven. Monsieur and the Guise, in their capacity as choral commentators, had argued this very point in *The Tragedy of Bussy d'Ambois* (v.ii.1–53), but there the argument is conducted on a lower level and without being satisfactorily resolved either at that particular point in the play or in the final apotheosis of Bussy that takes place soon after. Cato, in Chapman's Roman tragedy, speaks with assurance:

> the Consuls' souls
> That slew themselves so nobly, scorning life
> Led under tyrants' sceptres, mine would see.
> For we shall know each other, and past death
> Retain those forms of knowledge learn'd in life;
> Since, if what here we learn, we there shall lose,
> Our immortality were not life but time.
> And that our souls in reason are immortal
> Their natural and proper objects prove;
> Which immortality and knowledge are.
> For to that object ever is referr'd
> The nature of the soul, in which the acts
> Of her high faculties are still employ'd.
> And the true object must her powers obtain
> To which they are in nature's aim directed,

3. Compare *Tragedy of Bussy d'Ambois*, v.iv.149 ff., with *Hercules Oetaeus*, ll. 1940–88. And see T. M. Parrott, *Tragedies of Chapman* (London, 1910), pp. 560–1.

Since 'twere absurd to have her set an object
Which possibly she never can aspire. (v.ii.134–50)

There is a certainty here about the ultimate destiny of the soul
and the exact kind of its fulfilment, which is lacking in Chapman's other plays, but which reminds us strongly of the view so
confidently set forth by Sir John Davies in his *Nosce Teipsum*, some
of which parallels Chapman's material in the discussions between Monsieur and the Guise in the earlier play and that of the
more confident and elaborate assertions of Cato to his 'disciples'
in the concluding scenes of *Caesar and Pompey*.

Chapman therefore moves away from the original Senecan-
type heroic apotheosis. The Herculean figure is modified, for
example, in the Byron plays, where the hero plays Hercules:

I have Alcides-like gone under th'earth,
And on these shoulders borne the weight of France,[4]

but plays him without the Herculean apotheosis; instead,
Byron's death is the occasion for a note of elegiac finality:

Never more
Shall any hope of my revival see me;
Such is the endless exile of dead men.
Summer succeeds the Spring; Autumn the Summer;
The frosts of Winter the fall'n leaves of Autumn;
All these and all fruits in them yearly fade,
And every year return: but cursed man
Shall never more renew his vanish'd face.[5]

But we may suggest that the idea of a man being elevated to
supernatural honours because of his good deeds on earth is present in each one of Chapman's heroes. The interest lies in ob-
serving the way it is modified and developed from its first
appearance under the aegis of the *Hercules Oetaeus* in *The Tragedy
of Bussy d'Ambois* to the Catonian version of the heroized man in
Caesar and Pompey, heavily coloured with Christian and Platonic
ideas about the nature of the soul and its formal correspondence
with the heavenly sublimities. The modifications undergone in
the conception help to show the eventual inadequacy of the
Senecan example.

Chapman also seems to have discovered the inadequacy of

4. *Tragedy of Byron*, iii.i.151–2.   5. Ibid. v.iv.245–52.

Stoicism. It is true that his most integrated tragedy—*The Revenge of Bussy d'Ambois*—is a treatment in dramaturgical terms of the Stoic answer to that rather desperate appeal of Seneca's: 'Death is on my trail, and life is fleeting away: teach me something with which to face these troubles.' It seems also to be a treatment of this problem in specifically Stoic terms; Clermont d'Ambois is the most fully developed and convincing of the Stoic heroes. But the play tests very severely the suitability of the purely Stoic material. Its universe, like Seneca's, lacks that 'correspondence with an objective world': Chapman is here, like Marcus Aurelius, to adopt a phrase of Cochrane's, writing 'upon the cosmos a merely human rationality'. Like Seneca, too, Chapman appears to regard religion in this play not so much as a formality, but as a dead thing. For its reader, *The Revenge* suggests a refuge either in demonology or in Shakespeare. Artistically, too, Chapman's attempt, like Marston's feebler attempt, to graft a rigid Stoicism on to the conventions of the Elizabethan drama—and particularly those of the revenge drama—is not successful. It is no use making your hero an exemplar of Stoic calm and then rudely disturbing him with armed shades and the burden of the revenge for blood. In *Caesar and Pompey*, which was probably written not long after the revenge play, Chapman makes repairs and amends, doing abrupt violence upon historical likelihood in his anxiety to give us a doctrine of the soul more meaningful than that implied either by the Senecal man or the Herculean apotheosis. The gross body, as in *The Tragedy of Bussy d'Ambois*, must still be purged away, but Chapman can confidently assert with Davies that the soul has an 'end', that valour and learning are not merely the random gifts of nature, whose work is now seen as one of ordered creation. In Fulke Greville's words:

> She speaketh in our flesh; and from our Senses,
> Deliuers downe her wisdomes to our Reason.[6]

There is much else in Chapman besides this growth, much else in Chapman's tragedies alone more relevant and moving perhaps, and much in his poetry which needs to be understood

6. *Mustapha*, cho. v.28–29 (*Poems and Dramas of Fulke Greville*, ed. G. Bullough, Edinburgh and London, 1939, vol. ii, p. 136).

before anyone can seek to present a complete view of his exhaust-
less development. But his handling of the Senecan image shows
fairly clearly how, in this example at least, the Senecan mode
acquired a significance which was strictly not present in the
original.

Chapman and Jonson, then, can both be used in their different ways to show that it seems more sensible to regard the
influence of Seneca on Elizabethan dramatists as an aspect of
their contact with *romanitas* than as a curiously isolated and
distorted example of literary 'influence'. Study of the problem
must therefore be preceded by an attempt to distinguish not
only the broad differences between Imperial Rome and Jacobean England but also any resemblances which the dramatists
may have been in the habit of perceiving between the two cultures. Did, for example, the poets of James often see themselves
in an Augustan mirror, as Jonson appears to have done when
he wrote *The Poetaster*?

As to Seneca himself, his gift to Elizabethan drama has sometimes been seen as largely confined to the provision of a limited
number of technical devices, plain though it is that the dramatic
device cannot easily be separated from 'tone' and 'emotional
atmosphere'. In the light of recent work it is difficult to believe
that Seneca the dramatist had an effect in any sense profound
upon the general course of Elizabethan drama, although he may
have contributed a ghost, a sensation, or a bloody hand here and
there; he was certainly a model for academic theorists of the
school of Garnier, even though that most typically 'French
Senecan' play Daniel's *Cleopatra* begins with a speech very much
in the manner of the 'complaint'. If Seneca must yield much
ground in *The Spanish Tragedy* and *Gorboduc* to medieval classicism and the non-dramatic tragedy, so, in the later period, when
the curve of influence rises from technique to moral philosophy,
he must yield to the encroaching *romanitas* as that is modified by
its transmission through Renaissance hands and minds.

5

John Marston's *Sophonisba*: a reconsideration

Sophonisba (1606) was Marston's last tragedy (if we accept the view that *The Insatiate Countess* is in part the work of another hand). Nothing in Marston's reputation and little in his earlier plays prepares us for so curious a 'sport' as this austere and melancholy Roman tragedy, and the critics, consequently, have had some difficulty in placing the play. Mr Eliot praised it as the 'most nearly adequate expression of Marston's distorted and obstructed genius' and ascribed to it a tone different from that of any other Elizabethan play.[1] Ellis-Fermor could not concur with this judgement—to her the play is imperfect and negligible; nor could Marston's latest editor, Harvey Wood, who saw the play as an anticipation of the heroic drama of the Restoration.[2] The older critics greeted *Sophonisba* with a chorus of depreciation.[3] Some writers, though they deal with matters closely relating to it, omit all mention of it.[4] The critical difficulty suggests that the answers to three questions may help towards a reconsideration of the work: (1) What relation does *Sophonisba* bear to Marston's earlier plays? (2) What kind of 'Roman tragedy' is it? (3) What is the 'world' of the play? In a sense, none of these questions can be answered unless the others are; but they can be treated separately in an effort to relate *Sophonisba*

First published in *Durham University Journal*, NS, X, 1948–9, 81–90.

---

1. *Selected Essays* (London, 1932), p. 230.

2. U. M. Ellis-Fermor, *Jacobean Drama* (London, 1936), p. 96; H. Harvey Wood, *The Plays of John Marston* (Edinburgh and London, 1934–9), vol. iii, pp. xiii–xiv.

3. According to them it is 'pseudo-historical and romantic' (F. E. Schelling, *Elizabethan Drama*, 1910, vol. ii, p. 27); 'second-rate in both design and execution' (A. W. Ward, *History of English Dramatic Literature*, London, 1899, vol. ii, p. 481); 'a singularly feeble attempt to do justice to a powerful tragic theme' (W. Macneile Dixon, *CHEL*, vol. vi, 1910, p. 49).

4. As do Kastner and Charlton in their edition of Alexander; M. W. MacCallum in his *Shakespeare's Roman Plays*; M. Higgins in his 'Convention of the Stoic hero', *MLR*, xxxix, 1944.

more comprehensively to Marston's development and to contemporary plays of a similar kind. An answer to the third question may provide a clearer sight of the pattern which Mr Eliot
claimed to detect in the play—'the kind of pattern which we
perceive in our own lives only at rare moments of inattention
and detachment, drowsing in sunlight'.

The play deals, like several other much more celebrated
plays, with an episode found in Appian's *Roman History* (Book
VIII: 'The Punic Wars'). Appian relates that Scipio invaded
Africa from Sicily at the head of seven thousand men and found
Massinissa, 'son of the king of the Massylians, a powerful tribe',
at war with Carthage because the Carthaginians had cheated
him of his promised bride Sophonisba, the daughter of Hasdrubal. This Sophonisba had been given to Syphax, the principal
chieftain of Numidia, while Massinissa was away in Spain, because the Carthaginians hoped that Syphax would help them
against the invading Romans. When Scipio arrived, Massinissa,
therefore, allied himself with the Romans and together the
allies defeated the combined forces of Hasdrubal and Syphax;
the Massylian chieftain was reunited with Sophonisba. But the
captured Syphax, who had all along played fast and loose with
both sides, told Scipio that Sophonisba's refusal to join in with
the Romans, 'so strongly is she attached to her own country',
had been the cause of his own failure to give them the help that
he had at one time promised them; he went on to warn the
Roman leader that the fanaticism of Sophonisba would soon
divert Massinissa's loyalty also away from the Romans. Scipio
ordered Massinissa to deliver his bride up to him, but instead
Massinissa gave her poison which she drank with fortitude.
Syphax was taken to Rome and there presently died of grief.[5]
Marston somewhat alters the course of this history, but all the
main historical events of his play appear to be firmly founded
on Appian. The dramatist, however, expands and enriches the
characters, their relationships, and those of Appian's incidents
which were potential dramatic scenes: such as Hasdrubal's
abortive attempt to poison Massinissa,[6] the single combat be-

5. Appian, *Roman History*, vol. viii, pp. 7–28. For the connection with Livy's
version see Wood, vol. ii, p. xiii.

6. An incident perhaps expanded from Montaigne, *Essays*, III.i, although mentioned in Appian. See C. Crawford, *Collectanea*, Second Series (Stratford-upon-
Avon 1907), p. 46.

tween Syphax and Massinissa, and the death of Sophonisba. Syphax becomes the blackest of villains, with three attempts to rape Sophonisba and no credit given to him for his touching end, Hasdrubal a personal enemy of the ennobled Massinissa. Marston also develops some interesting scenes in which the Carthaginian councillors, led by Hasdrubal but opposed by the upright Gelosso, debate how Syphax may be encouraged and Massinissa crushed. ·

Sophonisba can be seen, then, as a departure from Marston's usual formula. That formula had entailed a romantic main theme, of the sort found in the *novelle*, laced with humour and satire, the latter sometimes integrally and sometimes only superficially related to the play's rationale. The growth of Marston's ability to present his world-view through the medium of satirical comedy and to develop from that to the writing of a satirical tragicomedy like *The Malcontent* forms a comprehensive enough basis for an account of his work up to 1604/5.[7] It is plausible also to regard *The Dutch Courtesan* and *The Insatiate Countess* as evidence for the deliquescence of his talent, and the loss of hard-won ground; it is disappointing enough, at least, to find that *The Fawne*, in spite of many brilliant passages, reverts at times to the celebrated clumsy and chilblained style of *The Scourge of Villainy* and that the satirical vehicle (the Duke of Ferrara) is much less successful a part of the dramatic action than had been Malevole in *The Malcontent*—in fact, to find that Marston, except possibly in the last-named play, never advanced in technique and dramatic artistry beyond the Jonson who wrote *The Case is Altered*. *Sophonisba*, however, is omitted from such a judgement, and *Sophonisba* is more than the exception which proves its general truth.

In writing a Roman tragedy Marston was deserting the Italian court and the London scene which had provided the milieux for all his other plays. But he was also going deeper, to the sources of the Stoic theme which had inspired his portrayals of Pandulpho and of Andrugio in *Antonio and Mellida*, Renaissance Italians though they are, and for once was writing a play about Seneca's countrymen and Epictetus' pupils set in that timeless or anachronistic landscape which was the Elizabethan classical world.

7. See O. J. Campbell, *Comicall Satyre* (San Marino, 1938), chap. vi, and M. S. Allen, *The Satire of John Marston* (Columbus, Ohio, 1920).

The same sort of interest therefore attaches to *Sophonisba* as to Chapman's solitary attempts in *Caesar and Pompey* not to impose the neo-Stoic pattern on Renaissance courtiers and scholars, but to portray the Romans in their habits as they lived. It is not improbable therefore that in *Sophonisba* there may be found a carrying to completion of the Stoic themes adumbrated in the earlier tragedies, which will establish a relationship between them and the later play. For practical purposes, of course, Marston makes no distinction between the African and the Roman characters; Massinissa goes through a Roman marriage ceremony, and Carthaginian councillors behave like Roman senators and impartially invoke the aid of Jove, and we are conveniently allowed to forget that Massinissa's face must have been, like Othello's, black. There is none of that sense of different cultures in conflict which Massinger managed to convey in *Believe as You List*. Indeed, Marston repudiates too exact a historical conscience in his address 'To the Generall Reader', which is generally taken to be an attack on Jonsonian scrupulousness in that respect:

Know, that I have not labored in this poeme, to tie myself to relate any thing as an historian but to inlarge every thing as a Poet, To transcribe Authors, quote authorities, & translate Latin prose orations into English blank-verse, hath in this subject beene the least aime of my studies.[8]

None the less Marston makes some approach towards a convincing portrayal of Roman habits. After Syphax has announced his abandonment of the Carthaginian cause, elaborate Roman marriage ceremonies occupy a scene. Later in the play Sophonisba prepares a sacrifice, of what kind is not specified, and prays to Jove; Scipio appears 'with the complements of a Roman general'; and Scipio adorns Massinissa at the end of the play with the Roman emblems of victory and honour. More significantly, for the most powerful scene in the play, that wherein the witch Erichtho deceives Syphax with the promise that she will bring Sophonisba to his bed, Marston went straight to Lucan (*Pharsalia*, VI) for a witch of the most severely classical kind, not a 'cunning woman' of the Mother Bombie sort, nor an Elizabeth Sawyer, nor a daemon with a Christian and neo-

8. The text of *Sophonisba* used throughout is that of Wood, vol. ii.

Platonic ancestry like the Weird Sisters, but a goetist with
affinities to Ovid's and Seneca's Medea. As such, she appears to
be the only fully-fledged example of her kind in Elizabethan
drama.[9] Having surrounded his figures with emblems of
romanitas, Marston was equally concerned to supply them with
an appropriate intellectual milieu, and, not unexpectedly,
this turns out to be largely Stoic in colour and character.

As there are two opposing military powers in the play, Rome
and Carthage, so there is a struggle between the protagonists in
the moral sphere. Scipio himself, it is true, is a colourless figure,
but the other characters divide sharply into the virtuous and the
vitiated. On the one side stand Hasdrubal, Syphax, and the
Carthaginian councillors including Carthalon; on the virtuous
side, Massinissa, Sophonisba, and Gelosso. This kind of morality-
play grouping (we are reminded of the good and evil counsellors in *Gorboduc*) suggests that the play is to be concerned
partly with the resolution of a moral conflict like *Gorboduc* itself.
The grouping is broken only by the figure of Scipio, and by the
two comparatively minor figures of Zanthia, Sophonisba's
maid, a shifty and trustless servant, who is simply amoral, and
the poisoner Gisco,[1] who is sent by Hasdrubal to dispatch Massinissa but recoils before his virtue and has his throat cut by
Hasdrubal for his pains. The virtues of both Massinissa and
Sophonisba are predominantly Stoic virtues. When the alarm of
Scipio's invasion is sounded on their wedding night they both
resign themselves to a postponement:

> *Vertue* perforce is *Vice*,
> But he that may, yet holds, is manly wise

is the *sententia* applied by Massinissa to the situation.[2] Sophonisba
is prepared even for her bridegroom's death in battle, fortified
with another *sententia*:

> Like wonder stand, or fall, so though thou die
> My fortunes may be wretched, but not I.

Sophonisba resists the threats and blandishments of Syphax

---

9. Less sinister parallels are to be found in the Medea of Greene's *Alphonsus of
Arragon* and the Melissa of his *Orlando Furioso*, the latter plainly derived from Ario-
sto, as is Spenser's Melissa in the *Faerie Queene*.

1. Marston did not look very far for his Carthaginian names—this one is, in
Appian, the name of Hasdrubal's father. 2. 1.ii, Wood, p. 17.

when he has her in his power ('Thou maiest enforce my body but not me'), nor for a moment admits his power over her living or dead.[3] Massinissa's speech in praise of her is in terms of the Stoic virtue well known to Marston from Montaigne, a celebration of an individual who is in herself a fortress of the moral excellences:

> *Lelius* . . . she is no god.
> *Massinissa.* And yet she's more.
>   I do not prayse Gods goodnes but adore.
>   Gods cannot fall, and for their constant goodnesse
>   (Which is necessited) they have a crowne
>   Of never ending pleasures: but faint man
>   (Framd to have his weaknes made the heavens glory)
>   If he with steddy vertue holde all seidge
>   That power, that speach, that pleasure, that full sweets
>   A world of greatnes can assaile him with,
>   Having no pay but selfe wept miserie,
>   And beggars treasure heapt, that man Ile prayse
>   Above the Gods. (III.ii, Wood, p. 41)

The contrast between the virtuous and the vicious is further developed in the actions of the two pairs, Gelosso and Carthalon, Massinissa and Syphax. Particularly in the council scene at Carthage the struggle between 'politick states men' and Stoic virtue is developed into an ethical *débat*. Carthalon and Hanno argue that the proposed betrayal of Massinissa is justified because the needs of the state demand it and because 'prosperous successe gives blackest actions glory'. Dishonesty is worth trying if it will save Carthage:

>   some must lie,
> Some must betray, some murder, and some all,
> Each hath strong use, as poyson in all purges:
> Yet when some violent chance shall force a state,
> To breake given faith, or plot some stratagems,
> Princes ascribe that vile necessity
> Unto Heavens wrath . . . states must not stick to nice.
>   (II.i, Wood, p. 21)

Gelosso counter-argues:

>   I am bound to loose
> My life but not my honour for my country;

---

3. IV.i, Wood, p. 45.

and urges that public and private morality are interdependent. Marston, of course, is here treating a well-known Renaissance debate, the debate that is reflected most favourably in those Elizabethan plays which deal with the nature and duties of the Prince and which generally set up the Stoic *exempla* as an argument against the Machiavellian compromise between morality and public interest—such as Chapman's Bussy and Byron plays, Jonson's *Sejanus*, Daniel's *Philotas*, Hughes's *Misfortunes of Arthur*, Fulke Greville's *Alaham* and *Mustapha*, and *Antonio's Revenge* itself. Greville, particularly, is fond of debating whether the prince is justified in abrogating morality in the interests of the state. In his *Mustapha*, for example, Soliman is urged by his evil counsellors, principally by his mistress Rossa (for reasons of her own), to put to death his virtuous son Mustapha. Mustapha is represented throughout as a perfectibilist who will not use bad means to achieve good ends. Soliman is unable to decide what to do, and is torn between the differing advice of Rossa and of his good counsellor Achmat (a Stoic type). The arguments that Achmat puts forward imply a profound recognition of the almost insoluble nature of the problem and a typically Stoic recognition that 'virtue' does not necessarily 'pay':

> For who doth wrest Kings mindes,
> Wrestles his faith vpon the stage of Chance;
> Where vertue, to the world by fortune knowne,
> Is oft misiudg'd, because shee's ouerthrowne.[4]

Compare this with Sophonisba's speech as she unwillingly obeys the Carthaginian order to deliver herself up to Syphax:

> I goe: what power can make me wretched? what evill
> Is there in life to him, that knowes lifes losse
> To be no evill: show, show thy ugliest brow
> O most blacke chaunce: make me a wretched story.
> *Without misfortune Vertue hath no glorie.* (ii.ii, Wood, p. 23)

Greville, of course, had thought deeper into the problems and developed them in a more complex form than either Marston himself or Chapman in the better-known discussions of the relations between private and public morality in *The Revenge of Bussy d'Ambois*, where Maillard, Clermont's treacherous captor,

4. *Mustapha*, ii.i.61–64, *Poems and Dramas of Greville* (ed. G. Bullough, Edinburgh, 1939), vol. ii.

gives a cynical exposition of the philosophy of Rossa without leading us to any recognition of the real difficulty, of which Achmat was thoroughly aware, that the antithesis between the Stoic and the Machiavellian codes presented to sixteenth-century statists.[5] Greville had no solution to the problem neat enough to be expressed by the kind of irony which Chapman puts into Maillard's mouth. Chapman, of course, is on the side of the Stoic angels; so is Marston, and he continues to develop the antithesis, particularly in his portrayal of Syphax and Massinissa. When the villain and the hero meet together in single combat, Marston takes the opportunity to make it crystal clear. Massinissa has already taken heart from the fact that Justice (in the sense of an absolute moral standard) is on his side:

> Justice is so huge odds
> That he who with it feares, Heaven must renounce
> In his creation. (III.ii, Wood, p. 42)

When he and Syphax fight, Massinissa cries.

> Of you my stars as I am worthy you
> I implore aide, and O if angels waite
> Upon good harts my *Genius* bee as strong
> As I am just.

Syphax, by contrast, makes a typical statement of what Greville calls 'selfenesse' and 'Opinion' (the Epictetan ὑπόληψις which Ben Jonson defined as without the 'tincture of *Reason*'[6]):

> Kinges glory is their wrong.
> Hee that may onely do just act's a slave
> My Gods my arme, my life, my heaven, my grave
> To mee all end. (v.ii, Wood, p. 55)

Syphax is also of the opinion that private morality must be motivated by 'selfenesse'. Thinking that Sophonisba has been won to his will, he congratulates her on her supposed abrogation of 'superstitious virtue':

> Shee that can time her goodnesse hath true care
> Of hir best good. Nature at home beginnes
> She whose integritye her selfe hurts sinnes.
> (III.i, Wood, p. 34)

5. *The Revenge of Bussy d'Ambois*, IV.i.47–76.
6. 'Discoveries' (in vol. viii, p. 564).

Syphax, Hasdrubal, and Carthalon between them turn topsy-turvy the world of moral order, private and public alike. Marston was dealing with problems which were in the atmosphere of the age, and one can shelter behind the broad back of Professor W. C. Curry if there be need to avoid the tracing of the exact sources of his moral philosophy.[7] In fact, and because of the labours of Crawford, we know that Marston took a good deal of his thought on the problem of the two kinds of justice from Montaigne (*Essays*, III.i). For a more sophisticated interpretation of the difficulties and one more closely integrated to current political formulas than can be found either in Montaigne's essay or Marston's borrowings from it, one must go to a writer like Greville (for instance, the Chorus Primus in *Mustapha*). But Marston was not on the side of sophistication, and his *exemplum* as set forth in *Sophonisba* has all the neatness and prettiness of the historical *exempla* in Montaigne. 'All things be not lawfull to an honest man for the service of his king . . . our countrey is not above all other duties', writes Montaigne,[8] and Marston echoes this with Gelosso's 'I am bound to loose my life but not my honour for my country', and Massinissa's.

> Men, be not foold
> With piety to place: traditions feare,
> *A just mans contry Jove makes everywhere.*[9]

Marston, indeed, had no difficulty in making his allegiance clear. 'There is no worse penalty for vice than the fact that it is dissatisfied with itself and all its fellows', wrote Seneca,[1] and with skilful irony Marston makes his politicians, when their plans go awry, coarsely upbraid one another, gathering the rags of their 'justice' awkwardly about their shame:

> *thus deedes*
> *Ill nourisht rot, without Jove naught succeedes.*
> (II.iii, Wood, p. 31)

7. Curry writes in *Shakespeare's Philosophical Patterns* (Baton Rouge, 1937), p. 23: 'Students of the humanistic period . . . must learn to think in terms of generally accepted traditions rather than always of specific and direct lines of reference.'

8. Everyman ed., vol. iii, p. 14.

9. III.ii, Wood, p. 40. For further discussion of the 'accepted tradition' see, for example, Ruth L. Anderson, 'Kingship in Renaissance drama', *Studies in Philology*, xli, 1944.

1. *Ep.* xlii.

But it is particularly in his study of lust in action, in the person of Syphax, that Marston completes his moral approach. Professor Spencer has pointed out how preoccupied Marston is with the theme of lust, carrying over into his dramatic treatment of the subject the morbid preoccupation (which takes the form of overt repulsion) that he shows towards vices and follies in *The Scourge of Villainy*.[2] Marston in that work may be consciously modelling his attitude on Juvenal's, and it is difficult to believe that Roman vices had eaten so deeply into the social fabric of the Elizabethan Renaissance as Marston there implies. In *The Dutch Courtesan* Marston had made a further study of the subject after the manner of Dekker's *Honest Whore*; and in *The Insatiate Countess* he devotes most of the play to a study of lust in action in the person of Isabella. Isabella is a truly Juvenalian figure; her nearest parallel is perhaps found in that strained portrayal of insatiate lust, the Messalina of Nathanael Richards's *The Tragedy of Messalina* (1640), who is a figure taken straight out of Tacitus and Juvenal.[3] The figure of Syphax, then, has relation to Isabella and to Freevil. He makes three separate attempts to rape Sophonisba: on the first occasion, she escapes by a trick; on the second, into which she is betrayed by the treachery of her maid Zanthia, even Syphax relents in the presence of her astonishing virtue (for the Stoic hero and heroine often had this power of amazing their enemies: Gisco's recoil before Massinissa may be compared). On the third occasion Syphax resorts for help to Erichtho, the Thessalian witch of the *Pharsalia*, who undertakes to exercise her magical powers in his favour. It is not quite clear from the text whether she deceives him by showing him a 'snowy image' of Sophonisba, like the image of the false Florimell in Spenser, but in any case it is Erichtho herself who benefits from Syphax's embraces. While Marston takes the details of Erichtho's appearance and habits out of Lucan, her function in the work of the Roman poet is quite different. In Lucan, Erichtho reanimates the corpse of a soldier in order that he may inform the younger Pompey of the issue of the Civil War: she is, of course, a sinister figure, no theurgist, but a practiser of 'magicke damned by all the gods above':

2. T. Spencer, 'John Marston', *Criterion*, xiii, 1933.

3. See A. R. Skemp, in *Materialien zur Kunde des älteren englischen Dramas*, xxx (Louvain, 1910), 32–39.

> And her detested secrets seeks to proove,
> Aide from the ghosts, and feinds below to crave,
> Thinking (ah wretch) the gods small knowledge have.[4]

Lucan's Erichtho is, however, in no way associated with sexual gratification. In so associating her, Marston is grafting a sixteenth-century conception of the witch on to the Roman idea because it exactly suited his moral purpose of showing the folly of trying to enforce free love. As Erichtho confesses:

> could thy weake soule imagin
> That t'is within the graspe of Heaven or Hell
> To inforce love? (v.i, Wood, p. 51)

Whether a 'cunning woman' could enforce love by the use of philtres and charms was one of the problems discussed in the rationalist George Gifford's *Dialogue concerning Witches and Witchcraft*; the harmless Mother Bombie of Lyly repudiated the idea. Not only this, but the high-raised 'sacred mind' of the Stoic has the power to vanquish the second attempt by Syphax; and Sophonisba's prayer to Phoebe and Mercury to preserve her chastity with a miracle is answered, though the miracle is assisted, it is true, by a soporific draught administered to the Negro guard.

The preoccupation with Stoicism, the discussion of 'policy' and its overthrow (a virtuous war is preferable to a politic peace is Gelosso's counsel, and much of the play is occupied with virtuous war), and the study of lust in action are three main ingredients in the tragedy; they are also the elements which help to relate the play to the rest of Marston's work as a carrying to completion of themes which he had already attempted. Mr Higgins has pointed out the dramatic inadequacy of Marston's attempt to incorporate the Stoic virtue into the revenge theme in *Antonio's Tragedy*:

4. *Lucan's Pharsalia . . . englished by Thomas May* (London, 1627), Book vi, Wood points out the parallels between May and the Erichtho passages. What more natural than that the author of *The Tragedy of Julia Agrippina* should have studied Marston's Roman play? Some differences between the verse of the Erichtho passages and the rest of *Sophonisba* might be explained by the supposition that Marston was incorporating work from a translation of Lucan which he might have had in his manuscript drawer, perhaps a postgraduate exercise: Marlowe had such an exercise. Three of the most impressively horrible lines are borrowed from Montaigne, iii.v (Everyman ed., vol. iii, p. 84)—a borrowing not mentioned by Crawford.

In Pandulpho [Marston] is content to add the moral dignity of the stoic to the popular figure of the revenger without attempting to harmonize the conflicting elements.[5]

But in *Sophonisba*, by his reversion to the Roman scene and by a more careful treatment of the figures, Marston does produce a much more convincing study in neo-Stoicism than either Pandulpho or Andrugio had been. The historical figure of Syphax is darkened and the Carthaginian leaders are made into exponents of the Machiavellian compromise in order to supply that environment of sin and moral chaos without which, as Higgins truly remarks, the Stoic figure loses its relevance. It is also in accordance with Marston's aim that neither Sophonisba nor Massinissa should display that traditional 'baroque character' and that indulgence in 'unheard-of eccentricities' to which Schücking has called attention in Marston's earlier plays.[6] In *Antonio's Revenge* Antonio's conduct when he hears Mellida's chastity impugned and Andrugio's death reported is dominated by a frantic alternation between the two passions of grief and fury, and when the standers-by urge him to 'keepe league with reason', Reason's voice is faint and immediately overwhelmed by the manifest tempest that floods Antonio's soul.[7] Not so does Massinissa behave in a similar situation. When the Massylian is told of Gelosso's death and the usurpation of his rights over Sophonisba by Syphax, Scipio expresses surprise that he makes no passionate display. He weeps for Gelosso, but—

> for the rest *silence* & secret anguish
> Shall wast: shall wast:—*Scipio* he that can weepe,
> Greeves not like me, private deepe inward drops
> Of bloud. (III.ii, Wood, p. 40)

The disasters merely encourage him in his belief that Sophonisba's chastity will be preserved and that virtuous and therefore successful war is the answer to the situation. A *sententia* confirms his resolve: 'Greefe fits weake hearts, revenging virtue men.' Similarly, Sophonisba wastes no time on frantic display in the midst of her battalioned troubles:

5. 'The Convention of the Stoic hero as handled by Marston', *MLR*, xxxix, 1944, 345.

6. L. L. Schücking, 'Baroque character of the Elizabethan tragic hero', British Academy Shakespeare Lecture, 1938.

7. *Antonio's Revenge*, I.iv–v, Wood, vol. i, pp. 80–84.

yet hath my constant toung
Let fall no weakenes, tho' my heart were wrung
With pangs worth hell: whilst great thoghts stop our tears
Sorrowe unseene, unpittied inward wears.

(III.i, Wood, p. 36)

This emphasis on the inward rather than the outward man was a
modification of neo-Stoic origin of the traditional baroque
character, a modification which occurs continually in the work
of Chapman and Greville. Indeed, evidence could be gathered
to show that it must have profoundly modified the idea of the
hero as a 'slave of passion', to use Miss Lily B. Campbell's too
well-known phrase, not only in respect of the dramatist's portrayal of the tragic hero but in regard to acting technique as
well. Gelosso in this play deliberately eschews what he calls
'a stage-like passion and weake heat'. The actor who wept
inward drops of blood or who was obliged, like Clermont
d'Ambois, to remain unmoved beneath Fortune's shrewdest
blows, could hardly behave like Antonio though he might
stiffen his sinews like Henry V. At least, in Marston, the change
from Antonio to Massinissa suggests that the dramatist has
worked out an old theme to a more austere and careful conclusion.

Similarly, the repulsive desires of Syphax relate to Marston's
previous preoccupation with the satirical treatment of the
theme of lust. In this case, it is the satire that is eliminated: there
are few traces of that ebullient lancing of the time's infirmities
which had added zest to the poetomachia plays. (A short
speech by Zanthia on women's love of ceremony, and the irony
of Massinissa's speech in praise of Carthage just before he learns
that Carthage has betrayed him, are only feeble reflections of the
satirical vigour.) Just as the Stoic virtues are more successfully
integrated into the character portrayals, so lust in action finds a
convincing embodiment in Syphax, which only the elimination
of satire made possible. The Erichtho–Syphax scenes convey
more powerfully than all the externalized *moralia* of *The Dutch
Courtesan* the darkness and vanity of lust, the 'expense of spirit
in a waste of shame' engineered by Erichtho, who is Lust personified: the moral allegory is fleshed by the conjunction between the real Syphax and Erichtho, part witch, part Lechery
from a moral play (for the method of the moral allegorist can

be the reverse of the method of the satirist, who sets up a different kind of relationship between the auditor and the object of his attack).

If we have established the kind of relationship which exists between *Sophonisba* and Marston's earlier work, from the analysis so far attempted should emerge also an answer to my second question: What kind of Roman tragedy is *Sophonisba*? It is plainly not the kind with which Garnier may have re-created the nuns of St Antony and their indulgent Abbess.[8] The characters in *Sophonisba* do not eliminate themselves from the dramatic action in order to indulge in lamentations of increasing fervour and Senecan propriety as do the characters in *Cornélie* (or in Kyd's 1594 version of that play). At the same time, we can hardly ascribe to *Sophonisba*, as Eliot did, a difference in tone from that of any other Elizabethan dramatist. If French Senecanism in its purer forms must be disallowed, some passages, especially those in which the politicians and Gelosso debate, are similar in material and tone to the plays of Greville. Marston eliminates the chorus (although there is one occasion in the play—Sophonisba's speech towards the end of Act I, when she addresses the attendant Lords—when we sense, as it were, the presence of an invisible chorus). Because of this, Marston has not the opportunity which Daniel made for himself in his *Cleopatra* and *Philotas* of expending great poetic power on choral observations on the course of the action. But he abandons the knotty prose of his comedies, which compares in excellence with the prose comedy of Shakespeare, just as he abandoned any attempt at comic relief, which he also does excellently, and is plainly thereby striving towards a sobriety and unity of tone of the kind that marks the work of Daniel and Greville. He had not permanently abjured the stylistic tricks and glibbery vocabulary which Jonson made fun of; but in *Sophonisba* he does abjure them, if only temporarily. At the same time, Marston was not concerned to produce a closet drama after the neo-Senecan model, although some approach to that model was more permissible in the case of a play for the private stage, such as *Sophonisba* was. Nor again was he attempting the kind of his-

8. Garnier's editor, Lucien Pinvert, finds 'quelque chose de pittoresque' in this incident, which involved the nuns' dressing up as men to represent the characters. See *Œuvres de Robert Garnier* (Paris, 1923), vol. i, p. xxx.

torical reconstruction which Jonson embarked upon in *Sejanus*. Marston's primary purpose remained the production of an effective stage play and there is no slackening of the familiar Marstonian interest in stage technique, as expressed in the form of elaborate and detailed stage directions; rather there is an intensification of it. Such moments as the entry of the wounded Carthalon into the bridal chamber (i.ii) or the black-suited Massinissa presenting the corpse of Sophonisba to Scipio (v.iii) remind us of the solemn and marmoreal splendours of *The Broken Heart* rather than of anything in immediately contemporary drama. That Marston should elaborate such moments throughout the play suggests a deliberate slowing-down of pace, a classical restraint in comparison to the hurry and pother of the Antonio plays, a use of the choric pause without the choric song. It suggests, in fact, that Marston, while avoiding what are from the point of view of the practical stage, the ineptitudes of the Senecan closet drama of Daniel and Greville, was nevertheless using his acquired skill as a practical dramatic craftsman to make an independent variation on their mode. In terms of literary history one cannot explain the regularity and the difference in tone by attributing to Marston a prophetic anticipation of the heroic drama of the Restoration, as does Wood:[9] to adapt a more famous remark to this occasion, *All for Love* can have had no possible influence on *Sophonisba*. Thus Marston uses the *nuntius* on three occasions because it has been shown to work; but he avoids for practical reasons the oppressively long speeches with their fully developed rhetorical stages, and devices, such as stichomythia and the chorus, cultivated by the English followers of Garnier, so that any resemblance perceived reduces itself mainly to a resemblance in tone and atmosphere. This is an admittedly vague criterion.

It can be made less vague by an examination of my third question: What is the world of the play and what is the pattern that is shaped by these tragic events? Marston has made clear for us in the 'Argumentum' which prefaces the play the outward pattern formed by the various involvements of the characters:

> A gratefull hearts just height: Ingratitude
> And vowes base breach with worthy shame persu'd.
> A womans constant love as firm as fate

9. Vol. iii, p. xiv.

A blamelesse Counsellor well borne for state
The folly to inforce free love, These know,
This subject with full light doth amply show.
(Wood, p. 6)

Our analysis has justified to a degree this antithetical view of the elements of the play—the framework of good and bad counsellors from which springs the treachery of Carthage, the sophistry of Syphax and his corrupted love, balanced against the incorruptible love of Sophonisba and the loyalty of Massinissa. From this aspect, the play has the four-square rationale of a moral construction like *Gorboduc*, and it is not therefore surprising that Marston should have found Senecan *sententiae* and the other characteristics which can be associated with the work of the English Senecans useful in conveying his subject. But if we look at the play not centrally, but in perspective, regarding it as a construction diminishing towards the point of tragedy, this kind of comparison becomes less adequate. The action which leads to the final tragedy begins not when Carthalon bursts into the bridal chamber, nor when Sophonisba in an ecstasy of Stoic abnegation permits herself to be delivered over to the power of Syphax; she survives a series of trials upon her honour and emerges from them triumphant; she meets a Libyan warrior whom she does not recognize because he has his helmet on and his gorget up; he reveals himself—it is Massinissa, and the lovers embrace. Massinissa has a not dissimilar fortune; betrayed by Carthage, he survives a series of trials by combat and emerges triumphant, his honour, and his Stoic philosophy intact. So far, indeed, the movement seems not a tragic movement at all. The rest of the fifth act can also be described in these terms. The lovers are put to a last trial in this series of trials. It is a choice between honour and love for both of them; for Sophonisba also is tempted to betray her country. It is not relevant here to adduce the clearer statement of Appian on Sophonisba's devotion to Carthage, for Marston makes no use of it, and there is no overt statement of the patriotic theme in Sophonisba's last speeches; but we know from two references in the play that Sophonisba is regarded as the Carthaginian *Palladium*, that is to say, as a sacred image on which the safety of her country mystically depends and which must not fall into the enemy's hands. She and Massinissa therefore decide that she must die. Put in this way, the final conflict looks very much like one of those love-and-honour conflicts which animate the Fletcherian mode, and which become sillier and more mechanical in the Caroline drama until, with an infusion of Gallic blood, they acquire in the Restoration the deadly vitality of formulae. From that point of view the final sacrifice of Sophonisba is a conventional trick, tacked on to the otherwise successful issue of her struggles so that the tragedy shall not 'want deaths', a surprising and ingenious twist in the plot; and the Stoic attributes are a mere garnish for a theme which shines like rotten wood.

To view the tragic action in this way is to misread the whole play. This misreading, so surprisingly frequent, omits consideration of that 'environment of sin and moral chaos' which really supplies the tragic rationale, and which is the background from which the Stoicism derives its justification. Syphax brings the sin and moral chaos to bear, and the tragic action begins in the first scene, which is why that scene is devoted to his lawless ambition and his betrayal of faith. It is Syphax and his fellows who measure by trial of lust and battle the virtue and devotion of Sophonisba and Massinissa, and it is the darkened Syphax who, by lying to the neutral Roman general, brings about the final tragedy, which is not a fortuitous trick, but the last demonstration of the fundamental dichotomy of the play world, and of the real world—the dichotomy which Marston is concerned to display and which is the justification of the Stoic theme. By this reading of the play, Sophonisba is seen not to die meaninglessly in order to make a playhouse holiday, but to move integrally towards a Senecan apotheosis. She escapes from the 'sublunary muckheap' into the region of fire:

> Thou whom like sparkling steele the strokes of Chance
> Made hard and firme; and like wild fier turnd
> The more cold fate, more bright thy vertue burnd,
> And in whole seas of miseries didst flame.
>
> (v.iii, Wood, p. 63)

If my reading of the play and the play's pattern be correct, it is probably of little use to try and decide whether Eliot was right in saying that *Sophonisba* was Marston's most interesting work, though it can be said with more confidence that the older critics misapprehended the play. It was certainly one which Marston seems to have taken seriously. The central meaning of the tragedy is not unrelated to his previous preoccupations, and it marks a stage of difference from the purely destructive ethos of *The Scourge of Villainy* in the sense that the dichotomy is finally seen to be irresolvable: there is in *Sophonisba* no adolescent disgust at the behaviour of the forked creature but instead what sounds like a final statement about the nature of man and the destiny of good men. *Sophonisba* therefore frees itself from the fundamental inconsistency of *The Malcontent* and from the morbidity of *The Dutch Courtesan* and *The Insatiate Countess.* How much further Marston could have gone is doubtful: whatever else official Christianity may have done for him, it proved hostile to the practice of poetry, and he had twenty-five years to meditate in country parishes on the deficiencies of the Stoic theme.

6

Cult and initiates in Ford's
Love's Sacrifice

Ford's tragedy *Love's Sacrifice* was probably written between 1625 and 1628; we do not know when it was first performed. It was printed in the same year as Ford's two masterpieces *'Tis Pity She's a Whore* and *The Broken Heart* (1633).[1] 'My ambition herein aimes at a faire flight', wrote the dramatist in dedicating the play to his 'truest friend', his cousin John Ford of Gray's Inn.

The central theme of the play is a triangular situation involving Phillippo Caraffa, Duke of Pavy, his Duchess, Biancha, and the young Fernando, described in the list of speakers as 'Favorite to the Duke'. The main events of the tragedy can be briefly told. Biancha was the daughter of a commoner of Milan raised to her exalted position owing to a chance meeting with Pavy (I.i.190–9).[2] When the Duke enters on the scene, he couples the name of Biancha with that of Fernando in a glowing apostrophe to his beloved and his friend, and justifies his marriage to those of his counsellors, and especially to his sister the widowed Fiormonda, who had opposed it as unfitting (I.i.211–19, 269–87). At a second meeting with Biancha, Fernando shows that he has been strongly affected by the beauty of the new Duchess; he has, in the meantime, been the unwilling recipient of the advances of Fiormonda. In the second act the favourite woos Biancha, although fully conscious of the way in which he is betraying his friend the Duke, and even unwittingly reveals his passion to the spy d'Avolos, an Iago-like figure who is in league with Fiormonda. On a second occasion (II.iii) Fernando is so

First published in *Modern Language Quarterly*, xi, 1950, 298–306.

---

1. M. Joan Sargeaunt, *John Ford* (Oxford, 1935), p. 24.
2. The text used is that of Bang in *Materialien zur Kunde des älteren englischen Dramas*, xxiii (Louvain, 1908). Act and scene references are given according to the Mermaid Edition, ed. Havelock Ellis (London, 1888), and line references according to Bang.

impressed by Biancha's horrified rejection of his suit that he undertakes never again to repeat the attempt. But the same night Biancha enters his bedchamber and offers herself to him on the strange condition that, should he take advantage of her offer, she will kill herself before morning. Together they swear, not to renounce each other, but to conduct a purely Platonic relationship (II.iv). Warned by d'Avolos of what is going on and urged also by Fiormonda, whose original hatred of Biancha because of her lowly birth is inflamed by her love for Fernando, the Duke heaps reproaches and threats upon Biancha. Next, he spies upon the Platonic lovers, who meet at night in Biancha's bedchamber after the approved fashion of such lovers. The sight is too much for the husband: he seizes upon Biancha as a 'shamelesse harlot' (v.i.2423) and finally stabs her to death. Fernando tells him in a later scene how groundless have been his jealous suspicions, and the Duke, now repentant, repairs to 'offer up the sacrifice of bleeding teares' at Biancha's tomb. Fernando emerges from the tomb in a winding-sheet and drinks off a phial of poison. Over the body of his faithful friend, and in the tomb which has now become an 'altar', the Duke concludes the action by stabbing himself, after giving directions that the three bodies should be interred together.

The theme (and on frequent occasions the style) of the main plot of the play is of the extravagant type which we associate with the Caroline courtly romances of such dramatists as Carlell, Cartwright, and Killigrew, although it antedates most of these, and never indeed attains to the high-minded dialectic and ethical complexities of the fully developed courtly drama.[3] It can be explained and criticized, like practically all Ford's extant plays except *Perkin Warbeck*, on two levels—as sensational and decadent, symptomatic of a 'moral collapse',[4] or as a problem play concerned with exploring the conflict set up between marriage and a love which falls outside marriage and changes the 'laws of conscience and of civil use', which are similarly defied by the incestuous lovers in *'Tis Pity* and by the 'strumpeted' Penthea in *The Broken Heart*.[5] More recently, in

3. The fullest account of the courtly romance is to be found in A. B. Harbage, *Cavalier Drama* (New York, 1936).
4. The phrase is Ellis's, p. xii.
5. This view is most clearly advanced by S. P. Sherman in his essay on 'Ford's contribution to the decadence of the *drama*' in *Materialien*, xxiii.xi.

The Tragic Muse of John Ford (1944), Professor Sensabaugh has produced an elaborate justification of the 'modernism' perceived by many critics in Ford's work. Sensabaugh analyses the character of the Duke as a clinical picture of jealousy drawn from Burton, who certainly did influence Ford in the presentation of many of his characters and one at least of his dramatic devices; and the conduct of the pair of lovers and indeed the whole Platonic creed by which they are affected is seen by Sensabaugh as an argument 'for unbridled individualism in matters of marriage and love'.[6] Sensabaugh also concludes from Ford's use of Burton, not only in *Love's Sacrifice* but in most of his other plays, that Ford shared Burton's 'scientific determinism' and that this is reflected in his conception of dramatic character:

What Freud seems to have done for Eugene O'Neill, Burton accomplished for John Ford; for both playwrights insist that character is determined by forces beyond human control. In this insistence upon the physical basis of character Ford removes human activity from the realm of ethical choice and, anticipating the exponents of modern thought, looks at life with amoral eyes.[7]

So far as concerns a reexamination of *Love's Sacrifice*, there would seem to be some danger of false emphases here. The relationship between Fernando and Biancha is certainly one variant of the Platonic cult. But this cult is nowhere elaborated by Ford to the degree in which it is found in the later Caroline drama. Ford's Platonism, whatever its nature, and whether or not the Platonic cult may be justifiably regarded as implying an ethic of unbridled individualism, never attains to that 'Platonism given a gallant and courtly twist' which may be found in the work of a Cartwright,[8] whose plays show a preoccupation with the metaphysic of love in its most advanced form.[9] The dialectic of a play like Suckling's *Aglaura*, where Platonic and anti-Platonic argue out the terms of the faith, the Platonic 'moral'

6. *The Tragic Muse of John Ford* (Stanford, 1944), p. 173.

7. Ibid., p. 70. Compare the summary on pp. 92–93 and the statement that Fernando 'runs to despair and confusion because of immutable physical laws'.

8. The phrase is A. H. Upham's in *The French Influence in English Literature* (New York, 1911), p. 331.

9. For example, the discussions between Atossa and Arsamnes in *The Royall Slave* and similar discussions in *The Lady Errant. Comedies, Tragi-Comedies with other Poems* (London, 1651), pp. 124 f., 25 f., 30 f., 59 f.

of Killigrew's *Prisoners*, the exquisitely disciplined acceptance of a rival in love which the courtly Platonic could and should practise[1]—all refinements of this sort are foreign to Ford's art. Ford it is true, makes use of the courtly love jargon, as Sensabaugh points out; he also makes fun of it, like the equivocal Davenant, and he does not use it for extended debates on the metaphysic of love, which are not found in his work.[2] *Love's Sacrifice* itself is too early, and Ford is not the kind of dramatist to exemplify the more recondite manifestations of the cult, which was not displayed to the outer world in all its elaborate artificiality until Montague's *Shepherd's Paradise* was acted at court in 1633.

The conduct of Fernando and Biancha is, however, worth examining in order that we may try to discover their exact relationship to the theme of Platonic love. At first, Fernando's love for the Duchess is almost violently normal and passionate. Before he meets her, her beauty is emphasized by both Petruchio and the Duke himself (and personal beauty, as the cult of the 'deformed mistress' shows, was sometimes considered disadvantageous by initiates), and it is this beauty that ensnares him:

> Oh had I *India's* gold, I'de giue it all
> T'exchange one priuate word, one minutes breath
> With this hart-wounding beauty. (I.ii.606–8)

Fernando soon becomes a prey to the carking cares of 'heroical love':

> Life without her, is but death's subtill snares
> And I am but a Coffin to my cares. (I.ii.673–4)

Biancha quickly realizes the physical direction of his passion and warns him:

---

1. The refinements mentioned and here taken as typical excesses of the fully developed cult when it is mirrored in the drama may be found in Suckling's *Aglaura*, I.v (*Works*, ed. A. Hamilton Thompson, London, 1910, p. 92), and cf. II.ii, of the same play (ibid., p. 100); Killigrew's *Prisoners*, IV.i (*Comedies and Tragedies*, London, 1664); Davenant's *Love and Honour*, IV.i (*Dramatic Works*, ed. Maidment and Logan, Edinburgh and London, 1872–4, vol. iii, p. 169).

2. Of the examples cited by Sensabaugh as debates in love jargon (*Lover's Melancholy*, III.i.1158–85; *The Fancies Chaste and Noble*, III.1170 f.; *The Lady's Trial*, II.1043–55), the first two are direct ridicule of the love jargon, while the third is merely an excessively flowery speech.

> It is the third time since your treacherous tongue
> Hath pleaded treason to my eare and fame . . .
>   if you dare
> To speake a fourth time, you shall rue your lust:
> 'Tis all no better . . . (II.ii.828–33)

But the Platonic note finds utterance in Fernando's next attempt, the exalted tone, the attitude of adoration toward the mistress-deity, the assurance that the love is chaste:

> *Biancha*. What meanes the man?
> *Fernando*. To lay before your feet
>   In lowest vassalage, the bleeding heart
>   That sighes the tender of a suit disdain'd.
>   *Great Lady* pitty me, my youth, my wounds,
>   And doe not thinke, that I haue cull'd this time
>   From motions swiftest measure, to vnclaspe
>   The booke of lust; if purity of loue
>   Haue residence in vertues quest; loe here,
>   Bent lower in my heart than on my knee,
>   I beg compassion to a loue, as chast
>   As softnesse of desire can intimate. (II.iii.1177–88)

In reply to this apostrophe, couched in language similar to that of the courtly jargon, Biancha herself shows that she has clearly misunderstood the new direction which Fernando's passion has taken in the interval between this and his previous attempt: she speaks of the 'baseness of his lust', his 'leprous mouth':

> We had much rather prostitute our blood
> To some inuenom'd Serpent, than admit
> Thy bestiall dalliance . . . (II.iii.1210–12)

One of the most puzzling features of the play is that Biancha should, after so firm a rejection of Fernando's plea, offer herself to him the same night and reveal that she has long loved him. Ford's dexterous use of the 'interval of silence' between scenes to indicate changes in the minds and hearts of his characters is here well illustrated. The dramatist intends to show that Biancha, in an interval of reflection, has realized the pure and chaste nature of the passion which Fernando has displayed in the previous scene. It is therefore safe for her to enter his chamber and even to indulge in the threat of self-destruction in her knowledge that Fernando, inspired by his new creed, will not

take advantage of her. The concluding lines of the bedchamber
scene forecast a long period of traditional Platonic dalliance:

> ... day comes on,
> What now we leaue vnfinish'd of content,
> Each houre shall perfect vp: Sweet, let's part. ... *Kisse*
>
> (II.iv.1375–7)

They exchange a Platonic kiss and swear to be faithful to one
another—'Your most faithful seruant', cries Fernando in part-
ing from her.

But Ford goes on to show that this Platonic situation, so
rapidly and perfunctorily attained, is threatened at the outset by
the weakness of Biancha, who is not the true courtly initiate
sometimes found in the later drama. The first sign is when we
see Biancha, losing control over her emotions, wipe Fernando's
lip with a handkerchief and threaten to 'steale a kisse' (III.ii.1604)
in the very presence of the Duke and the watchful d'Avolos. On
the next occasion, much later in the play, when we see Biancha
and Fernando alone together, they are in the approved attitude
of Platonic dalliance, but Biancha is on the verge of breaking away
altogether from her previous vows:

> Why shouldst thou not be mine? why should the laws
> The Iron lawes of Ceremony, barre
> Mutuall embraces? ...
>   I had rather change my life
> With any waiting-woman in the land,
> To purchase one nights rest with thee *Fernando*,
> Then be *Caraffa's* Spouse a thousand yeares.
>
> (v.i.2353–62)

The mutual kisses which they now exchange are interrupted by
the entry of the enraged Duke. In the final interview with her
husband, Biancha proudly avows the physical nature of her
passion for Fernando. The 'unbridled individualism' of Biancha
is shown not in her obedience to the Platonic love ethic but in her
disobedience to it. Physical intercourse, except in the eyes of the
numerous satirists of the fad (and one can never be quite certain
when Davenant, for example, is writing as cultist or as satirist),
is not the end towards which the Platonism of the coterie
tended: it only seemed to non-initiates that this might be its
end because so much physical dalliance could be involved in it as

well as the possibility of one woman having any number of 'servants'. To the idealists of the coterie whom we find mirrored in the later drama this misrepresentation of their creed as something which led to unbridled individualism, expressed in promiscuous love affairs was often a matter of indifference, since it was the ignorant blasphemy of laymen. Biancha's feeble attempt at the Platonic relationship breaks down at an early stage, and after that her love is eager to follow the accepted course of an adulterous passion. She may consider, like Giovanni or Penthea, that her love is superior to the marriage tie and the 'laws of conscience and of civil use', but this is consequent upon her abandonment of the 'chaste freedoms' of the Platonic cult.

Closely related to the Platonic cult, in *Love's Sacrifice* and in scores of other plays, is the romantic relationship between male friends.[3] There are, of course, many expressions of this in the drama prior to the play we are considering: Fletcher, for example, makes it a continual source of dramatic interest and conflict in *Valentinian*.[4] The friendship theme expands and revivifies in the congenial atmosphere of Platonic *préciosité*: plays like Heywood's *Challenge for Beauty* (?1635), Brome's *Love-Sick Court* (?1640), or Shirley's *Court-Secret* (1642) treat the theme with a ludicrous extravagance of expression which is nearly as foreign to Fletcher as it is to Ford. In *Love's Sacrifice* Fernando is the protégé of the Duke, and this fact at first inhibits his passion for the Duke's wife:

> she's bosomed to my friend:
> *There, there*, I am quite lost . . . (II.ii.866–7)

It is the recollection of this friendship which makes the tortures undergone by the jealous Duke so exquisitely painful (IV.i. 1928 ff.). The relationship in which he stands to the Duke may well be considered Fernando's primary motive for refraining in the crucial scene from profanation of the 'sacred temple' which is Biancha with his 'wanton appetite'. Biancha, too, assures the

3. It is not surprising that the themes of friendship and Platonic love should be frequently found in conjunction when we consider that in their origin in the *Symposium* they can be said to be identical.

4. The most extended example of the conflict is to be found in Maximus' speech in *Valentinian*, III.iii, *Plays of Beaumont and Fletcher* (ed. A. R. Waller, Cambridge, 1906, vol. iv).

Duke that it is this friendship which has acted as a restraint upon Fernando:

> I must confesse I mist no meanes, no time,
> To winne him to my bosome; but so much,
> So holily, with such Religion,
> He kept the lawes of friendship, that my sute
> Was held but, in comparison, a iest;
> Nor did I ofter vrge the violence
> Of my affection, but as oft he vrg'd
> The sacred vowes of faith 'twixt friend and friend.
>
> (v.i.2485–92)

And with almost her dying breath she pleads with her husband to 'spare thy noble friend'. If Biancha's statement is true, the Duke's slaughter of her is therefore a double injury—to her 'chastity' and to heroic friendship as well. The point is important because, if rightly emphasized, it makes the whole play less of a 'remarkable instance of confusing moral values' than it has generally been taken to be.[5] The claims of friendship, which were apparently binding on Fernando after all, taken in conjunction with the allowance that must be made for the fact that it was accepted practice for Platonic lovers to meet in situations and attitudes which to a non-initiate like d'Avolos or the jealous Duke, might suggest wantonness, imply that Biancha's chastity is not so much a technical matter as a state protected by formidable moral restraints on the part of Fernando. We are, therefore, forced to conclude that only Biancha had attempted to bring the dalliance to a physical consummation, and that Fernando had continually proved unwilling—the reverse of an 'unbridled individual'.

This point can be made clearer by a reexamination of the vital interview between the lovers before the Duke's entry in the first scene of the fifth act. The crucial lines are as follows in Bang's text:

> *Biancha* . . . I had rather change my life
> With any waiting-woman in the land,
> To purchase one nights rest with thee *Fernando*,
> Then be *Caraffa's* Spouse a thousand yeares.

5. The phrase is that of F. S. Boas in *Introduction to Stuart Drama* (London, 1946), p. 342.

Fiormonda. Treason to wedlocke, this would make you sweat.
Fernando. Lady of all, what I am, as before,
   To suruiue you, or I will see you first,
   Or widowed or buried; if the last,
   By all the comfort I can wish to tast
   By your faire eyes, that sepulcher that holds
   Your Coffin, shall encoffin me aliue:
   I signe it with this seale.——*Kisses her.*
Fiormonda. Ignoble strumpet.
Biancha. You shall not sweare, take off that oath againe,
   Or thus I will inforce it.——*Shee kisses him.*
Fernando. Vse that force,
   And make me periur'd; for whiles your lips
   Are made the booke, it is a sport to sweare,
   And glory to forsweare.
Fiormonda. Here's fast and loose;
   Which for a Ducat, now the game's on foot.
   Whiles they are kissing, Enter Duke with his sword drawne.
                             (v.i.2359–80)

The lacunae at the beginning of Fernando's first speech are unfortunate and confusing, but, if my interpretation of his character is correct, Fernando has not threatened to murder the Duke
but to wait until Biancha is a widow in the natural course of events
before he attempts to consummate his love. Should she die
before the Duke, he swears to die with her, and seals the oath
with a chaste and Platonic kiss, like that given and bestowed in
ii.iv.1378, whereat the spying Fiormonda, misunderstanding as
usual, thinks the kiss a lascivious one. Biancha, urging, as she
puts it later, the 'violence of her affection', cries to him to for-
swear his oath (that is, the oath that he will maintain a purely
Platonic relationship with her until, if ever, she is free to marry
him) and returns his kiss, but not after the manner of Platonic
dalliance. Fernando's response is equivocal, but does not really
imply any departure from the stand he is taking. He is in a
position somewhat similar to that of the unfortunate Paris, in
Massinger's *Roman Actor*, who almost yields to the kisses of the
wanton Empress just after he has declared his absolute unwill-
ingness to betray his master's faith: the Emperor breaks in
upon them at the same moment that the Duke breaks in upon
Fernando and Biancha.[6]

6. *Roman Actor*, iv.ii.

It seems, then, that Biancha only is the would-be adulteress. We are now in a position to examine the final crisis of the play, the deaths of the three main protagonists. Why is Biancha a voluntary sacrifice? She dies willingly because, since she cannot satisfy her passion for Fernando, further life is without meaning. She is thus a true example of 'unbridled individualism', running on death as a release from her vain suffering. Her own attempts at Platonic restraint and her later attempts to overcome the similar restraints on the part of Fernando have both failed. Fernando's appearance in his winding sheet and his death within her tomb are an exact fulfilment of his oath to be encoffined alive in Biancha's sepulchre. Two lines in his last speech, crowded though it is with reproaches to the Duke, his false friend, show quite clearly what has been his guiding principle:

> Had eager Lust intrunk'd my conquered soule,
> I had not buried liuing ioyes in death.
>
> (v.iii.2773–4)

That is, to expand and paraphrase, 'If lust had really overcome my soul, and destroyed the purely Platonic nature of my love for Biancha as intercourse between two souls, I would not have died; but my death proves that it was not carnal enjoyment ['liuing ioyes'] that I sought but intercourse between souls.' The implication is that Fernando's soul will now rejoice to find Biancha's in another sphere ('I come Biancha', are his dying words). The slowness of his death by poison is perhaps insisted upon by the dramatist because it emphasizes the destruction of the corporeal integument, the body that, in Chapman's words, is 'but a thick cloud to our souls', and the consequent release of the pure soul. Fernando, then, emerges as a Platonist of a sort, although he is at no time the polished dialectician found in the plays of Cartwright or Davenant. As for the Duke, in his last speech he recollects too late the virtues of friendship which he now sees had animated Fernando, and ends his life as friendship's sacrifice as well as love's.

There are three kinds of sacrifice in the play: Biancha meets the end appropriate to the adulteress in intention, if not in act, in that she is punished by her husband; the Duke, who is no Platonic initiate, punishes his own faithlessness to his friend and the supposed wrongs done to his wife and goes to his grave without understanding either the wantonness of Biancha or the purity of Fernando, which are set forth against a background of the Platonic cult; while the true love's sacrifice dies as an idealistic practitioner of the closely related ethics of friendship and Platonic love, not as an individual running to 'despair and confusion because of immutable physical laws'. The play therefore preserves in the separate fates of the main protagonists a consistent ethical scheme, although it is not one which is either so complete or so complex as many found in the true courtly drama of the metaphysic of love. It is significant that, at the end of the play, the bridegroom Roseilli announces to his bride Fiormonda, whose misunderstanding of the Platonic code has been a principal cause of the tragedy, his intention to 'dismisse / The mutuall comforts of our marriage-bed'. And Fiormonda sadly replies:

> . . . since lust hath made me foule,
> Henceforth I'le dresse my *Bride-bed* in my soule.
>   (v.iii.2885–6)

7

Fulke Greville's dramatic characters

Their conscience fir'd, who doe from God rebell,
Hell first is plac'd in them, then they in Hell.
SIR WILLIAM ALEXANDER, *Doomes-Day*: the first Houre

I

The work of the Elizabethan French Senecans is 'coterie literature', and Fulke Greville may well be a bat flying in the twilight
between *The Spanish Tragedy* and *Hamlet*. But coterie literature
may explore very thoroughly the minutiae of human conflict,
while its closely woven texture sometimes demands painfully
precise analysis. Since Professor Croll remarked, 'There is
probably no play in the language in which it is harder to understand continuously what happens than *Alaham*',[1] it cannot be
said that either *Alaham* or *Mustapha* have been subjected to the
continuous understanding that they deserve. A recent judgement that Greville's plays are 'really rhymed political treatises'[2]
may take its origin from Greville's own remark in the *Life of
Sidney* that his purpose in his tragedies was to 'trace out the
high waies of ambitious Governors, and to shew in the practice
that the more audacity, advantage, and good successe such
Soveraignties have, the more they hasten to their owne desola-
tion and ruine'.[3] But Greville has done himself an injustice if
this well-known passage has led some critics to take too simple a
view of his dramatic methods—although Greville did go on to
declare that the arguments of his tragedies were not 'naked, and

First published in *Review of English Studies*, NS, i, 1950, 308–23.

1. M. W. Croll, *The Works of Fulke Greville* (Philadelphia, 1903), p. 40.
2. Laurence Michel, *The Tragedy of Philotas* (New Haven, 1949), p. 10.
3. *The Works of Fulke Greville* (ed. Grosart, printed for private circulation, np, 1870), vol. iv, p. 220.

casuall' but 'nearer / Level'd to . . . humours, councels, and practices'. The subtlety and skill with which Greville levels to humours require, to be fully valued, a closer examination of the plays' textures than can be given here. For his own action in separating his overgrown choruses from the plays for which they were originally intended shows that he was aware of the differences between a play and a rhymed political treatise. Although Greville rejected the 'strangeness or perplexedness of witty Fictions', he did not reject προαίρεσις. His business is to explore the 'unbound, raging, infinite Thought-fire'[4] of his *personae*. He is preeminently the dramatist of the 'inward man' and the correlator of the 'inward discord' with the 'outward wayes'.

The emphasis on the inward man was a modification of what Schücking has named the 'baroque character' of the Elizabethan tragic hero. It is the difference between Marston's Antonio and Kyd's Hieronimo on the one hand, unpacking their hearts with words and frantic gesture, and Chapman's Senecal man on the other. Marston's own Gelosso in *Sophonisba*, who eschews what he calls 'a stage-like passion and weake heat', and the conduct of the other characters in the same play, illustrate in the work of a single dramatist the contemporary change in method from the baroque to the Senecal.[5] In Chapman and Marston one of the agents that helps to effect the change is neo-Stoicism: both evil and good have become inward matters—'our euill is not extrinse-call, it is within vs, and is setled in our intrailes'[6] and (in Lodge's significant mistranslation of Seneca's 'Bonus vero sine deo nemo est') 'There is no good man but hath a God within him'. It is not surprising that the neo-Stoic man weeps, like Marston's Massinissa, 'private deep inward drops of blood' in silence and secret anguish.[7] It is part of Chapman's purpose in some of his tragedies to describe what happens when man, so conceived,

---

4. *Alaham*, v.iv.26. All references to Greville's plays are to *Poems and Dramas of Fulke Greville, First Lord Brooke* (ed. Geoffrey Bullough, Edinburgh and London, 1939), vol. ii.

5. See Chapter 5.

6. Seneca, *Workes* . . . (trans. T. Lodge, London, 1614), p. 242. 'Non est extrinsecus malum nostrum: intra nos est, in visceribus ipsis sedet', Seneca, *Epistolae Morales*, 50.4.

7. *Sophonisba*, III.ii (*Plays of John Marston*, ed. H. Harvey Wood, Edinburgh and London, 1938, vol. ii, p. 40).

comes into contact with the outward world and corrupt society. This is the theme of *The Revenge of Bussy d'Ambois*; it is Byron's tragedy, too, that he has made the error of 'building himself outward', and has trusted his blood in others' veins.[8] As presented by Chapman, Pompey's story in his *Caesar and Pompey* is also that of a man who forsakes his own 'God-inspir'd insight' and disregards Cato's warning that greatness which is not the product of an inward order is doomed to fall, but who later recovers his neo-Stoic balance with the resolution that he will 'build all inward'.[9] The philosophy of Chapman's poems frequently exploits the contrast between the inward order and the outward ways.[1]

Chapman's awareness of the inward man is analogous to Fulke Greville's; but where Chapman tends to grasp the harsh dichotomy in its simpler forms, Greville is more alive to the disconcerting antinomies that arise from it. Chapman's attitude is inspired by his neo-Stoicism. Croll writes:

The kind of truth that the Stoics chiefly had in mind was moral and inward. It was a reality not visible to the eye, but veiled from common observation; hidden in a shrine toward which one might win his way, through a jostling, noisy mob of illusory appearances . . . It is . . . possible to depict the effort of the athletic and disciplined mind in its progress toward the unattainable goal. And this effort of the mind was the characteristic theme of the Stoics, and the object of their rhetorical art.[2]

Greville, too, turns inward in a way that is characteristic of the contemporary mood, and serves to show his affinities with Chapman. But while the inspiration of neo-Stoicism is central to Chapman, Greville tends, at least in the works in which he overtly speculates on the nature of man, towards a repudiation of the theory of human nature which lay at the basis of Chapman's ethic. Chapman's *Eugenia*, which is almost a treatise on the life of

8. *The Conspiracy of Byron*, I.ii.140.   9. *Caesar and Pompey*, v.i.203.

1. See, for example, in *The Poems of George Chapman* (ed. Bartlett, New York, 1941); 'To the High Borne Prince of Men Henrie . . .', ll. 4–5; 'To . . . Robert, Earle of Somerset', first prose passage, 1–9; *Euthymiae Raptus*, ll. 8–14, 36–37; *Eugenia*, ll. 638–43, 810–11; 'A Hymne to our Saviour', ll. 41–43, 265–7; 'To the Viscount . . . Rochester', ll. 2–4; 'To yong imaginaries in knowledge', ll. 5–9; 'To live with little', ll. 47–48; 'Virgils Epigram of a good man', ll. 9–10; 'A great man', ll. 38–46.

2. M. W. Croll, '"Attic Prose" in the seventeenth century', *Studies in Philology*, xviii, 1921, 112–13.

sound religion in the guise of an epicede on the death of Lord Russell, exhibits a temper different from that of Greville's 'Treatise of Religion'.[3] Although Greville's description of the true religious life (stanzas 64–67) resembles Chapman's (ll. 471–84), Greville's writing is filled with precise theological implications (and terminology) that are quite foreign to Chapman's; and while Chapman emphasizes the correspondence between God and man's soul (ll. 423–30) and the 'Analogia Mundi & Corporis Principum partium' (ll. 721–45), Greville declares that any hope, such as is implied in Chapman's lines, that man might 'in flesh and blood / Grow happily adorers of the Good' is checked by 'natural corruption' (stanzas 12–13). In phrases which he borrowed from Plutarch's *Moralia*,[4] Chapman celebrates the *stabilis animi sedes* (ll. 678 ff.). It is this very doctrine of εὐθυμία that Greville chooses to attack, the 'heathen vertue', as he names it,

> Where sublime Religion seems to refine
> Affection, perturbation, every thought
> Unto a *Mens Adepta*.

The powerful stanzas that follow set out Greville's case against the ethic of neo-Stoicism and use the characteristic antithesis:

> For in this work, man still rests slave to Fame,
> To inward caution, outward form and pride,
> With curious watch to guard a rotten frame
> Safe undiscover'd from the piercing ey'd,
>   Assidious Caution tyrannizing there,
>   To make frail thoughts seem other then they are.
>
> Under this mask, besides, no vice is dead,
> But Passion with her counter-passion peaz'd;
> The evil with it self both starv'd and fed,
> And in her woes with her vain glories eas'd;
>   The work and tools alike, vain flesh and blood,
>   The labour great, the harvest never good.[5]

Greville and Alexander were perhaps the only French Senecans

3. References are to the texts in Bartlett, and in *The Works of Fulke Greville* (ed. Grosart), vol. i.

4. See F. L. Schoell, *Études sur l'humanisme continental* (Paris, 1926), p. 241.

5. Grosart, vol. i, p. 251.

so conscious of the rubble in the Stoic bastion; the awareness accounts for the difference in Greville's plays of his treatment of the 'unbound, raging, infinite Thought-fire' from that
of Chapman or Daniel. For Calvinism was much more than a
variant on Stoicism, although the *De Clementia* may have shown
Calvin the way. Calvin could restate the Lutheran *imperium
spirituale*, the 'striving for inward freedom and independence of
the world' which has been claimed as characteristic of Christianity in all ages,[6] in terms which made for a *rapprochement* of the
Christian to the Stoic ethic; for the Stoics, too, had declared that
virtue was a state of mind in their attempt to supersede an
antique system of taboo,[7] just as the Lutherans attempted
to replace χαρίσματα and 'outward holiness'[8] with 'outward
decency . . . [and] . . . inward spiritual righteousness'.[9] But the
Institutio stresses other aspects of the system which make any
easy synthesis that may—by the author of *Eugenia* or by others—
be effected between Reformation thought and Stoic ethics not
applicable to Calvin's share in the rediscovery of the inward
man. It is these aspects that compel Greville's poetic imagination, throughout 'Of Religion' and the later *Caelica* sonnets
especially. If redressing the balance of Aquinas with Augustine
meant to some Reformation neo-Stoics discovery of the God
within, *deum in corpore humano hospitantem* of Marcus Aurelius
and Epictetus, it was another God whom Calvin found dwelling
within us on the evidence of the continual working of his power.[1]
Calvin and Montaigne might both help to diffuse the psychological method,[2] but while Montaigne emphasizes that 'study
of his own inner strength and weakness' through which man
can learn to discover himself,[3] for Calvin the rediscovery of the
'labyrinthine' inward man is itself the immediate source of that
'variety of fictions', the 'immense crowd of [false] gods [that]

---

6. Heinrich Boehmer, *Luther* (London, 1930), p. 277.

7. E. V. Arnold, *Roman Stoicism* (Cambridge, 1911), p. 287. Cf. R. D. Hicks, *Stoic
and Epicurean* (London, 1910), p. 92. 'The deepest thought of Stoic ethics is that
virtuous or vicious life is not to be regarded as a sum of isolated virtuous or vicious
actions, but as an inward unity governed by a single principle.'

8. The phrase is Boehmer's, p. 284.

9. Calvin, *Institutes of the Christian Religion* (trans. Henry Beveridge, Edinburgh,
1845), vol. i, p. 434.

1. Ibid., p. 75.

2. P. Villey, *Les Sources et l'évolution des Essais de Montaigne* (Paris, 1933), vol. i, p. 9.

3. Douglas Bush, *The Renaissance and English Humanism* (New York, 1939), p. 93.

have issued from the human mind'.[4] Realization of how excellent is the human person, 'a magazine stored with treasures of inestimable value' (which is not, however, the same phrase as 'a God within'), concludes in sinful pride,[5] whenever human pollution is not measured against the refulgence of God.[6] In Greville and Calvin another kind of false religion is born of superstitious fear (which must be distinguished from voluntary reverence), issue of that inward weakness which cannot bear the contemplation of the divine majesty:

> when Fear's dim eyes look in,
> They guilt discern; when upwards, Justice there
> Reflects self-horror back upon the sin . . .

For fear

> Fashions God unto man, not man to God:
> And to that deity, gives all without
> Of which within it lives and dies in doubt.[7]

Fear and self-horror are consistently revealed in Greville's explorations of the inward man in *Mustapha* and *Alaham*; Chapman's confidence that 'As we are men, we death and hell controule' is in Greville negatived by an awareness that 'flesh and blood' may itself become 'hell'.[8] In *Caelica* and in the treatises on Fame and Learning this awareness gives the lie to the whole Stoic–Christian *rapprochement*, trailing after it a scepticism which in the dramas, since they are set in no Christian milieu, directs itself not towards fideism, but towards an

---

4. Calvin, vol. i, p. 77. Cf. Greville, 'Of Religion', stanzas 16 ff. Greville here differs from Duplessis-Mornay (*Trewenes of the Christian Religion*, chap. iii) who calls upon antiquity to testify that, notwithstanding appearances, men have always been monotheists at heart (*Complete Works of Sir P. Sidney*, ed. Feuillerat, Cambridge, 1923, vol. iii, pp. 292–311). Greville's religious temper seems generally different from that of Duplessis-Mornay: one suspects that the tendency to associate Greville with the Huguenot humanist is a matter of biography rather than of much intellectual kinship.

5. Calvin, vol. i, p. 68.   6. Ibid., p. 49.

7. 'Of Religion', stanzas 22–23. Cf. Calvin, vol. i, pp. 59–63. For other reactions by Greville against classical humanism see 'An inquisition upon fame and honour' (stanza 23: 'Within our selues, they seat Felicities') and also the passages cited by Professor Ellis-Fermor in her chapter on Greville in *Jacobean Drama* (London, 1936).

8. Compare Chapman, 'A Hymne to Christ', l. 200, and the Epictetan confidence of Clermont d'Ambois (*Revenge of Bussy d'Ambois*, iii.iv.66 ff.) with Greville, *Caelica*, cii (Bullough, vol. i, p. 146).

investigation, at once savage and melancholy, into the 'diverse world', seen as 'a stage for blood-enammeld showes'.[9]

Greville in his plays, therefore, shares the contemporary tendency to look inward, but the entrails of his beings, when they are examined only in the strong light of his own faith, contain not a God but corruption, and are 'the ugly center of infernall spirits'.[1] Such examination is not always vouchsafed to them. For Greville the dramatist is too steeped in the affinities of his French Senecan form to the Senecal philosophy to be able to present a dramatic picture darkened by Calvinism to the degree that Chapman's is illuminated by Stoicism. We are conscious of a willingness to conform to certain dramatic methods which is irreconcilable with the rigorism displayed in 'Of Religion'. To these dramatic methods the looking inward and the correspondence between inward state and outward action are important. This fact suggests that current emphasis on the 'monarchall' aspects of his tragedies has sacrified, for the sake of what is typical and documentary in his plays, that which is personal and valuable in them as a contribution to literature.[2]

II

Greville's dramaturgical exploitation of the rediscovery of the inward man may be stated as follows: his plays, and especially *Alaham*, contain together, and in unresolved conflict, both the

9. *Alaham*, cho. 3.82.

1. *Caelica*, xcix. It is in *Caelica*, lxxxvi, c, ci, cii, cvi that we are most conscious of Greville's case against the heathen virtue in his handling of the inward-outward antithesis. A pleasant kind of Stoicism, but hardly one felt in the blood, is observable in parts of the monarchy treatise and in the rather worldly treatment of the antithesis in 'A Letter to an Honourable Lady' (*Certain Learned and Elegant Workes*, London, 1633): 'My counsell is therefore Madame! that you enrich yourselfe upon your owne stocke, not looking outwardly, but inwardly for the fruit of *true Peace*, whose rootes are there' (p. 273, *et passim*). The tone of parts of the 'Letter' is that of Daniel's 'Epistle to the Countesse of Bedford', and even involves praise of the *mens adepta*. For a 'normal' Stoic–Christian handling of the antithesis see also Joseph Hall, *Heaven upon Earth* (ed. Rudolf Kirk, New Brunswick, 1948), sect. iii (a definition of Christian εὐθυμία), with an interesting introduction on Hall's Christian neo-Stoicism.

2. In any case, Greville's political views (which are unexciting) are best seen in the monarchy treatise, and have been set out by M. Kuppfer, *Fulke Greville's Poems of Monarchy als Spiegel seiner politischen Ansichten* (Riga, 1929). Miss Kuppfer gives no explanation of Greville's obsession with the 'weak tyrant', as distinct from the danger of monarchy degenerating into tyranny—a commonplace of the *Politics* sharpened by Machiavellian *Angst*—and it does not seem to be reflected in writers like LeRoy, Hurault, or Grimaldus.

neo-Stoic and the Calvinist idea of man's inward nature and its relationship to the outward world and God. Neo-Stoic and Calvinist views, when put in conjunction, may be represented thus: inward, the neo-Stoic finds *nihil aliud quam deum hospitantem*, potential εὐθυμία (Chapman's 'inward peace'); the Calvinist finds corruption, the hell of flesh and blood, the 'ugly center' (Greville's 'inward discord', Calvin's shadow-producing 'labyrinth'). This corruption is qualified—and the qualification is responsible for blurring the distinction between the two systems—by man's own awareness of an apparent excellence (when that is not compared to God's) and by the natural conviction of God's existence which man finds on examining his heart.[3] Outward, the neo-Stoic sees the corrupt, fortune-dominated world (Chapman's 'gaudy light', Greville's, Chapman's, and Daniel's 'Opinion');[4] for the Calvinist, too, the world is corrupt, but the aetiology of this corruption is not Stoic, for the world contains the false outward Church and the other shadows which man's inward corruption spins out of itself:

> A play of Sunne-motes, from mans small World come,
> Vpon the great World to worke heauy doome.
> *(Mustapha, cho. 2.175–6)*

The Stoic τύχη is superseded by the idea of the Fall.

This is a diagrammatic statement of the antitheses, and consequently an oversimplified one. But it is the business of literature, and especially of drama, to be more complex than the most complicated diagrams. Greville's plays are built up from interactions between neo-Stoicism and Calvinism as complex as are the affinities of Calvin with Seneca and of the Reformation with the Renaissance of classicism. 'A Treatie of Humane Learning' and 'A Treatie of Warres' are created with the resultant paradoxes as their sustaining basis, so that it is always hard to say, in examining Greville's writings, where Calvinism retreats or compromises before a neo-Stoicism that is often itself but a mirror

---

3. Duplessis-Mornay makes much of this conviction in his first chapter, pp. 263 ff.

4. The frequent use of this word with a special pejorative meaning in these writers derives from the Stoic belief that 'opinion' (δόξα or, in Epictetus, *Discourses*, II.ix.14, ὑπόληψις) is 'unworthy of the sage' (Hicks, p. 69). Cf. also the signification of the word as used by Jonson in *Hymenaei* and *Discoveries*, *Ben Jonson*, vol. viii, p. 564; by Charron, *De la Sagesse* (Paris, 1836), p. 80; by Guilpin, *Skialetheia*, satire VI; by Selden, *Table-Talk*, XCVI; by Cornwallis, *Essayes* ('Of Opinion'); by Drayton, *The Owle*, *Works* (ed. Hebel, Oxford, 1932), vol. ii, p. 492.

image of the *Institutio*. In the plays, Greville's creation of character and situation is affected by this ambivalence, although, since his scenes are Turkish, the elimination of specifically Reformation ideas is compensated for by a tendency to weight the scales in favour of the view that fallen man (and Mohammedan man at that) can hardly escape from his ugly centre. By stressing the antinomies Greville compels his characters to live to themselves and to one another. Three kinds of approach to the plays may lend support to this view—a demonstration of how vital to the life of the characters is their consciousness of their inward potentialities and discords, some examples of the way the antitheses are made vivid in passages of dialogue (which may also show that such interchanges have vitality, although not of a kind acceptable on the stage), and an evaluation of Greville's treatment of the supernatural world. For Greville's interpretation of the powers of the supernatural is relevant to the distorted beings whom he portrays.

It is convenient to discuss *Alaham* first, although it may be substantially the later play,[5] because in it Greville's idiosyncratic method is more identifiable. In *Alaham* it is not the outward action[6] which is of interest but the self-analyses of the characters and the manoeuvring of Alaham and Hala in relation to each other's corrupted ambition. Greville's method is to inform their colloquies, which seem largely composed of lofty *sententiae*, with all the skill and passion resident in Alaham's and Hala's inward natures.

These are unfolded chiefly in soliloquies or in interchanges with persons indifferent to the main conflict. A continual tortured life goes on beneath the surface; 'all things are corrupt with doublenesse' (Prologus, 149). When the play opens, Alaham is in

5. Bullough, pp. 57–58.
6. The action of *Alaham* falls into two divisions which may be entitled: (1) A palace intrigue: I.i–III.iii. The ambitious Alaham succeeds in disposing of two Pashas, Mahomet and Caine, who stand between him and the throne occupied by his weak father. But Caine had been the lover of Alaham's wife Hala, a fact of which Alaham was aware, and Hala herself, who hoped to advance to power with Caine at her side, his deadliest rival; (2) Hala's revenge: III.iv–end. Alaham seizes the throne and destroys the King, his daughter Caelica, and his eldest son Zophi, a half-wit. But Hala's revenge has kept pace with Alaham's ambition: this woman has two children, one Alaham's and one Caine's. Alaham, dying of a poisoned robe, Hala's gift, is forced to witness the slaughter of his son; but when Alaham is dead, Hala finds she has killed the wrong child.

despair because his plans have so far failed; but rather than 'watch for change of times or Gods revenge' (i.i.179) he resolves to strike all into hazard, since his 'State' is not bound to what Ford calls 'the laws of conscience and of civil use' but rests in his own well-being (214). Thus far we have been peering into the mind of an ambitious favourite. Alaham now switches to the outward policy with which 'ambition of revenge' (187) has inspired him by changing his tone from one of brooding introspection to a series of hypocritically uttered slogans: we must read i.i.221–6 and i.i.233–51 as private rehearsals of public 'policy'. But policy is on two levels, the slogans in which it is dressed, and the real intention behind it. It is this real intention, displayed in one aspect—the future conduct of the state church —that animates the instructions which Alaham now gives to the priest (258–84). Lastly (315–25), Alaham invokes the Evil Spirits to work the ruin and change which he desires. Throughout the scene Alaham's conduct is delineated on four levels, which succeed one another: internal confusion and introspection, a display of outward hypocrisy, a controlled interpretation of the purpose of the hypocrisy, and an invocation to demons. The change from confusion to resolution is suddenly worked by 'visions' (185): it is one of those irruptions of supernatural evil which bring the action of the play throughout into contact with the Evil Spirits of the Chorus and the prologuizing Ghost. Alaham's 'character' is thus a complex four-dimensional world, ranging from 'inwardness' to supernatural visitings.

Hala's character has the same proportions. She, too, labours with an inward war, a struggle between her hatred for Alaham and her love for Caine (ii.i.2 *et passim*); her motives include lust as well as ambition and express themselves in an outward policy which is urged upon her by Alaham—and which she hypocritically embraces (ii.ii, iii)—but her real intention is the destruction of Alaham and the exaltation of Caine. Later, after Caine has perished, the inward war is between her hatred of Alaham and her love for her children (iii.iv.23 ff.); her outward policy is acceptance of Alaham's *fait accompli*, but her real intention is revenge, to which her whole being becomes narrowed down, thus superseding the inner conflict (iii.iv). She appeals to the supernatural spirits, including Caine's ghost (iii.iv.97–104; cf. v.iii.130–6).

Since none of the other characters in the play is the mainspring of the action, but merely instrument, confidant, or victim, they are less complex. In them the level of outward action is precluded. We observe only their inward struggles, which are not, generally, struggles to perform any outward deed but to master the 'images of self-confusednesse' with which their human nature charges them. Thus the old King's misfortune is simply that he cannot do anything: he is 'one that hath lost / Himselfe within; and so the world without' (v.ii.54–55);[7] by his confusion all laws have lost authority (iv.i.113). Act iv, scene i shows the continual inward movement by which he hopes to escape from the exercise of his legitimate authority and from life itself. Zophi the half-wit is in a similar condition (iv.ii.20). Mahomet, unlike these victims, has achieved an inward control which allows him to consult his own heart before taking action (i.ii.184); while he, too, is racked with an intestine war (ii.iv.63–66), he has a special power of insight which enables him to see into the hearts of Alaham (i.ii.102–10) and Caine (ii.iv.120 ff.).[8] Caine himself shifts from the absorption of his whole being in his love for Hala, so that 'It is not I that liue in me, but you' (ii.iii.100), to the 'inward discords' of remorse (ii.iv.99–104) and back again through an inability to sustain the mood of repentance (ii.iv.158–72). Caelica alone is exempted from these wearisome conditions.[9]

Greville's confrontation of Hala and Alaham has, beneath its sombre trapping of *sententiae*, an unexpected subtlety, not least because the *sententiae* themselves are dragooned into working their passage. The difficulty of applying a continuous understanding to ii.ii, for example, may well be due to the unlooked-for convolutions of its texture.[1] Alaham, in the first lines of the scene, uses his state of inner confusion for dialectic's sake: his cry that Chance must be his guide, since his heart has run away from itself (ii.ii.8–9), shifts, in response to Hala's hypocritical offer of advice in the form of three *sententiae* (10–14), to the observation

7. The dying Alaham's condition is the same (v.iii.54–55).
8. That Greville let this promising character disappear after ii.iv shows his determination to rig the balance in favour of the infernal spirits.
9. We need not accept the Ghost's gloss upon her conduct (Prologus, 119–25), but her unanswered prayer (iv.ii.66–73) and her death by torture make her, like another Servetus and like Mahomet, a sacrifice to rigorism.
1. Unlooked for, because the plays of Garnier, Daniel, Brandon, or Alexander are innocent of such sophistication. Since I am here concerned to trace only the dominant antithesis, I do not carry my commentary beyond a few scenes.

that advice offered from without is likely to be of less use than reliance purely upon a man's inner counsel. Hala's reply—

> Who trusts his passion multiplies his care;
> *All paines within, all cures without vs are*

shows that the two enemies are manoeuvring within the limits of the characteristic antithesis (Inward, corruption or εὐθυμία; Outward, the help of others or of God, or 'Opinion', the 'casting of one's blood in others' veins'.) In reply, Alaham warns Hala that if she herself is 'captiued' by inner passions, then, by taking her advice, he will merely be exchanging his confusion for hers (19–20). This is indeed true, and we, as witnesses of Hala's re-solution to deceive in the preceding scene, know it; but Hala assures Alaham that her whole state of mind is directed towards subserving his ends, and that her 'selfe-loue', the *quidditas* of her being, 'payes tribute' to his will (21–23). By changing the meaning of 'love' in his reply Alaham pierces through the mask of hypocrisy:

> If loue haue power to leaue, and breake her vow;
> How can I trust to that you promise now?
> If loue change not; how can I trust, and know,
> That you loue *Mahomet*, my ouerthrow?

This sudden thrust, an index of Greville's skill in using *sententiae* for toppling down as well as building up, leads to a further stage in the dialectic. To Hala's plea that Alaham had not forbidden free and 'indifferent' association with Mahomet, Alaham re-plies with a *sententia* to the effect that forbidding merely pre-vents a thought from manifesting itself in outward action and does not destroy it; further, forbidding is that which must be imposed by 'violence' on those who have no inward powers of inhibition (a hint here that such is Hala's case—Alaham sees into her heart). He adds a lie—that Mahomet had traduced her character, proclaiming 'deceipt to be thy state of mind'. To this Hala answers lightly that in that case she may 'freely hate all men, but thee' (28–45). She is far from meaning this, for we know that Hala really loves Caine, hates Alaham himself, and is in-different to Mahomet except as he blocks her way to power. But Alaham exploits the remark: Hate, he declares (46–47), is merely resident *in* the heart, nothing if not bodied forth in the outward form of revenge. He relentlessly leads Hala to agree that she must be revenged on Mahomet; he urges on her that she cannot execute the act of revenge herself but must entrust it to Caine. This is the very impasse that Hala wishes to avoid, for she fears that Caine, as executant of the revenge, may be trapped by Alaham; she is therefore forced to make an unequivocal declaration of her intention to kill Mahomet (74–76). This declaration convinces Alaham himself that Hala is really his ally. (He has overreached himself—for, although he has himself forced Hala to make the promise—which she does only to save Caine from a suspected trap—he none the less becomes convinced of Hala's love. This trust in Hala brings about his death.) In his moment of triumph he invokes, in an aside (77–82), the abstracts of evil to prosper the work now set on foot. In the succeeding lines (which must all be given to Alaham)[2] he promises Hala future glory, while she listens in an attitude of silent hatred or hypocritical gratification (83–104).[3] None the less he will send Caine to her. Hala's inward war in the final soliloquy enables her to reach a decision; it is a decision conforming to her literary ancestry—she ends the scene as a Medea.[4]

It is a text which, in Hoskins's phrase, has as many hands as a Briareus: 'It is very true that a sentence is a pearl in a discourse; but is it a good discourse that is all pearl? It is like an eye in the body; but is it not monstrous to be all eyes?'[5] The criticism may be modified, in Greville's case, if we recollect how the *sententiae* in this and other scenes are made to subserve the movement of minds, the duckings and twists of the corrupt hearts.[6]

With this sample of Greville's method in *Alaham* before us, *Mustapha* must be treated more briefly. In *Mustapha*, the alignment of man seen through neo-Stoic eyes with man seen through Calvinist eyes is clear. 'Inwardness', too, is everywhere to be perceived: man may be a bee sucking honey or a spider drawing poison from the selfsame flower—which, depends on

2. In Bullough's printing of l. 83 'Hala.' (as speech prefix) is a misprint for 'Hala!'
3. The line 'Ruine, the *power* (not *art*) of Princes is' (72) is a good example of Greville's aculeate style and his habit of squeezing the meanings of words.
4. Bullough, l. 135, misprints 'Oh' (for 'Of').
5. J. Hoskins, *Directions for Speech and Style* (ed. Hudson, Princeton, 1935), p. 39.
6. With II. ii can be compared III.iii.39–96, where Hala accepts the outward situation (Alaham is seated on the throne by III.ii.1) and uses *sententiae* as slogans to conceal her inmost mind. The scene proceeds on the level of outward action and only one glimpse of the involutions (Hala's aside, 32–37) is given.

his heart (II.ii.160–1). Solyman experiences an inward war on a more extended scale than that of any of the characters in *Alaham*: it is waged between his duty of preserving his power as degenerate king and his love for his son Mustapha:

> Two States I beare; his Father, and his King;
> These two, being Relatiues, haue mutuall bonds;
> Neglect in either, all in question brings (II.ii.15–17)

Fear for his power and his Love for his son are the fighting abstracts which the *sententiae* overlay. (These are also the motives which the charitable Camena (II.iii.135–52) sees influencing Rossa.) But Solyman is also blinded and 'captiued' by his love for Rossa, and has delivered over the kingdom of his mind to her (I.i.73); as he is man, his humours are delicately balanced (I.ii.18, and cf. Chorus Primus 1–22), but as he is King and the axis of the State they are even more sensitive and intricate (I.ii.21–35, and cf. Chorus Quartus, 85–110). He cannot reconcile his powers and passions as King, man, and father (II.ii. 82–83). Solyman is finally being trapped, as Achmat explains, because he cannot perceive that his belief in his son's imaginary treason has been purposely made dependent upon, and the direct issue of, his love for Rossa (II.ii.136–7). By murdering his son, he will really be murdering himself—all such unnatural acts are the product of Fear (II.ii.147–8). The causes of Solyman's ruin are as complex as the relationship of his various inner debilities to the strong forces pressing from outside. Rossa's task would have been easier if he had been, like Rossa herself, a creature of extremes, willing to 'plant confusion in the powers above' by forsaking the laws of nature. Solyman's whole difficulty is in moulding the inward motions of his mind into an outward policy which will be congruent with kingship, manhood, and fatherhood. Like Alaham, he experiences supernatural visitings (IV.i).

Rossa is already a 'Monster growne within', and her outward actions are, unlike Solyman's, entirely congruent with her inward wickedness ('My selfe! What is it but my desire?' III.ii.24). After she has twice tried and twice failed to persuade Solyman to execute Mustapha, she realizes that she is building her hopes on the quicksand (III.i.54; cf. I.ii.84–86) of the King's temperament. In an important scene (III.i), she rejects Rosten's advice to continue her previous policy of teaching 'Power to doubt' (III.i. 112). Instead of trying to work from within upon the King, she must commit some outward act of violence and cruelty whose pressure of proof and horror will arm the King with a resolution he does not normally possess. This act is the murder of her own daughter Camena, after whose death she produces a tapestry supposed to be evidence that Camena has been conspiring with Mustapha. The King is convinced and Mustapha is slain. But both Solyman and Rossa have forgotten (as Rosten in III.i had not, and as we are continually being reminded by the Chorus) that the people, who favour Mustapha, are also an order in the State of which the tyrant's temperamental humours must take account; they revolt, and ruin threatens the kingdom.

Another element in the final ruin is Zanger's suicide. Zanger, Mustapha, Camena, and Achmat are built on neo-Stoic lines, although all their εὐθυμία is powerless to prevent the Rossa–Solyman relationship of inner weakness and determined evil from issuing in disaster; only Achmat, a 'soule loving Nature, Dutie, Order' (v.iii.109), survives to draw the moral and attempt by manoeuvring with τύχη (v.iii.120), to save the state. For Achmat is a Stoic ('I first am Natures subiect, then my Princes', II.i. 75) who is prepared, unlike Chapman's Cato, to 'wrestle his faith vpon the stage of Chance' (II.i.62) and contend with the 'heap of digested villainy' that is Cato's world, although he does not attain the resolution to pursue this virtuous course without an inward struggle. Virtue is in labour with chaos in Camena, whose soliloquy (II.iii.1–66) manipulates the antithesis of ἀρετή and τύχη, and aligns her, as Stoic heroine, with Marston's Sophonisba. Mustapha himself is a Stoic of single-minded virtue (IV.iv.123–39).

The fact that these contrasts form the life-blood of the play means that it is irrelevant (and probably wrong) to identify Achmat or any other character as the 'projection of the author's own moral philosophy'.[7] Nor, perhaps, is it useful to say with Orsini: 'Tutti i personaggi sono . . . condannati dal severo giudizio dell' autore.'[8] The overweighting is there and must be recognized (most notably in the choruses) in both *Alaham* and *Mustapha*, but the peculiar interest of Greville's plays lies in the

7. Croll, *The Works of Fulke Greville*, p. 42.
8. N. Orsini, *Fulke Greville tra il Mondo e Dio* (Milan, 1941), p. 61.

strength and sincerity with which, beneath the crust of *sententiae* and the often rather jejune political speculation, the characters beat with their inward life and their effort to correlate action with desire.

In both *Alaham* and *Mustapha* the supernatural plays some part in the waging of the inward war. We are undoubtedly meant, in *Mustapha*, to look upon Rossa as a woman in some sort possessed by the vicious abstractions which are continually in her mouth: Rage, Envie, Desire, these passions are also Furies, half-way between the Eumenides and the Calvinistic *Tartari* of *Alaham*. Rossa ends the play completely possessed by them—let the religious and the humble-minded rejoice, since, like the scapegoat, she will rid the land of them by bearing them all away with her (v.iv.116–24), but let them also beware for she has become a vessel charged with their power to harm (v.iv.125–6). Rossa's hatred of 'Mediocrity' in passions (III.i.75), which leads to her being ultimately possessed by 'Furies of choyce', which override the inward war and the outward sanction (v.iv.48),[9] is combined with deliberate invocation of the 'ugly Angells of th'infernall Kingdomes' (III.ii.10–14). She offers her daughter up to Avernus (III.ii.39–41) and describes herself to Solyman as a microcosm of Hell (IV.iii.30–34).

The tendency in *Mustapha* for the wicked passions either to become objective infernal spirits or to be directly attributed to the activity of such spirits is accelerated in *Alaham*. In this play Greville is interested in the objective manifestation of supernatural evil, the 'metaphysical aid' with which Lady Macbeth was infatuated. For neither are the angels 'nothing but good motions or inspirations which God excites in the minds of men' nor the devils 'nothing but bad affections or perturbations suggested by our carnal nature'.[1] The 'Furies', too, the passions seen in their objective aspect as tormenting man from without, are still further objectified in the 'Chorus Secundus of *Furies*: Malice. Crafte. Pride. Corrupt Reason. Evil Spirits'. Here the Evil Spirits *are* the Furies. In another Chorus the Evil Spirits are identified with the fallen angels, 'exiles out of heauen' (Chorus

9. v.iv.48 reads: '*Furies of choyce, what arguments can moue?*' The difficulty of interpretation presented by this line is so typical of Greville that I have preferred, in this and similar instances, to let the interpretation I have chosen stand in my text without unfolding possible alternatives.

1. Calvin, vol. i, p. 209.

Tertius, 176), just as the abstract 'Fury', Corrupt Reason, has herself fallen (Chorus Secundus, 18). The Evil Spirits, including the prologuizing Ghost, perform the Calvinistic function of 'exercising believers' by warring against them, but can never overcome them (Chorus Tertius, 101–8);[2] created though they were by God, their sinful nature, like that of Calvin's Devil,[3] comes not from creation, but from 'depravation' and privation (Prologus, 21–33). 'They hold the wicked in thraldom, exercise dominion over their minds and bodies, and employ them as bond-slaves in all kinds of iniquity.'[4] Hence Hala's and Alaham's invocations and possessions. In all this the inactivity of the Good Spirits is noticeable. The dramaturgical problem is here mixed with the theological. As a Calvinist, Greville holds to the doctrine of predestination,[5] but it is difficult to write a drama of the inward war in which the nature of the *personae* is already so irrevocably determined. (The defects of *The Atheist's Tragedy* as a drama of *spiritual* struggle illustrate this contention.) It was perhaps because Greville wished to avoid too neat a division of his characters into the elect and the unregenerate that he chose a non-Christian milieu, since he is thereby freed from the obligations imposed by his theological convictions. This choice faced Greville with another difficulty, one which he has by no means completely solved: for all 'Mohammedans' are likely to be synonymous with the 'unregenerate' and the possibility of inward conflict is again destroyed. Greville partly solves this problem by discovering neo-Stoicism amongst the Pashas, and partly the solution was ready-made in the French Senecan form, the approximation of Hala and Rossa to the Medea type. But more importantly, and despite the affinities of his supernatural spirits with the Calvinistic devils and angels, Greville avoids too rigoristic and undramatic a milieu by a blurring of the distinction between the objective evil Spirits and the 'Furies' of the human heart. The wickedness of Alaham and the rest thus becomes not merely a question of their not enjoying Grace, with the Devil and his angels free, in Calvin's phrase to 'exercise dominion' over them: the 'Furies' are as much a subjective product of the characters' inward evil as they are participators

2. Cf. ibid., pp. 203, 207.
3. Ibid. 205. Cf. Greville's lines on the Fall, *Mustapha*, cho. 4.1–16.
4. Calvin, p. 207.   5. 'Of Religion', stanzas 95 ff.

in, and allies of, the objective evil activity of the Devil and his spirits. For to be possessed by and to invoke the evil spirits with the confidence of an Alaham implies more than a simple objectification of their mode of being. In 'A Letter to an Honourable Lady' Greville writes:

These extremities of good or euill will not easily be beleeued to raigne in these middle natures of flesh and blood: in respect that God hath decreed the angels to heauen, the diuels to hell; and left the Earth to man, as a meane creation between these two extremes. So that he must be a kind of diuell himselfe, that can easily beleeue there should be diuels raigning within or amongst vs.

Greville managed to avoid, for the sake of depicting the inward war, a Manicheism which would have been objectionable to him as a Calvinist, and a Calvinism which might have been frustrating to him as a dramatist. That Greville does not, in spite of this compromise, succeed in convincing us that he has not rigged the balance in favour of scepticism and pessimism is as much due to his choice of the Senecan form, with all its monstrosities of parricide and infanticide, as to the fact that his mind was coloured and his imagination fired by a contemporary belief in human corruption.

The compromise accounts for the ambiguity with which we view Hala's end (*Alaham*, v.iii.128–46). This terrible passage, so powerfully written that it almost justifies French Senecanism, is very difficult to understand. Perhaps it is a prelude to a physical descent into Hell, or perhaps Hala's wits have gone. What is certain is that Hala is here accorded no sort of triumph in Medean fashion, and that behind Greville's variation on the Senecan finale lies the whole weight of a new period's discovery of the potentialities for good or evil of the inward man. In this case, for evil; for it is Hell itself that, in Alexander's phrase, has been placed within Hala.

Greville is more vividly aware than most of his contemporaries that those things which we identify as outward evils, abstract or Furious, and their formulation in institutions, wars, false Churches, and great crimes, are manufactured out of the evil within, motes from the heap of dust and corruption that the 'Paradise' of the unregenerate human heart has become; the

Devil, however objectified, can never absolve man from punishment for his own 'uncreated' sin. Neither the theory of 'Fortune's shoures', nor the *mens adepta*, nor 'outward holiness' can
avail to cancel that dreadful bond. The emphasis on the corre-
lation between outward weakness and crime and their origin
within the creature is the essential psychological principle upon
which Greville's *personae* are constructed. Greville, therefore,
could not trust his steps to the clew which guided Chapman and
Daniel through the human labyrinth. For Greville, it cannot be
the confusion between old decrees and later institutions, of
which Drayton wrote in *The Owle*, that accounts for the founder-
ing of the Elizabethan achievement; man's iniquity runs deeper
in his blood, inaccessible to the lancing of any satirist: 'an infinite justice is offended', said Hall. But Greville did find that
the Stoic emphasis on the inward order and the kinds of outward
iniquity made popular by Seneca were materials which he could
charge with fears and hatreds discovered by quite another tradition. In *Mustapha* and *Alaham* the outward ways by which such
evils proceed are merely paths leading back and back to the
new Avernus in the human heart:

> All what the world admires comes from within;
> A doome, whereby the sinne, condemnes the sinne.

8

The main outline of
Chapman's Byron

Swinburne found that the portrait of Byron in *The Conspiracy and Tragedy of Charles Duke of Byron* was 'overlaid with so many touches that the main outline is completely disguised'.[1] Chapman's plain and didactic manner, according to Mr Wyndham Lewis, leaves his thinking starkly apparent. Mr Lewis went on to show that Byron is 'a "Machiavel" of the Chapman pattern in the making... whom subsequently you see dying in a very confused state indeed'. Dr Praz denies this: Byron, he declares, borrowing a phrase from M. Schoell, is imagined by a 'Chapman spell-bound by the moralized image Plutarch had sketched of Alexander'. We owe to M. Schoell our knowledge of the connection between Chapman's great double play and Plutarch's *De Alexandri Magni Fortuna aut Virtute*, but Schoell's work does not yield quite the implication that Praz makes it yield. More recently, Professor Hardin Craig has read Byron as an exemplification of an ethical confusion in Chapman which prefigures that of Beaumont and Fletcher and the 'decadents': Byron is used by Chapman to 'justify rebellion in the nature of his creation'. Chapman, says Craig, 'goes further than ethics permitted in sympathizing with sin'.[2]

The figure of Byron is like those Renaissance toys of pleated

First published in *Studies in Philology*, xlvii, 1950, 568–88.

1. *George Chapman: A Critical Essay* (London, 1875), reprinted in 'Contemporaries of Shakespeare', *Complete Works* (London and New York, 1926), vol. xii, p. 195. [In fact the words quoted are given by Swinburne as what 'has been observed' and he replies to the criticism they convey.]

2. Lewis, *The Lion and the Fox* (London, 1927), pp. 266, 273; Praz, 'Machiavelli and the Elizabethans', *Proceedings of the British Academy*, xiv, 1928, 73; Schoell, *Études sur l'humanisme continental* (Paris, 1926), p. 85 *et passim*; Craig, 'Ethics in the Jacobean drama: The case of Chapman', in *Parrott Presentation Volume* (Princeton, 1935), pp. 42–45.

paper, the pictures wrought to th'optike reason, 'one way like a shade / Another monster like':[3]

> And till you stand and in a right line view it,
> You cannot well judge what the main form is.[4]

The fascination which these devices exercised upon Chapman suggests something about the nature of his dramatic art. He has the ability to place his spectator in a number of quite different relationships with his dramatic characters. Those who are most his compeers, Marlowe, Daniel, and Fulke Greville, used the classical chorus itself as one means of providing an extra 'point of view'. Chapman avoids the formal adoption of what was by his time a somewhat archaeological device; but in both the Bussy plays his need for some such central viewpoint was satisfied by imposing the function of choric moralization on some of the characters in such a way that the action is deliberately suspended, for the true image can never be discerned by 'passers-by, and such as make no stay'.[5] Furthermore, Chapman enriches our apprehension of the central figures by giving us different accounts of him by different persons, accounts often moulded out of language elaborately figurative, whose poetic tone tells us something about the speaker's approach to the subject. This 'indirect method'—if a phrase and a meaning may be borrowed from Percy Lubbock's critique of Henry James—is also a highly 'dramatic' method, again in Lubbock's sense. We obtain an understanding of the central character's account of his own dilemmas, as well as a dramatized and objectified account of him as he appears to those who surround him. 'I delight in a deep-breathing economy and an organic form', wrote James.[6] Chapman has the reputation for delighting in the qualities most opposite to these; but are his plays—and in particular the Byron plays—really 'large loose baggy monsters, with . . . queer elements of the accidental and the arbitrary'?[7] Chapman's reputation for severe learning will not go with the attribution to him of too much of the accidental and the arbi-

3. 'Eugenia', 174–5, *The Poems of George Chapman* (ed. Bartlett, New York, 1941), p. 276.
4. *The Tragedy of Chabot*, I.i.71–72. Compare 'Ovid's banquet of sense', stanza iii, *All Fools*, I.i.47–48, and Parrott's note.
5. 'Eugenia', l. 176.
6. *The Art of the Novel* (New York, 1934), p. 84.   7. Ibid.

trary; his use of the shifting viewpoint, the indirect and the dramatic method, suggests that the 'right line' in which to view his optic pictures is the one which Asall recommends for viewing the Admiral in the opening scene of *The Tragedy of Chabot*: 'Judge him', says Asall, 'by no more than what you know, Ingenuously.' This means judging Chapman's play characters in strict relation to the rationale of the plays in which they appear, not constructing an account of Chapman's mind and art by means of passages stripped of their often complex relationships with the business of the play world. It means also paying close attention, within the play, to *how* we learn about Chapman's central character and from whose lips, and to the nature of the figurative language by means of which the information is conveyed. 'What makes [his poetry] most poetic is what makes it most dramatic', wrote Mr Eliot of Shakespeare.[8] The maxim holds good for Chapman too.

The problem may be brought closer to the Byron plays and to the observations that have been made, notably by Professor Craig, about Chapman as a 'case' of ethical confusion, by my anticipating here some conclusions that I reach later in this essay. For example, one point where an 'improper' sympathy with Byron's inversions appears most strongly reflected in Chapman's own attitude might show itself in the way Byron is made to state his case against Henry's employment of La Fin as spy and informer. We were introduced to La Fin in *The Conspiracy* by Henry himself, who was in the act of banishing him for his behaviour in a speech which strikingly reveals the degree of La Fin's corruption (*Conspiracy*, I.i.148–62). Yet, later, the King has used this man to entrap the Marshal. In the light of this conduct of Henry's, which derogates considerably from his reputation as the 'ideal monarch',[9] Byron's cry 'Is it justice / To tempt and witch a man to break the law, And by that witch condemn him?' (*Tragedy*, v.ii.156–8) has the appeal of truth. There is good dramaturgical justification for the use of La Fin— the confrontation of Byron with the 'intelligencing instrument' makes a theatrically effective scene. One could also justify the Prince's use of such an instrument out of the *specula*, although it seems doubtful if that kind of justification was in Chapman's

8. *Selected Essays* (London, 1934), p. 52.
9. The phrase is Parrott's, p. 596.

mind.[1] The problem is really one involving the relationship between Chapman's method of character portrayal and the total moral scheme of the play. That the relationship is a very loose one does not, in fact, make the moral scheme any the less firmly delineated. A small illustration of the inconsistency in 'characterization', the carelessness as to whether each portrait is psychologically coherent and decorous, is seen in the minor figure of Janin, who in the *Tragedy* (III.i.162–225) is represented as a grave counsellor giving good advice to Byron, and yet in the next act (IV.ii.29–47) is the mouthpiece of the political doctrine that Henry rejects as a mark of tyrant rather than of king. On a larger scale, the King himself *is*, within the politico-moral scheme which the play illustrates, the ideal monarch; and within the Virtue–Fortune dynamic, which, as we shall see, activates the play, his is the exemplar of Virtue. But in the historical scheme which Chapman is also employing, the King does not maintain this aspect. There are only two ways of making a dramatic character completely 'plausible' and self-consistent— the one is the method of naturalistic character presentation, the other is the method of moral allegory. Chapman's method avoids both these, or rather it combines them both, so that the resulting product retains the sort of interest which is attached to the moral play, the struggle between vice and virtue, and yet is presented in a way consistent with the changed ideas about actual history and observed psychology. This is not confusion, but transition. The split which runs up the character of the King is the sign of the grafting of the moral play tradition on to a growing naturalism. But that split is a matter of dramatic method which need not affect our view of the parts played by Byron and the King in the ethical *débat*. In that dialectical scheme the King is the arbitrator between Byron and the politically infamous conspirators: as such he is the exemplar of political wisdom. Byron himself is the Alexander-hero, whose virtue has become corrupted, with all the implications that corruption in such a man has for contemporary political *moralia*. But both Byron and Henry—and, indeed, all the characters

1. R. H. Murray writes, referring to Bodin's compromise with the Machiavellian doctrine: '. . . when men attack Machiavellianism, they do so on general grounds. When, however, it comes to a particular point, some of the expedients might readily have come out of the pages of the *Prince*', *Political Consequences of the Reformation* (London, 1926), p. 137.

(including La Fin)—are used by the dramatist on several levels: on the level of the moral scheme; on the level of the dramatic action, as persons who behave on occasion naturalistically and historically;[2] and on the level of comment, or as vehicles of choral moralization—as when Byron comments on the corruption of courts, a comment applicable to the generality of courts but not applicable to Henry's court as that court is presented to us on the level of the historical and dramatic action. (Thus Byron's comments in this kind are not to be read as Chapman's way of excusing Byron's personal behaviour, or as signs of an ambivalent attitude in the dramatist towards his hero.) It is because we are continually being switched from one level to another that the figure of Byron gets overlaid and its outline becomes disguised; and for the same reason the ethical scheme has the appearance of being confused too.

In what follows I am concerned to explore what Byron is, on the level of what I have called the dialectical scheme, that is, to examine the double play as an exercise in politico-moral thinking expressed in dramatic form. It is this last, the dramatic form, which makes for difficulty, since it is unfair to read the work as though it were a treatise, because it is a play; and equally unfair to read it purely as a play, applying to it vague criteria such as are summarized in modern formulae like 'coherent dramatic structure' or 'characterization'. These criteria, even if kept at the very back of the critic's mind, cannot illuminate Chapman's probable way of planning his play, while the large extent to which the play does partake of the characteristics of a political or moral treatise makes them seem less useful. A hostile critic of Chapman could say that a moral treatise and a play lie buried together in *The Conspiracy and Tragedy*, draining the life from one another. This examination of Byron's character is rather intended to show that Byron's function in the politico-moral world of the play is clearly defined in a series of dramatic contexts. This at least should absolve Chapman from any very damaging ambiguities in regard to his ethical scheme. It does not follow from that absolution that Chapman has created in Byron a dramatic character necessarily convincing, plausible and consistent, as those terms are applied in dramaturgy; but, in the criticism of Elizabethan drama (with a possible exception

2. Parrott cites some examples of such behaviour, p. 595.

in the case of Shakespeare criticism) such terms are still applied far more widely and with far more conviction than the uncertain degree of their relevance warrants.

Plutarch's orations *De Alexandri Fortuna*, and their importance in shaping what has been called Chapman's political testament, provide a starting-point for an analysis along these lines. Plutarch uses Alexander as an *exemplum* to illustrate his idealistic view of the triumph of ἀρετή over τύχη in Alexander's person. The Virtue by whose aid he triumphs in the face of Fortune's bitter hostility is made up of a selection of virtues, which include 'courage and justice ... restraint and mildness together with ... decorous behaviour and intelligence ... sober and sane judgement'.[3] Alexander's 'disciplined virtue . . . pronounced invulnerable to the buffets of time and circumstance'[4] conforms to a Stoic principle that Chapman restated in 'Eugenia' (Vigilia Prima):

> Each action that a wise man makes his fruit,
> He doth with all the virtues execute.
> Some one, the ground-worke laying; All the rest
> Flow in as fellowes, with their interest.[5]

It is the Virtue-Fortune antithesis that animates both plays. The way it is handled is to a large extent the key to what the plays are about. Byron moves in a world where the Plutarchian Fortune and Virtue are waging their ancient *débat*. Chapman makes Byron appear conscious of a relationship between himself and Alexander, most strikingly where Byron declares his intention of having a mountain fashioned into a colossal image of himself: in the statue's left hand a city will be built and a river will pour from its right hand (III.ii.140–77).[6] Plutarch tells us that a similar project had been proposed to Alexander but rejected

---

3. Plutarch, *Moralia* (trans. Babbitt, Loeb ed., London and Cambridge, Mass., 1936), vol. iv, p. 415 (332 A).

4. Cochrane, *Christianity and Classical Culture* (London, 1940), p. 168.

5. 'Eugenia', ll. 371–4. Cf. Schoell, p. 240. It is not irrelevant to our view of Byron that the one virtue which is the groundwork of all the others in the character of William, Lord Russell, is, according to Chapman, 'Religion'—a term given specifically Christian meaning by the marginal gloss. It is Religion which seasons the Fortitude, Humanity, and Continence which go to make up the Nobilitie of the hero.

6. See Plutarch, *De Alexandri Fortuna*, p. 433 (335 D). And cf. Castiglione, *Courtier* (trans. Hoby, Everyman ed.), p. 289. See Schoell, pp. 208 ff., for these and other indebtednesses of Chapman to Plutarch.

by him. Even Byron's eyes and the 'something-stooping carriage' of his neck are like Alexander's. Byron's emphasis on his
personal achievements in the wars (for example, in *Conspiracy*,
v.i.130–54) and his valuation of the 'dear price of five and thirty
scars' (*Tragedy*, v.iii.182) are a reminder of Plutarch's praise of
Alexander:

> How, then, think you, did he glory in his own wounds, remembering by
> each part of his body affected a nation overcome, a victory won, the
> capture of cities, the surrender of kings? He did not cover over nor hide
> his scars, but bore them with him openly as symbolic representations,
> graven on his body, of virtue and manly courage.[7]

Byron is in this sense an Alexander figure. But Byron is also in
the habit of seeing himself in the guise of other heroes of antiquity, most significantly, perhaps, as Alcides, frequently allegorized in Renaissance literature as Heroic Virtue:[8]

> I have Alcides-like gone under th'earth,
> And on these shoulders borne the weight of France.[9]

He also compares himself to Achilles, and France becomes
'French Ilion' (*Conspiracy*, II.i.151–3); La Fin, his tempter, is
called by Savoy the 'French Ulysses' (ibid. II.i.52); and to Curtius,
who saved Rome (*Conspiracy*, III.ii.66–73), to Pompey (*Tragedy*,
v.ii.232–49), and to Orpheus, when he is intoxicated with the
entirely mistaken impression that his judges have been won over
by his eloquence (ibid. v.iii.7–10).

   In all these passages we seem to see Byron claiming for himself the special kind of *virtus* associated with the heroes of classical antiquity. And although Hercules, Alexander, Curtius, and
the rest are but figures of poetic speech, they are also the elements of a heroic mythology with which Byron is associated
in his own mind. That Chapman has the deliberate intention of
indicating that Byron's equation of himself with the classical
hero and his consequent implication that he shares their special
quality of virtue (ἀρετή) in the Plutarchian sense is part of a

---

7. *De Alexandri Fortuna*, p. 409 (331 C).
   8. See for example Jonson's gloss to the speech of Heroic Virtue in the *Masque of
Queenes*, vol. vii, p. 302.
   9. *Tragedy*, III.i.151–2. For the relation of Byron's invocation of the Hercules
figure to the Senecan treatment of the Herculean apotheosis, see Roy Battenhouse,
'Chapman and the nature of man', *ELH: A Journal of English Literary History*, xii,
1945, 96.

process of self-deception (encouraged of course by his own very substantial achievements) is suggested when we refer the incidence of these images to their dramatic contexts. For example, the speech in which Byron projects the mountain statue is the climax to a situation carefully engineered by the conspirators La Fin and Savoy: they have been, to use Philemon Holland's phrase, cogging and soothing up the hero with the grossest flattery. In particular, they have employed a painter to take his picture—this, as Savoy elegantly expresses it in a whispered conversation just before Byron appears, is to be 'a state potato', a 'high cullis and potion' to excite the lust of his ambition (*Conspiracy*, iii.ii.16–18). In his chapter on 'How the Prince must avoid Flatterers' Erasmus writes:

There is a tacit sort of adulation in pictures, statues, and honorary titles. Apelles flattered Alexander the Great in this manner by painting him hurling a thunderbolt; and Octavius took great pleasure in being painted in the likeness of Apollo. The same thing applies to those huge statues of colossal proportion, far greater than human size, which were formerly set up to the emperors.[1]

Byron's megalomania is excited by the poison of flattery, and as a result he equates himself with Alexander; but Chapman's own attitude to the central figure is not ambiguous, but ruthless. What was fitting for Alexander (though Plutarch made Alexander say 'let Athos remain as it is') is only a wild impropriety on the part of a conspiring noble.[2] Similarly the Alexander-like percussion of Byron's sounds in *The Conspiracy*, v.i, and *The Tragedy*, v.iii, illustrates the rebel's perversion of the Alexander theme: on the first occasion the speech is made as a bombastic answer to the King's revelation of his precise knowledge as to the extent of Byron's treachery; on the second Byron has become an 'altering vapour', as Harlay calls him (v.iii.187), and the tender and submissive note of ll. 132–47 yields to a declaration, voiced with fury, that the King should have pardoned him for his past services. But the Chancellor has already pronounced the last word on that plea in his likening of Byron's fate to that of Manlius, another saviour-hero:

---

1. *The Education of a Christian Prince* (ed. L. K. Born, New York, 1926), p. 197.
2. In *Bussy d'Ambois* (i.i.15–17) 'those colossic statutes, / Which, with heroic forms without o'erspread, / Within are nought but mortar, flint, and lead', symbolize a like perversion. Cf. Schoell, p. 197.

Yet for his after traitorous factions
They threw him headlong from the place he sav'd.
(v.ii.293–4)

And it is just after we have heard this judgement soberly pronounced that the deluded Byron compares himself to Orpheus.
In short, Byron is continually making claims to be the exemplar
of a virtue which is not his.

Because of this, Chapman makes him mediate in terms of the
Virtue–Fortune antithesis, which is, indeed, a dynamic of the
plays. But the working of this theme must be studied in close
relation to the dramatic contexts and the play world. For Chapman is not merely imposing a formula, disinterred from Plutarch, on his character relationships: he is revivifying a theory of
human nature and *la condition humaine*, reapplying it, and reor-
ganizing it into the pattern of Renaissance France. It is time therefore, to attempt a complete statement of what Byron is and does.

The opening discussion *de regimine principum* in the first scene
of *The Conspiracy* and the 'state criticism' indicate with firm
strokes the kind of world we are entering; it is against this background that we have our first point of view on Byron.[3] We learn
that to Savoy's counsellor he appears to have many attributes of
heroic virtue (matchless valour, the capacity for hard work, a
chastity like Alexander's), but that these are accompanied by
bragging ('he is past measure glorious'), ambition, which at
present takes the form of imagining that France cannot subsist without him, and an immense susceptibility to flattery. These
flaws appear to Roncas and Savoy as merely the handles which
will allow them to grasp Byron and use him for their own purposes, but to us and to Chapman they are plainly the dram of
evil which ruins all the noble substance. They are, indeed,
qualities quite unlike those of the Plutarchian Alexander. The
theme of Byron's proneness to flattery will, for example, occupy
much of the play; from Plutarch to Erasmus and Machiavelli
citizens and princes were warned at tedious length to eschew this
vice.[4] It is Machiavelli's name which introduces appropriately

3. The thickly scattered *sententiae* in this scene enhance the impression that we
are in a world of 'statists', of persons whose constant study is the *specula principum*.
4. Plutarch, 'How to tell a flatterer from a friend', *Moralia* (trans. P. Holland,
London, 1912, Everyman ed., pp. 36 ff.; Erasmus, chap. ii; Machiavelli, *Prince*,
chap. xxiii. And see A. H. Gilbert, *Machiavelli's Prince and its Predecessors* (Durham,
North Carolina, 1938), pp. 186–9.

the whole complex tissue of deceit that Byron now becomes involved in. Picoté is in the vanguard; after Byron's
ambition has been blown to a flame by the spreading of a carpet
beneath his feet patterned with the history of Catiline—Byron
may miss the intentional ambiguity but the audience cannot—
Picoté's sophistical arguments are deployed to show that in
'state criticism' there is nothing really good—all is but 'flourishes
of form':

> simple loyalty,
> Faith, love, sincerity, are but words, no things,
> Merely devis'd for form. (I.ii.116–18)

To this pure 'Machiavellianism' Byron's reply is, in one sense,
ambiguous, but, dramaturgically speaking, perfectly clear and
effective. It is ambiguous in that Byron plainly has not made up
his mind, for Chapman's purpose is to show his gradual de-
generation into a conspirator, and this speech, within the
necessary time-scheme and architectonic of the play, stands for
him in his unperverted state (I.ii.137–64). We learn from it
Byron's awareness of the world of nature, reason, and virtue
which he is later to forsake, as well as his knowledge of the
dangers which attend upon that forsaking. The figurative
language of the speech expresses with a 'deep-breathing economy' Byron's elegiac awareness of the possibility of Fall—a
possibility to which his mind, when fully perverted, is shown as
being almost entirely closed.

La Fin, in the next act, takes over the task of perversion from
Picoté. La Fin is the complete Machiavellian, the politic villain
of the kind whom even Dr Praz admits may fitly be regarded as
a product of the Elizabethan versions of Machiavellian teaching;
in addition, he claims that he possesses the traditional powers of
the witch to 'tumble nature's germens' in a speech which reads
like a précis of Rémy or Wier (II.i.107–27). When La Fin has
finished, Byron's soliloquy (II.i.145–74) shows that the Marshal
has learnt precisely what Picoté and La Fin had wished him to
learn. To the air he gives back their doctrine: 'How fit a sort
were this to handsel Fortune,' he exclaims, 'And I will win it
though I lose myself.' He will experiment with Fortune, but
what has happened to Virtue? It is buried in the Achilles image,
and in the context that becomes perverted from Plutarchian

ἀρετή, the Heroic Virtue, to something much closer to the Machiavellian *virtù*.

In the next scene (II.ii) we learn from Henry's lips of Byron's choleric nature; the King's first thought is to send him to be cured by 'temperate English air', for the King wishes to save Byron from himself, while the conspirators are eager to exploit his defects for their own ends. And Savoy, carrying out his plan of trying to inflame the King against Byron, presents a picture of Byron which makes him out to be like Plutarch's Alexander: 'Fortune to him was Juno to Alcides' (II.ii.93). La Fin's attempt to re-erect the Alexander image of Byron must be valued in the light of the Machiavellian's declared objective (to arouse the jealousy of the King); and what La Fin says was true of the old Byron, the 'admir'd Byron' who 'touch'd heaven with his lance' (Prologus, l. 17), but who now fusts unused in what Marston's Chrisoganus called the 'ill-nurs'd age of Peace'.

Byron's relaying back of La Fin's own doctrine in the first scene of Act III is meant to show not only how exact a pupil of the Machiavellian Byron has now become but also how intellectual understanding of the political teaching is in him a concomitant of the political action.[5] This appears to be the dramaturgical function of the scene, which cannot be justified in terms of the 'plot' as such, and suggests that Chapman's main interest is in giving us an absolutely clear and full portrayal of the nature and motives of the central figure. The next scene (III.ii) shows the climax of Byron's vanity and folly: puffed up with persuasion that he is a god in worth, as the King puts it, he assumes the giant's robe of Alexander. It is against the effect of this scene, in which Byron has attempted to climb to the height of Alexander's style, that we must balance Byron's behaviour in the succeeding scene (III.ii.215–43) and his virtual rejection of the King's advice. The King warns the Marshal against La Fin, and Byron replies:

> Be what he [La Fin] will, men in themselves entire
> March safe with naked feet on coals of fire:
> I build not outward, nor depend on props . . .
> (III.ii.227–9)

This reads very like the declaration of the unperverted Byron in

5. III.i.25–46, 48–62, and 67–74 are elaborate summaries of the hated doctrine.

his first soliloquy: when men forsake the 'natural clime of justice',

> To seek without them that which is not theirs,
> The forms of all their comforts are distracted . . .
> (I.i.158)

The difference lies in the dramatic context: we now know enough (and the King suspects enough) to realize that Byron's profession of the right faith (as that is set out, for example, by Chapman in the *Hymnus ad Cynthiam* in almost identical terms)[6] is a hollow profession, belied by his actions, and indeed by the lines of implied reproach against the King which follow. Byron can still gloss his treasons with the doctrine of Virtue, which he has abandoned, just as La Fin has them on his tongue in the opening passage of Act III (i.6–23) when he wishes to deceive Byron with a feigned passion. These people are acquainted with each other's worlds and aware of the issues, so that the conduct of Byron and La Fin is shown as a deliberate choice of *deteriora*. The King, indeed, replies on this occasion with what reads like a summary of Plutarch's teaching on how a flatterer may be discerned from a friend,[7] while his figurative description of the foolish, flattered man:

> his head is napp'd with bays,
> His lips break out with nectar, his tun'd feet
> Are of the great last, the perpetual motion,
> (III.ii.256–8)

seems intended to recall to us Byron's first temptation, when the carpet of Catiline is spread before him:

> They follow all my steps with music
> As if my feet were numerous, and trod sounds
> Out of the centre with Apollo's virtue . . .
> (I.ii.457)

The scene with the astrologer La Brosse (III.iii) requires to be justified in terms of its relevance to the total scheme of the play, as that has been exposed so far. It is true that it allows Byron to make his first display of 'adust and melancholy choler', but it

---

6. *Hymnus ad Cynthiam*, ll. 130–7 (*Poems*, pp. 33–34).

7. La Fin is notable for his professions of friendship in the approved fashion of the flatterer. See *Conspiracy*, II.i.135–7.

has a relevance more vital than that, a relevance which seems to
run counter, in this instance, to Hardin Craig's generalization
that 'Chapman has shifted the blame from the individual to
fate, not the nemesis of the ancient world, but to a sort of psychological determinism' and his conclusion that 'Chapman has, in
the process, let his sympathies come over to the side of sin'.[8] For
the subject of this scene is not Byron's choler; it is the Virtue-
Fortune theme. It was not necessary for Chapman to incorporate
the astrological anecdote from Grimeston merely to show us
Byron in a rage. Byron's soliloquy (III.iii.20–36) develops the
theme of the prince's favourite who is raised up by Fortune; his
very success, as well as the fact that it depends on Fortune alone,
grubs up his root, makes his fall more likely. These are familiar
ideas. 'All human business Fortune doth command,' writes
Jonson, 'Without all order.' And Jonson, like Chapman and
Plutarch, wishes his Prince's conduct to be based on an alliance
between Fortune and Virtue in which virtue shall take the precedence.[9] Related to the discipline of virtue is another theme—
one often pondered on by Chapman[1]—which replaces in Byron's
soliloquy the emphasis on Virtue itself: 'In my late projects,'
Byron declares, 'I have cast myself Into the arms of others.'
He has sought outside himself, and we know that 'The worth
that weigheth inward should not long / For outward prices'.[2]
As we have learnt from his first soliloquy (I.i.137–64), conspiracy
involves not only trusting one's blood in another's veins, but,
for the conspirators, 'Forsaking of all the sure force in themselves / To seek without them that which is not theirs'. Byron's
response to the danger—and his awareness of it is characteristically made vital by being linked with observations *de regimine
principum*—is the wrong response. Instead of retreating to the
inward practice of Virtue, Byron consults the asterisms of
Heaven. When he learns his fate the Alcidean images of his
choleric outburst show that Byron has become, for the time, a

8. Craig, p. 35.

9. Jonson, *The Poetaster*, v.i (vol. iv, p. 291).

1. And by Fulke Greville. Cf. 'Of Religion', stanzas 14–16 (*Works*, ed. Grosart,
1870, vol. i, pp. 243–4); *Caelica*, LXXXIV; *Alaham*, I.i.313; II.ii.18; IV.i.42; etc. (*Poems and
Dramas*, ed. Bullough, 1939). Greville's *Letter to an Honourable Lady* emphasizes the
inward re-creation which is an essential principle of the Stoic hero in Chapman (eg,
in *Caesar and Pompey*, v.i.203–15). Cf. Seneca, *Ep.* xli, *Workes* ... (trans. T. Lodge,
London, 1614), p. 230.

2. 'Euthymiae Raptus', ll. 57–58 (Bullough, p. 174).

Hercules Furens—the ἀρετή which he claims for himself in association with the mythical hero has turned to madness, a disease of the 'burnt blood'. This is followed by a resolution:

> I'll change my course,
> I'll piece-meal pull the frame of all my thoughts,
> And cast my will into another mould:
> And where are all you *Caput Algols* then?
>
> (III.iii.116–19)

This is something other than the old adage *Sapiens dominabitur astris*.[3] 'If one could change one's nature with time and circumstance, fortune would never change', wrote Machiavelli,[4] and Byron is at this moment shown to be his pupil. Machiavelli lays no great emphasis on the idea that Virtue may provide a means of overcoming, in the Stoic sense of inwardly dethroning, Fortune.[5] And in Byron's unstable world the remedy he proposes is not the practice in Virtue—in short, in this context, the abandonment of his treasonable plots—but a policy of ἐνέργεια, of *vigore*, regardless of heaven (III.iii.132–4). So the scene closes with the most quoted lines in the Byron plays (ll.135–45), in which Byron declares himself the master of his fate through his *virtù*. Byron in this scene cannot be read purely as a dramatic formula of the choleric man, as Tamburlaine has been,[6] driven to act as he does by the current of a 'psychological determinism'. He is shown at the end of a process which has involved the deliberate eschewal of virtuous action.

Lest we should misread this point, it is not unfair to say that the dramaturgical justification of Act IV, so far as our understanding of Byron's character is concerned, lies in the way it brings Byron's rejection of Virtue home to our apprehension. The advice given him by the English counsellor is a very clear handling of the Fortune theme in the manner and phraseology of Plutarch's *De Alexandri Fortuna*; and, though ostensibly applied to the relations between states, it has a direct reference to Byron's personal position. Virtue has built Byron up into an Alexander; Virtue only can overcome Fortune; and not to proceed by Virtue is in reality to 'put the roof to Fortune' (IV.i.179),

---

3. For the distinction between this adage and the new turn that Machiavelli gave it, see Cassirer, *The Myth of the State* (1946), p. 159.

4. *Prince*, chap. xxv.   5. Gilbert, pp. 204 ff.

6. See J. Parr, 'Tamburlaine's malady', *PMLA*, lix, 1944, 696–714.

to leave the completion of the work to the hand of chance. This advice which is particularly pertinent to Byron's state because, as we know from the preceding scenes, especially that with La Brosse, Byron believes that a mere Machiavellian twisting of will, a damming of banks and streams, the exercise of *vigore*, will cause Fortune 'never to change'. Here, is anywhere, Chapman is speaking unambiguously to his own hero through the Chorus— and Byron turns a deaf ear.

How far does Chapman intend to convey that Byron's choice of *virtù* rather than Virtue is forced upon him by the determinants of his temperament, by his choleric blood? The question becomes of greater importance as the drama advances, for, after Byron's return from England at the beginning of the fifth act of *The Conspiracy*, not a great deal that is fresh is added to the factors that have already been seen at work building up the dramatic portrait of Byron. We contemplate not the addition of new factors to Byron's inner drama, but the gradual obfuscation of his faculties.

It is true that Chapman employs a psychological formula to help him and us in the reading of Byron's character—the formula of the 'choleric man'. But it is nowhere in the play suggested that this accident of his temperament controls his *choice*, and that it is intended to be seen as a choice I have attempted to show. To read Chapman's creative understanding of Byron as 'sympathy' for a creature whose conduct is determined by his mental perturbations and to infer from that Chapman's own reading of *la condition humaine* is a too ready invoking of 'Elizabethan psychology': it is calling up Timothy Bright to exorcize Hamlet.[7]

These remarks can be expanded into a consideration of the last part of the double play. In *The Tragedy* we learn little more of the *data* of Byron's character; we learn a good deal more about his situation. And what we have already learnt about his character is confirmed and sharpened by the opposites that are now ranged against him and the alternatives that still remain open to him. His great opposite is the King; the alternative that still remains for him is that of overcoming Fortune by Virtue, instead of attempting to overcome it by *virtù*. The latter, Chapman

7. See L. C. T. Forest, 'A caveat for critics against invoking Elizabethan psychology', *PMLA*, lxi, 1946, 651–72.

believes (if the English counsellor is to be trusted), is, in reality, but 'putting the roof to Fortune'.

It is the King who is the real Alexander of the play. The theme of Virtue triumphing over Fortune is activated in his person, characteristically in combination with contemporary doctrines *de regimine principum*. It is the King who sets out in summary form all that we have learned so far about Byron (an 'Achilles' and a 'Ulysses' as he calls him) as well as the extent of his fall, the inward danger that menaces him, in the first act of *The Tragedy* (1.i.55–86). It is the King who shows himself the correct— or Plutarchian—analyser of the relation of Fortune and Virtue in his prayer for his son: 'Let him by virtue quite [cut] off from Fortune / Her feather'd shoulders and her winged shoes' (1.i. 141–2). It is in the light of this solemn interview between the virtuous King and the infant Dauphin (who has been born since the play began)[8] that we must view the ensuing scene. In this scene Byron is shown making a characteristically false analysis of the real situation of the kingdom (1.ii.14–42), with himself cast for the role of Rebel Creator, a 'Roman Camillus' laying claim to an ἀρετή which he has forsworn. His speech is of course received by La Fin and the rest with flattering exclamations: La Fin even calls him 'learn'd'—the vivid misapplication of Chapman's favourite adjective suggests very forcibly that the confusion and inversion of vice and virtue which Byron affects to see in the kingdom is resident only in his own soul. The masque or entertainment, which closes the act, feeble though it is, contains something in the nature of a reply to Byron's pose as the neglected peacetime soldier (ll. 5–10), and the whole theme of the masque is an answer to his charge that sensual vice informs the kingdom —a charge which Chapman, by adopting this device, perhaps intends us to see as wildly out of accord with the true state of things.

In the succeeding acts Byron is given several opportunities to repent and seek the King's forgiveness by confession. How far is his failure to do so represented by Chapman as psychologically determined in such a way as to suggest an ethical confusion? Byron's conspiracy is, unequivocally, a league with foreign princes to overthrow Henry and deliver the crown of France into

8. In *Conspiracy*, 1.ii.200 we learn of the King's marriage, in 1v.i.144 of the Dauphin's birth.

Byron's own hands (*Tragedy*, III.i.53–56); his evasions and pro-
testations in the scene with D'Escures (III.i.60–115), his lies to
Janin and his politic excuses in the next scene (III.i.161–225), his
final decision to go to court not because the King commands
him but because of his receipt of a letter from La Fin (III.i.248–51)
must be measured against the good advice given him by the
various messengers. In these messages the hand of a good and
virtuous King is seen at work. D'Escures offers him further
command and honours from the King's hands and meets with a
sophistical refusal ('Does he think / It is an action worthy of my
valour / To turn my back to an approaching foe?'); Janin's appeal
is much graver and more personal. It lays no emphasis on the
new tasks which the King wishes Byron to undertake but only
on his chance of clearing himself in a personal interview. It is
not till this too has failed that the King resorts to a trick and La
Fin's letter is delivered. There is no sign of Byron's choleric
nature here. The explanation is more old-fashioned: Byron's
conduct is guided by 'admiration of his [own] pride and folly'
(III.ii.9), or, as Janin says, 'a *will* by giddiness to fall [rather] /
Than to descend by judgment' (III.i.192–3). Vitry comments in choral
fashion on the likely fall of this fortunate man—but Virtue is
not one of his powers, although he is granted 'valour, wit, and
smooth use of the tongue / Set strangely to the pitch of popular
likings' (III.ii.14–15). And, by way of contrast to Byron's conduct,
we have in III.ii one of the most extended portraits of Henry as
the virtuous Prince after the manner of the *specula*.[9] Indeed, as
Byron's tragedy draws towards its end, the trajectory of his fall
crosses the ascension of the King. Epernon's remark,

> Farewell for ever! So have I discern'd
> An exhalation that would be a star
> Fall, when the sun forsook it, in a sink.
> Shoes ever overthrow that are too large,[1]
> And hugest cannons burst with overcharge,

9. Chapman makes much of one technical detail: Henry has avoided the building
of internal fortresses on the well-known Senecan principle that 'We need not build
strong Citadels, on high hills, nor fortifie vnaccessible places . . . Clemencie will
secure a King in the open field. His only inpregnable fortresse is the loue of his
Cittizens' (*De Clementia* I.xix, in *Workes* . . ., p. 598). Cf. Isocrates, *Ad Nicoclem*, 21,
and Machiavelli, *Prince*, xx.

1. I prefer the Quarto reading of 'shooes' (for 'shoes') to Parrott's emendation
'shows'. [Ure argues for this in *MLR*, liv, 1959, 557–8.] See Parrott, p. 627.

must be referred to the King's words:

> Now I am settled in my sun of height
> The circular spendor and full sphere of state.
>
> (v.i.138 ff.)

Special emphasis is laid on the King's refusal to do other than prosecute Byron by 'law's usual course', his complete rejection of the theory that because 'princes . . . are masters of their laws', therefore 'they may resolve them in what forms they please / So all conclude in [the appearance of] justice' (IV.ii.31–33).[2] The King is another Chabot, an embodiment of justice; in both, the soul's eye is sharpened with the sacred inner light of the almighty wisdom.[3]

Byron's conduct during his trial and the preparations for his death form the subject of those final portions of the play in which Chapman's creative understanding and dramaturgical exploitation of his central figure are most likely to be mistaken for a confusion of ethical values, a sympathy with Byron's 'sin'. But the figurative language which is used of Byron suggests the relationship which Chapman sees him as holding to the kingdom, orderly, peaceable, and well ruled, whose order he has tried to disturb. We may set aside Henry's description of him as 'a foul and damnable atheist and traitor', a leper 'buried quick in ulcers' (IV.ii.250–4), as merely Henry's point of view within the dramatic context as it shapes itself at that moment. But it is possible to distinguish between this kind of utterance, which belongs to the level of the dramaturgical 'business' and the kind which is woven deeper into the dialectical scheme and which, by flashes of imaginative figures, lights up the face and bearing of the dramatist himself. Byron is the air-drawn hawk that 'stoops in a puddle' (Janin, III.i. 207–11), the blinded horse, dulled by a senseless apoplexy (Captain, IV.i.106–10), the overcharged cannon and the rotten exhalation (Epernon, IV.ii. 291–5), the savage boar (D'Escures, v.iii.229–35).

At the trial Byron holds out as long as he can; but when all is revealed upon La Fin's testimony, he takes refuge in the defence that he has been bewitched, that, in short, his conduct

---

2. Compare the King's refusal to break the treaty and his remarks on the King and the Law in v.i.48–68.

3. Compare IV.ii.77–79 with *Tragedy of Chabot*, I.i.93–107.

has been psychologically determined—'... this damn'd enchanter
... took into his will my motion' (v.ii.264–5). We have heard
little about witchcraft in the play since La Fin's claim in *The
Conspiracy* (II.ii.110–27), but we have heard a great deal about
'Machiavellian' practice; the two are equated in the person of
La Fin (cf. the King's description of him in *The Conspiracy*,
I.i.154–61). Byron's claim that he has been bewitched by Machiavellian practice is true enough;[4] but the whole course of the
play runs counter to his plea that he could not have helped
himself. The *sententiae* of the judges (v.ii.174–7) may sound
hollow, but that is perhaps in the nature of dramatic *sententiae*
when they sound in our ears. They must be balanced against
Byron's wild criticism of the King ('politic and thankless royalty',
v.ii.182–3), which cannot be accepted if the King, as we have already seen him delineated, means anything at all in the politico-
moral scheme, and also against Byron's characteristic claim to
be an exemplar of virtue accompanied by a characteristically
wrong analysis of the relation between Virtue and Fortune:

> Virtue in great men must be small and slight,
> For poor stars rule where she is exquisite.
>
> (v.ii.186–7)

The fact that Byron has been bewitched by the Machiavellian
does not of course diminish Chapman's case against the political
practices associated with La Fin and so emphatically rejected by
Henry. Indeed, Byron's fall is an illustration of the fascination
which is an agent of their dangerous power. Moreover, even in
this scene Byron's outburst of choler is the consequence of an
external check rather than the antecedent which determines his
way of behaving. Just as he raged when he found the stars adverse, or when he came up against the King's conception of his
kingly duty and justice in the refusal of the fortress, so now when
he is faced with the inescapable truth about his own actions, his
choler bursts forth, reaction rather than determinant. Against
Death, the last factor in *la condition humaine* which he cannot
evade, he rages in the same way.

Byron's dying speeches show him gradually passing out of the
politico-moral world altogether, so that the themes of Virtue
and Fortune are superseded, as well as the contrast between the

4. Though the judges tend to disbelieve him (v.ii.282–3).

real and the corrupted Alexander. Instead, the personal agony
domineers. The dimensions of the play expand, and Byron
changes from the rebellious noble, rightly condemned for his
treason, to an archetype of the dying tragic hero. The only
element that connects him with the Byron that has gone before
is his choler, always the characteristic least connected with his
activities on the politico-moral level. Nothing in the rest of the
play prepares us for Byron the neo-Platonist (v.iv.32–37) or for
the entry of Religion (v.ii. 205–14). That the dying Byron fails to
be integrated with the living Byron should not suggest that the
moralia of the political drama in which he has been performing
are rendered nugatory. Chapman has, however, led his hero
beyond the political drama and the moral treatise buried in it,
and is writing on the level of poetic symbolism. This shifting of
viewpoint and change of tone is only 'confusing' if we have remained unaware that the play is written on the assumption that
such shifts may legitimately be made: from and to the levels of
political and moral philosophy, expressed in dramatic form of
impartial choral commentary, and of dramatic and poetic
symbolism. As in the Bussy plays and *Caesar and Pompey*, it is
the task of writing the dying scenes of his heroes that most
strikingly serves to recall Chapman to the business of poetic
drama away from this preoccupation with moral philosophy.
Byron's death, however greatly executed, cannot be intended to
justify retrospectively his ambition or his treason. His final
speech seems rather to place the whole world of ambitions,
treason, good kings and bad, even Plutarchian Virtue, in the
perspective of Religion poetically expressed:

> Fall on your knees then, statists, ere ye fall,
> That you may rise again . . . see in me
> How you are pour'd down from your clearest heavens.

'Statists' suggest that Byron is referring to 'politicians' in the
contemporary pejorative sense; but the image of the 'clearest
heavens' reminds us even of Henry's 'circular splendour and full
sphere of state'.[5] But this final moral of the play, if final moral it
be, lies outside, or above, the play as a 'political testament'.

Nor is Byron's tragic end and the sympathy which is active in
Chapman's description of it so detached from the Byron who

5. Henry's use of the adjective 'circular' connects his phase with Byron's reference of the Heavens. See *Poems*, p. 425.

has gone before as might at first appear. Throughout the play
the new, or Machiavellian principle that politics is a science, a
body of rules and 'arts', fights with the older idea that the right
of Nature and 'simple virtue' are the proper nourishment of an
imperial line.[6] Either view presupposes its own analysis of the
nature of man. Since Chapman holds the older view, he conceives man as describable in terms of Virtue and the virtues
(Fortitude, Humanity, Continence, and so on),[7] not in terms of a
sceptical analysis of man as necessarily perverse and depraved.[8]
It therefore follows that he conceives Byron in terms of the
virtues and his fall as an inner corruption of these virtues. But
Byron remains describable in terms of Virtue and virtues (or
their corruption) throughout all his vicissitudes: it is this fact
which allows Byron to be, dramatically speaking, 'rescued' at the
end of the play, to have his apotheosis. Byron's description of
his soul rousing itself like a falcon and stretching its silver wings
(v.iv.29–30) is neither a display of sympathy on the part of the
dramatist for Byron's wilful corruption of his virtues nor a denial of the political moral of the play as embodied in the Henry–
Byron–La Fin relationship. It is merely an admission that Byron
is still a man as Chapman, and not Machiavelli, analysed men.
Not even Lady Macbeth, though physically possessed by demons, could become wholly evil, as Professor Curry has pointed
out. No one even attempts to describe Byron, bewitched though
he is, as 'fiendlike'. Moreover, the persistence of the old analysis
of human nature allows Byron's corruption to appear as tragic:
we have not been watching the overthrow of an allegorical
personification of political depravity (such as La Fin very nearly
is), but that of a man whose virtue had corrupted—even corrupted into a belief that he *could* act like a Machiavellian and according to the Machiavellian analysis of human nature.[9] Such a spectacle only ceases to be tragic if, by neglecting the political moral
of the play, we allow ourselves to share the view of man's nature

6. As stated by Byron (acting as 'Chorus') in *Tragedy*, III.i.10 ff.

7. Cf. the passage from 'Eugenia', quoted on p. 128 above.

8. Machiavelli wrote: 'Whoever desires to found a state and give it laws, must
start with assuming that all men are bad and ever ready to display their vicious
nature . . . men act right only upon compulsion; but from the moment that they
have the option . . . they never fail to carry confusion and disorder everywhere',
Discourses, I.iii. Cf. Cassirer, pp. 148–9. Contrast the choral passage from *Tragedy*,
cited in n. 6 above.

9. See *Conspiracy*, III.i. 25 ff. and III.iii.115–45.

which Chapman was indirectly attacking, to see, that is, Byron's fall in terms of a failure to become an effective statist; or if, by paying too much attention to the political moral and not enough to the human and dramatic contexts in which Byron moves, we expect Byron to behave with the inhuman consistency of an allegorization, the dramatist's sympathy withdrawn from him because he has fallen from virtue. Byron could not become wholly evil and therefore 'unsympathetic' if Chapman is to be true to his original analysis of human nature, just as Henry, and not Byron, must be shown to be the really virtuous man, if Chapman is to be true to his championship of political conservatism against political Machiavellianism. Chapman maintains both truths, which, in his philosophy, were interdependent. Thus he was able to give Henry his triumph, and Byron his tragedy.

9
Marriage and the domestic drama in Heywood and Ford

I

The new murder play, so formlessly topical, and the old prodigal son play, with its didactic symmetries, both help to compose the Elizabethan domestic drama. If the citizen rank of the characters and 'the sensibility of ordinary people in ordinary life'[1] are looked upon as characteristic of this kind of drama, it is difficult to deny the claims of *The Glasse of Governement* and *Arden of Feversham* to be included in the discussion every time a consideration of the domestic theme is attempted. And if the 'common man as hero' is the criterion, as it is for Mr Adams,[2] we will be constrained, like him, to include not only *'Tis Pity She's a Whore* but also perhaps *The Roman Actor* and even *Romeo and Juliet,* and countless others, in the genre. What is of interest here is not so much to define more precisely a kind whose shifting edges leave the historian uneasy as to find some central characteristic which, even if it severely limits the number of plays to be considered, will permit the revaluation of some fine plays that have, from time to time, been accepted into the category. If we add to the three criteria already mentioned a fourth—that the play concern itself with the relationship between husband and wife—we arrive at a convenient limitation. This is not to propose the use of another label—the 'marriage play' or some such term—with the threat of another formula lurking beneath it. The term, used as a label, would obviously take us far outside the domestic genre—to *Othello* and beyond— and its edges would be as indefinite as any. But it suggests that

First published in *English Studies*, xxxii, 1951, 200–16.

1. Mr Eliot's phrase, *Selected Essays* (London, 1934), p. 175.
2. H. H. Adams, *English Domestic or Homiletic Tragedy 1575–1642* (New York, 1943), p. 1.

the strength of the three plays, written at different times between 1603 and 1630, and to be considered here in each other's
light, lies in the way that they dramatize husband and wife.
This eliminates most of the murder plays, too, where the interest is in the murder and not in the marriage; it gives us some
chance of escaping from the pressure of various kinds of homi-
lectic tradition—best exemplified in the prodigal son plays—
and allows us to read the plays as something less unscrupulously
formalized than mere versions of homily. For, while it is a code
of marriage that lies at their basis, the tragedies (for such they
mainly are) could not have occurred without that order being
disturbed by the aberration of one or other partner. A play as
impressive as *A Woman Killed with Kindness* is not simply, as
Mr Adams would have it, a *pièce à thèse*.

It is true that a playwright would be sustained in his use of the
theme by common agreements about marriage amongst his
audience. Chilton Powell and L. B. Wright have shown the variety and wide distribution of popular books on marriage: the
citizen doctrine of marriage is already settled before the earliest
of the plays appears, nor does it alter much in the years that
follow.[3] There is little trace in these decent and godly treatises of
those preoccupations of the courtly literature for which the
Elizabethan period is justly renowned: the conventions of
passionate love preserved in the sonnet, the impossible shees,
the 'Platonic' masquerades, the Phillidas and Coridons—all
these are inconceivably remote from the interests of the authors
of *The Glasse of Godly Loue*, *A Discourse of Marriage and Wiving*,
and *A Happy Husband: or Directions for a Maid to Chuse her Mate*.
Not quite so remote, perhaps, are the ecclesiological discriminations of sectary and Catholic about the doctrine of matrimony.[4]

3. L. B. Wright, *Middle-Class Culture in Elizabethan England* (Chapel Hill, 1935),
p. 226. Wright is speaking of a period of citizen treatise-writing extending from 1558
to 1640.

4. The current argument between Puritans and sectarians on the one hand and
Catholics on the other as to whether marriage is a necessary evil (the Catholic view)
or an 'honourable and natural association between men and women of which children were the proper result but not the prime cause' (the Puritan view) is discussed
by Chilton Powell, *English Domestic Relations 1487–1653* (New York, 1917), p. 120.
And cf. William Haller, *The Rise of Puritanism* (New York, 1938), pp. 120 f., and
Wright, pp. 203, 226. But neither domestic play nor middle-class domestic conduct
book is much concerned with the ontology of marriage; they are practical affairs
which very often confine themselves to formulating sensible *post factum* rules for
domestic living in a bourgeois milieu. Nor do the plays argue the current contro-

There are many points where a particular play may read like a version of the conduct books, as when Mistress Arthur in *How a Man may Choose a Good Wife from a Bad* refuses to divorce her termagant husband and he, repentant, draws the moral at the conclusion:

> he that will chuse
> A good wife from a bad, come lerne of me
> That haue tried both, in wealth and miserie . . .[5]

The ethical basis of the play is the doctrine, reiterated everywhere in the treatises, that the wife should win her mate with mildness:

> for each *crosse*
> Answer'd with *anger*, is to both a losse[6]

—a theme of the two *Patient Grissell* plays, just as the husband's duty of ungrudging tolerance is emphasized throughout Henry Porter's entertainment *The Two Angry Women of Abingdon*. A distich in Field's *Amends for Ladies*:

> Who fals, because her husband so hath done,
> Cures not his wound, but in herselfe makes one,[7]

is, applied to either partner, the unshakeable doctrine of marriage play and domestic conduct book alike.[8] But even such plays as these are not simply homiletic, since the playwright's purpose is not the same as the treatise-maker's. Niccholes and Hannay and the others who write on marriage wish to advise their readers on choice and instruct them in conduct; they have, as Haller writes of the Puritan John Dod, 'the practical utilitarian [purpose] of directing behaviour to moral ends . . . in plain straightforward prose [or pedestrian verse], neither eloquent nor inspiring but apt and well salted'. The playwright, although

---

versy about the relative importance of the civil contract and the ecclesiastical solemnization (on which consult Powell, p. 37), or delve into the question that agitated Calvin (*Institutes*, trans. Norton, London, ?1599, IV.xix.34) whether marriage was or was not a sacrament.

5. Ed. A. E. Swaen, in *Materialien zur Kunde des älteren englischen Dramas*, xii (Louvain, 1912), 2721–3.

6. 'A Wiues behaviour', *The Poetical Works of Patrick Hannay* (Hunterian Club ed., Glasgow, 1875), p. 172.

7. II.ii.122–3 (*The Plays of Nathan Field*, ed. W. Peery, Austin, Texas, 1950).

8. Cf. for example Niccholes's *Discourse* (Harleian Miscellany, London, 1809), iii.280 f. It was not of course necessary for play to borrow from treatise or treatise from play: the ideas in both are 'the reflection of current thought rather than an influence from one field to another' (Powell, p. 205).

he accepts the morality from which the treatises proceed, is concerned with more complex problems. No matter how closely we juxtapose the plays with their analogous treatises, we are obliged to remember, even in considering the meagre excellences of Porter or Field, that the dramatists had to handle character and incident before an audience, and have, therefore, the right to be judged as dramatists and not as homilists. This absolves us from indicating all the points where play matches treatise. We need remember only that the plays belong to the same world as the middle-class treatise—a world that is not very interested in nice discriminations about the theology of marriage that tends to reject 'Platonic' and passionate love as impartially as an ascetic or suspicious attitude to marriage; a world, indeed, that is no satellite of the aristocratic culture that produced Donne's love poems, the antilogies of the curious Burton, or the insinuating realism of Bacon's essay on marriage. As Burton remarked, 'What cares *vulgus hominum* what they say?'[9]

II

That the play should be looked at without the intrusion of too many preconceptions about ruling formulas is particularly important in the case of what has always been justly considered the finest example of the genre, Thomas Heywood's *A Woman Killed with Kindness*. It is apposite that in this play the theme of marriage is handled in a way that contributes immensely to the dramatic force of the work, yet without any departure from an accepted code. It is the agreement about this code, which Heywood could assume in his audience—an agreement reinforced by the powerful appeal of the theme quite apart from any conscious formulation of it—that contributed to its effect and can still contribute today.[1] Those who have written on this play have not

9. *The Anatomy of Melancholy* (London, 1881), p. 624 (part 3, sect. 2, mem. 5, subs. 5).

1. Powell (p. 124) says that marriage as an institution was not so highly valued then as nowadays. Certainly neither the Anglican Catholic view of marriage as a necessary evil nor Calvin's equation, proceeding from a quite opposite principle, that 'it is a good and holy ordinance of God, so tillage, carpentrie, shooemakers craft, barbers craft, are lawful ordinances of God' would be very sympathetically received nowadays. But whatever the theory may have been, it is surely safe to assert that the depiction of suffering husband or wife betrayed would have an appeal to an audience of husbands and wives and their children quite unaffected by the relatively low value which churchmen continued to set on the institution of matrimony right up to the time when post-Calvinistic Puritanism began to glorify it.

done it justice. It is worth while to reconsider the whole work with special attention to the objections that it has had to meet.

The relation between the main plot, the story of the Frankfords and Wendoll, and the subsidiary action has always caused difficulty.[2] We may agree that an underplot should not merely distract our attention with a set of irrelevant events thrown in for good measure, which even constrict the dramatist's freedom in his handling of the main action. Dr Clark makes a double objection that this underplot is distracting in just that way and that the appearance of a Lucrece in the fields of Yorkshire is an incongruity sharply pointed by the domestic realism of her setting. Miss Townsend has discerned, in answer to this objection, the thematic unity which binds the two plots together in the form of a contrast between Mistress Frankford's easy yielding of her honour and Susan's Roman staunchness.[3] Even more striking than this play upon honour is the way the underplot takes up the paradox of the drama's title. Sir Charles must discharge the burden of moral debt which his enemy's kindness has laid upon him;[4] similarly, Mistress Frankford must find a way to repay with interest the kindness of Frankford after his discovery of her adultery. Cheated of her rightful punishment,

---

2. See the various observations of Courthope (*History of English Poetry*, Oxford, 1910, vol. iv, p. 215), A. M. Clark (*Thomas Heywood*, Oxford, 1931, p. 230), McIlwraith (*Five Elizabethan Tragedies*, London, 1938, pp. xvii–xviii), and others cited by Miss Townsend in 'The artistry of Thomas Heywood's double plots', *Philological Quarterly*, xxv, 1946, 97 f. Since Clark says of the sub-plot that 'We endure it, but it escapes the memory', I give a summary. It is the story of Sir Charles Mountford who quarrels with Sir Francis Acton, another member of the Yorkshire squirearchy, during a hawking match. Mountford and his men fight with Acton and his men, and Mountford kills two of Acton's retainers. He is put on trial and acquitted, but the legal expenses ruin him. All he has left is a small house and garden to which he retires with his sister Susan. He falls into a moneylender's power and is finally deprived of his remaining estate and thrown into the counter. Acton, who up to now has been implacable, falls in love with Susan, and for her sake secretly pays her brother's debts and releases him. Mountford is shamed by this kindness, and, unable to repay Acton in any other way, offers to prostitute his sister Susan to him. As in *The Rape of Lucrece* and Webster's *Appius and Virginia* (which may be partly Heywood's work), we have a scene in which Susan prefers death to dishonour. But Acton greatly refuses his opportunity and takes the hand of the penniless girl in marriage, himself providing the dowry. Mountford gives up the unequal battle with his enemy's kindness and the two men are reconciled.

3. Townsend, p. 101. She adds the balance of Wendoll's dishonour with Acton's honour.

4. v.i.63. The text used is that of McIlwraith in *Five Elizabethan Tragedies* (London, 1938).

in which she expects to suffer the part of a Tamyra or a Penthea (IV.v.90–91), she must herself inflict upon herself the appropriate penalty in order to discharge the mounting debt to husband and conscience. Frankford's improper kindness has surcharged her and in the end kills her—it is the paradox at the heart of the play, suitably pointed by the concluding lines of the fifth act. Both plots thus explore this strange paradox and run a concurrent course: Sir Charles suffers under the monstrous burden of being forgiven by a bitter enemy and is driven to an immorality (the prostitution of his sister) in order to free himself of it; Mistress Frankford, pardoned by a deeply injured husband, has to rid herself of the debt by an act of contrition that proceeds far beyond Christian penitence. She starves herself to death. In the conclusion, Acton's magnanimity to Susan is balanced by Frankford's passionate compassion as his wife dies. Both men have been consistently kind and these final mercies are a consummation of their virtuous Magnificence. Heywood was not writing a problem play, and it is true that the stark unusualness of Mistress Frankford's action and fate is softened by the conventional lines of the sin-repentance-forgiveness scheme which is all that Adams sees in the play. But Heywood *was* concerned, as his title suggests, to exploit a paradox which perhaps ran deeper than he knew. It is at least difficult, in the age of Ibsen, to refrain from asking why the increasing disproportion between the kindness of Acton and the indebtedness of Sir Charles should cease to worry the latter at the point it does, or to forget that the depiction of a justifiable self-slaughter in *Samson Agonistes* led even Milton into some obliquity and wresting of doctrine.[5] Heywood, of all writers, had least wish to divellicate such problems. The fact, however, that his play evades the question goes closer to an explanation of why it is not a *very* great work than any attempts by later critics, applying criteria never very clearly articulated, to charge its author with dramaturgical incompetence.

If the thematic unities of Honour and Kindness hold good, the point satisfies, at least, the requirement that an underplot should help to give structure, solidity, and verisimilitude to the architecture of the play world and underpin our understanding of the principal action. We can, in that case, derive some added

5. H. J. C. Grierson, *Milton and Wordsworth* (Cambridge, 1937), pp. 146–7.

pleasure from the shapeliness of the correspondences; we can recognize that Mistress Frankford's attempt to discharge her debt is not so incredible when we view the motive operating with strange results in a man of honour like Sir Charles. But an underplot may also be asked to give us a different kind of pace and rhythm from that of the main plot. In *A Woman Killed with Kindness* we cannot, by any abrupt removals from banqueting hall to porter's lodge, enjoy the relief that clownish gambols supposedly afford to the tensions engendered by princely circumstance. Though the source be ultimately in the *novelle*,[6] the story of Susan has, in every sense, been domesticated. Heywood does seem, however, to have tried to make the Susan story go faster than the Frankford story: the great trajectory of Sir Charles's descent from prosperous country gentleman, whose fall stands not in the prospect of belief, to hind and prisoner, and his recovery from these declined conditions, contrasts, in the rapidity with which we absorb it all, to the slow working of the other tale—the arrival of Wendoll the seducer, his honourable resistances, Nick's suspicion of him, Nick's discovery, followed by the slow-dropping agonies of the central scenes. This may be an impression difficult to substantiate, but it bears closely upon another, and final, question about the relationship between the two plots: why it is in the nature of the subplot, admitting its thematic correspondence with the main plot, that it should end happily, and in the nature of the main plot that it should end solemnly. The difference can be explained thus: what happens to Sir Charles is something external to his deeper self, the kind of misfortune that can be spoken of plainly in terms of debts, land, and gentle status. Although he twice hovers on the verge of dissolution, when conscience-stricken after the falconry affray and when he meditates the surrender of his sister's honour, his agony never marches with Frankford's—Heywood does not trench him to the heart. He can mount aloft and resume gentility by a mere twist of Fortune's wheel. But Frankford has been flung from the wheel. His is a burrowing grief, inward and slower, like Geraldine's in *The English Traveller*; he is betrayed in a point of deepest consequence, his marriage, and when he recovers he is a changed man, existent in a world he had not formerly known, the world of repentance, exalted pardon, and

6. As Clark indicates, p. 230.

imminent death. Thus, though thematically the two plots encourage understanding of one another, the contest between the
way Mountford's character is sketched and Frankford's graved,
is one feature which helps to keep the subsidiary plot, as it should
be, decorously subordinate to the main plot, which has digged
deeper in love's mine. The cohesion between the two plots is
one of moral themes which increases our understanding of the
play's rationale; the difference between the two characters is
the point where the dramatist's (as distinct from the moralist's)
task begins. And in the Frankford story we are inducted into a
world where the profound theme of marriage, unknown to the
underplot, is stated not in terms of moral formulas but by the
more potent agencies of dramatic character and poetic speech.
We look in it not for understanding but for catharsis.

When we enter upon the main plot, we have to dispose of one
more objection. Heywood was not the first writer of domestic
dramas to handle the theme of a virtuous woman fallen. The
author of *A Warning for Faire Women* (1599) had simply fobbed
his audience off with a dumb show,[7] and Heywood himself
made no attempt to represent the seduction of Wincott's wife by
Delavil in *The English Traveller*. In *A Woman Killed with Kindness*
he was ill-advised, or courageous, enough to put the incident on
the stage. The sudden breakdown of Mistress Frankford's
resistance to Wendoll in II.iii.152–4 is condemned as, by modern
standards, psychologically implausible—the result according
to Clark, of the constriction of the main plot by the underplot—
or hardly justified as a fragment of obsolete psychology having to
do with old beliefs about man's dominance by a single passion
and the debility of virtuous women placed in Eve's situation.[8]
It may be that we must gulp down these dry morsels; but it is
fair to Heywood to remember the necessary time-scheme and
architectonic of the whole play. The three great incidents of
the Frankford story, the seduction, the discovery, and the death,
to all of which the wedding scene is an important prologue, are
three blocks of time dramaturgically handled. To the first
naturally belong the struggle of conscience, the seduction, the

---

7. *A Warning for Faire Women*, ii (ed. Simpson, *The School of Shakespeare*, London,
1879, vol. ii, p. 269).

8. See Hardin Craig's remarks on the play in *The Enchanted Glass* (New York,
1936), pp. 128–36, and cf. Wright on 'The controversy over women', chap. xiii.

yielding. Seduction and surrender are the *données* of the succeeding incidents on which Heywood's special interest and the
originality of the play are centred. Heywood could not delay
with this early effect without disrupting the structure, which is
in itself quite satisfying, and, because the audience are not
baulked, much more satisfying than the reticence of *The English
Traveller*. Further, since the play so utterly disregards the
unity of time in the interest of extracting full pathos from the
marriage theme, it was all the more desirable that Heywood
should achieve a shape for it by a forthright representation of
the main incidents of the marriage's chequered course, each
being allotted only that share of stage time proportionate to
its importance in the total scheme.

That scheme, and its moving effect, depend very largely upon
the marriage theme, for the tragic powers of *A Woman Killed
with Kindness* derive from the broken marriage. It is a domestic
play in this narrower sense, as well as in its setting and literary
affinities. The first scene opens with the wedding festivities,
with Mistress Frankford already cast for the part of the dutiful
wife favoured by the makers of conduct books:

> A perfect wife already, meek and patient;
> How strangely the word 'husband' fits your mouth,
> Not married three hours since! Sister, 'tis good;
> You, that begin betimes thus, must needs prove
> Pliant and duteous in your husband's love. (i.i.37–41)

Sir Charles's next speech celebrates in what is perhaps the finest
of all passages of homespun domestic verse the happiness of the
marriage and the rightness of Frankford's choice (i.i.55–72). It is
of these scenes, of the country measures—

> Hark, they are all on the hoigh;
> They toil like mill-horses, and turn as round,—
> Marry, not on the toe. Ay, and they caper,
> Not without cutting; you shall see, tomorrow,
> The hall-floor peck'd and dinted like a mill-stone,
> Made with their high shoes . . . (i.i.85–91)

and of the footing in parlour and yard that we are reminded
during the discovery scenes of the fourth act. For a key to these
scenes is recollection, the desire to undo what has been done and
to return to the former happy state (iv.v.51 f.). The strongest

emphasis is placed upon the way this early happiness has been destroyed by the breaking of the marriage bond:

> This is the key that opes my outward gate;
> This is the hall-door; this my withdrawing chamber;
> But this, that door that's bawd unto my shame,
> Fountain and spring of all my bleeding thoughts,
> Where the most hallowed order and true knot
> Of nuptial sanctity hath been profan'd;
> It leads to my polluted bed-chamber,
> Once my terrestrial heaven, now my earth's hell,
> The place where sins in all their ripeness dwell.
>
> (IV.v.8–16)

And, later, it is his desire not to suffer the unbearable tension between what is and what was that urges Frankford to rid the house of everything that may remind him of his wife (v.ii.1–11) and that leads to the famous scenes with the abandoned lute (v.ii and iii), scenes of an artistry not less great, though more extended, than that moment in *Othello* where the Moor remembers that he can no longer speak of 'my wife'. In all these scenes Heywood's mastery is complete, displaying a perfect control of stage effect and timing and a complete reconciliation between character and theme—that is, we are enabled to feel with Frankford's sufferings and yet contemplate the firm development of the moral tale of the broken marriage. It is a point where the social seriousness with which the marriage contract is viewed expertly supports the *agon* in the individual before us. To realize the extent of Heywood's achievement here we need only compare it with the management of the discovery scene in *The English Traveller* (IV.iii): in Young Geraldine's long speech we find the same trajectory from happiness to misfortune described —the lover's fond recollection of his contract, the discovery, the suppressed movement of revenge, and the sudden stripping of the man of all his comforts. Yet the scene is less commendable because the audience are as unprepared for the surprise as Geraldine himself. It is an effective stage situation, a thrilling jolt, but we are not able, as we are in the earlier play, to bring our previous knowledge of the broken contract, and the moral and social gravity which that theme has engendered in us, to bear at just that point where it is stated in terms of a particular individual's endurance of it in his own life—where, in fact, the moral theme becomes incarnate in the suffering husband. (The surrender of Mistress Frankford herself in II.iii, which is the ground of these scenes, is, rightly, not felt as they are: there we are merely presented with the act itself, the datum only of the theorem of tragic consequences which are the substance of drama as distinct from morality. Consequently, our reaction there is one of regret, tinged with moral reproof, and an acceptance that this is a part of the unfolding of the story.)

The discovery scenes in Massinger's *The Fatal Dowry* (which may have been written with Field's help) are also a means of measuring Heywood's distinctive quality. Massinger, too, is able to sound the note of irrefragable loss in Beaumelle's speech:

> While I was good I was a part of you,
> And of two, by the virtuous harmony
> Of our fair minds, made one; but, since I wander'd
> In the forbidden labyrinth of lust,
> What was inseparable is by me divided.
> With justice, therefore, you may cut me off . . .[9]

But this speech bears almost the relationship of an afterthought to the discoveries of the previous scene. The story is not unlike Romont playing the part of Nick in *A Woman Killed with Kindness*, and Novall Wendoll's role. But Massinger is interested not in any such humanized category as the suffering husband, but in the betrayed Friend and the knightly Revenger: these are local and temporary masks, *personae* derived from aristocratic cults. *The Fatal Dowry* might well, when we remember what Rowe did with it, go in the catalogue for domestic drama, but nothing could illustrate more sharply the difference between this kind and Heywood's kind of domestic play, based on the morality of ordinary men and undisturbed by the currents from an aristocratic troposphere.

The discovery scenes are the part of the play where we feel most deeply the tragedy of the whole affair, because it is in them that the fate of the individual marches with the fate of the marriage, and both are broken. But Heywood carries his play further, bringing to bear the scheme of repentance and forgiveness which Adams has matched with the homiletic teaching of the

9. IV.iv (*The Plays of Philip Massinger*, ed. W. Gifford, 3rd ed., London, 1840, p. 334, col. 2).

day. We can also trace, perhaps more significantly, because closer to the heart of the dramaturgical business, the way the marriage is resuscitated together with the individuals who have sunk with it. It is a theme touched upon, in hugger-mugger fashion, by Field in *Amends for Ladies*,[1] and obtruded into *The Miseries of Enforced Marriage* as a tag for happy ending.[2] But the fullest treatment of it is in Heywood's own earlier play *King Edward IV* (printed in 1600). Here, in the domestic story of Jane Shore, the breach of wedlock and the ruin of wife and husband are studied at some length.[3] The fall of Jane is darkened by recollections of the happiness of her former union,[4] although there is no point in the play where these are focused to the degree of intensity found in *A Woman Killed with Kindness*; and, like Frankford, Shore is kind, though until Jane's final repentance unforgiving.[5] When that final repentance comes, the husband and wife, after their sufferings, rise to a state of exalted sublimity and are new-married in death:

> *Jane.* Oh, dying marriage! oh, sweet married death!
>   Thou grave, which only should'st part faithful friends,
>   Bring'st us together, and dost join our hands.
>   Oh, living death! ev'n in this dying life!
>   Yet, ere I go, once, Matthew! kiss thy wife![6]

In the same way, in *A Woman Killed with Kindness*, though not with Juliet's tragic irony, Mistress Frankford's cold grave is her nuptial bed, and she dies upon the word 'wife':

> My wife, the mother to my pretty babes!
> Both these lost names I do restore thee back,
> And with this kiss I wed thee once again.
>   (v.iv.116–18)

This triumphant flaring-up of the marriage theme is in key with the exaltation of the happy pair; once again Heywood has fused the profound appeal of his domestic theme with the new state of the dramatic characters. Heywood's constant play upon the marriage both as a social institution with 'audience appeal' and

---

1. *Plays*, p. 480.
2. Hazlitt's Dodsley, vol. ix, p. 576.
3. *King Edward IV, Part 2*, ii.i (*Dramatic Works of Thomas Heywood*, ed. Collier, Shakespeare Society, London, 1853, vol. i, pp. 129–30). Cf. iv.iii, p. 176.
4. *King Edward IV, Part 1*, v.iv, p. 84.
5. *King Edward IV, Part 2*, v.ii, p. 184.   6. Ibid., p. 189.

as a means of happiness and grief to individual husband and wife not only bestows a firmness of structure upon the whole story—happiness (the wedding prologue), grief (the discovery of the broken contract), happiness (the remarriage in death)—but also allows him to define the second happiness as something new in kind, wrested from sorrow and penitence. This adventure cannot be, in the common sense, tragic, and not only because it is too busy a confirmation of the moral code. The play is not a tragedy, because the fracture which was felt to possess a tragic quality—the breaking of the contract and of Frankford—is allowed to mend before the conclusion. This mending is, indeed, a natural growth, fundamental to the play's whole scheme, not a hasty splinting as it is in *The Miseries of Enforced Marriage*.

III

If this is a true description of some aspects of Heywood's play, it is worth while to consider, however briefly, a later example of the domestic kind which may be aptly related to it. Middleton's *Women Beware Women* which is a new kind of domestic drama, in which the marriage theme is sophisticated by the playwright's design of showing the impact of court immoralism upon citizen morality. The play therefore provides a useful link between Heywood's and Ford's versions of the theme, for it seems to have been in the nature of the domestic drama that it should extend outwards, grasp, and finally become assimilated to the romance. The extent of this assimilation in the last part of *Women Beware Women* makes its scheme, compared with that of Heywood's play, confused.[7] But the first three acts of the play are impressive, because they too depict the slow dissolution of the marriage bond incarnate in Leantio and Bianca. At the opening of the play the citizen Leantio gives his version of wedded happiness in a scene which, although it is a coarsened and extended version of the wedding prologue in *A Woman Killed with Kindness*, sets the note as firmly. It is repeated in I.iii against the darkening background of the purely courtlike immorality

---

7. Thus, in the last two acts, we have only the voice of the Cardinal, a mere hypostasis of the doctrine of the marriage treatises, and Bianca's dying words ('Now I feel the breach of marriage / At my heart breaking') have become a moral intrusive to the Italianate intrigue.

of the underplot. The theme of the disrupted marriage (after Bianca has been seduced by the Duke) is most articulate in III.i, when Leantio finds Bianca in a condition of peevish dissatisfaction with her middle-class poverty.[8] But it is not until Leantio has been appointed, so to speak, official cuckold to the Duke that the bitterness of his loss really overcomes him, and he develops the 'so strange, so insupportable' theme of Bianca's broken troth in accents of a domineering agony. As a tragic figure Leantio belongs here with Frankford in the discovery scenes.[9] Lastly, in the terrible quarrel between the pair in the fourth act, the marriage is finally and cruelly shattered, the irony and vanity that has so far sustained Leantio breaking down in abuse and threats. Up to this point Middleton maintains the conjunction of moral theme and dramatic business, drawing, like Heywood, on the profound appeal of the marriage relationship and simultaneously matching it with the individual fate. After it, nothing but an intrusive moral links the many deaths with the divorce that has already been accomplished.

IV

The original criteria of the domestic drama—the 'sensibility of ordinary men', the common man as hero—if they are strictly applied, simply confirm the impression that the drama, after passing through the stage represented by *Women Beware Women*, has, in the hands of a playwright so late and sophisticated as Ford, become finally assimilated to a kind quite alien to the middle-class domestic. Ford's work has, however, elements in it which are more congruous with that tradition than his reputation and his almost exclusive devotion to Italian and Hellenic milieux might suggest.[1] It is true that none of Ford's characters,

8. The scene is enclosed within two speeches, III.i.82–109, 271–95, the one expressing Leantio's absolute content as a husband, the other completely reversing his former mood.

9. Though there are other elements in him besides that of suffering husband: consult Professor Ellis-Fermor's remarks, *Jacobean Drama* (London, 1936), pp. 143–4. Bianca, who has attracted more critical supervision than Leantio, is a character belonging much less to that world of domestic grief which is most brilliantly seen in Heywood's play: after her brief appearance as a loving wife in the first scene she is much closer to that part of *Women Beware Women* which explores the impact of an alien morality.

1. The Thorney scenes of *The Witch of Edmonton* conform to most definitions of the kind. The story of Auria and Spinella in *The Lady's Trial* is a notable treatment of

outside *The Witch of Edmonton*, is a common man like Frankford or Leantio; the citizen rank of Annabella and Giovanni is a mere accident. Yet in the case of one play, *The Broken Heart*, a continuity can be suggested. The clue to it is the marriage theme as it is worked out in this play. To establish the continuity is certainly not to attempt to enlarge the definition of domestic drama by adding anything of Ford's to the kind. But if the marriage situation which is buried in *The Broken Heart* is seen in conjunction with other treatments of the theme in the regular domestic drama, it forces us to modify the emphasis which has been laid on Ford's 'revolt against the established order' and the 'unbridled individualism' of his supposedly decadent ethic.

In the opening scene of the play we learn that Penthea had originally been intended for marriage with Orgilus, who describes what followed:

> A freedome of conuerse, an enterchange
> Of holy, and chast loue, so fixt our soules
> In a firm grouth of holy vnion, that no Time
> Can eat into the pledge; we had enjoy'd
> The sweets our vowes expected, had not cruelty
> Preuented all those triumphs we prepar'd for . . .[2]

The cruelty was the marriage of Penthea, enforced upon her by her brother Ithocles, to an insanely jealous nobleman called Bassanes. His brutal follies and her continuing love for Orgilus finally drive her to madness and death. Penthea is at first a meek and dutiful wife (ii.i.656–67); but it soon appears that she rejects Orgilus' appeal in the palace garden (ii.iii.975–8) not because she is faithful to Bassanes but because she regards herself as merely strumpeted to him (iii.i.1195–8; iv.i.1894–9, 1951–5). Her real 'marriage' was with Orgilus—that 'enterchange of holy, and chast loue', the marriage of minds prescribed by the domestic conduct books; she will not offer a prostituted body to her

---

the relations between husband and wife, which, though overlaid with the conventions of friendship and the formal 'trial', is not deflected by them, as *The Fatal Dowry* is, quite away from its centre in the domestic crisis. For the best discussion of the puzzles in the important scenes (iii.iii and v.ii) consult M. J. Sargeaunt, *John Ford* (Oxford, 1935), pp. 87–91. In *Perkin Warbeck* Katherine's faithfulness to Warbeck the husband, after Warbeck the Plantagenet has been discredited, is all that Niccholes or Hannay could have desired.

2. Text in *John Ford's Dramatic Works* (ed. H. de Vocht, in *Materials for the Study of the Old English Drama*, NS, I, Louvain, 1927).

'husband'. Instead, she becomes a '[self-] murthresse' (IV.i.1966) and starves to death to purge what she considers the 'plurisie' of her blood (IV.i.1956–60). Her death is received with terror and despair by the lookers-on, with change of kingdoms and multiple murders.

Professor Sherman's comment on *The Broken Heart*, although nearly half a century has passed since it was made, is still not unrepresentative:

It presents clearly and sharply the conflict between the world's conventions and the heart's desire. It is a plea for the rights of the individual against the tyranny of the matrimonial bond. It powerfully suggests that obedience to the promptings of the heart would conform to a higher morality than passive acceptance of the fetters which conventional morality decrees must be worn and borne. It has, perhaps, the unique distinction of being the first problem play in English.[3]

For Professor Sensabaugh, who does not depart from the general lines laid down in Sherman's critique, Penthea's lament over her wrack'd honour is a 'plea to posterity', an aspect of Ford's modernism:

In backing up this subtle attack upon institutional rights with Burtonian science Ford creates dilemmas which are in every sense real and which smack of the ethical impasse present in modern thought.[4]

According to Sensabaugh, Penthea dies because she suffers from the disease of heroical love, which, frustrated, brings about love-melancholy; she loses her reason and droops into her grave because convention forbids her to love Orgilus, while Bassanes, besides being very jealous, is sexually impotent into the bargain.[5]

We may certainly concede that Ford relies a good deal on Burton's gigantic case-book and that he handles the matrimonial crisis in this play with characteristic vitality and originality. But this originality is of a kind that requires narrower definition; nor is the view that interprets the 'conflict between the world's opinion and the heart's desire',[6] which Havelock Ellis, Sherman, and Sensabaugh read into the play, as ultimately part of an 'insidious' and 'subtle' attack upon institutionalized values an

3. *John Fordes Dramatische Werke* (ed. Bang, *Materialien*, xxiii, Louvain, 1908), xi.
4. *The Tragic Muse of John Ford* (Stanford, 1944), p. 181.
5. Ibid., pp. 65–66.
6. Havelock Ellis, *John Ford* (Mermaid ed., London, 1888), p. xiv.

inference perfectly allowable. If we recur to the opening scene of *The Broken Heart*, we find that Orgilus is describing to his father a contract of love between himself and Penthea which they both consider binding; Crotolon hears sympathetically the tale of Penthea's enforced marriage. There follows immediately, as if to emphasize what should be the proper conduct of a brother towards a sister, the scene with Euphrania. Orgilus undertakes that he will exercise no tyranny in the matter of his sister's choice (1.i.195–200).

This scene lays open the ground of the play's proceeding. It is plain that the 'enterchange of holy, and chast loue', the 'holy vnion' between Penthea and Orgilus, approved by the parents of the couple, was very near to being a precontract of marriage of the kind legally known as spousals *de praesenti*. Such spousals corresponded to a civil marriage ceremony and took the form of a mutual plighting of faith and troth, preferably with a priest as witness. Sexual union sometimes followed after a spousals, although it was considered better to wait for the solemnization in church as well.[7] Orgilus does not declare that he and Penthea had actually exchanged the prescribed words of troth-plighting,[8] and there is no description of the ceremony such as we find in *Twelfth Night*,[9] but his words suggest that Ford thought of the death of Penthea's father as having intervened between the contract and the solemnization, or as having occurred just before the precontract had been virtually accomplished:

> we had enjoy'd
> The sweets our vowes expected, had not cruelty
> Preuented all those triumphs we prepar'd for,
> By *Thrasus* his vntimely death. (1.i.123–6)

The union between Penthea and Orgilus was, then, viewed by Ford as no secret and unconventional marriage of souls, but as something conforming very closely to a public and approved

---

7. Powell, pp. 3–5. Writing about 1600, Henry Swinburne said of spousals *de praesenti* in his *Treatise of Spousals*: 'Albeit there be no witnesses of the Contract, yet the Parties having verily (though secretly) Contracted Matrimony, they are very Man and Wife before God; neither can either of them with safe Conscience Marry elsewhere, so long as the other party liveth.'

8. They are given by Powell, and another example by C. J. Sisson, *Lost Plays of Shakespeare's Age* (Cambridge, 1936), pp. 28–29, who also cites Lyly's *Mother Bombie*, IV.i.

9. *Twelfth Night*, v.i.150–5.

civil contract of marriage. The later behaviour of the pair must
be examined in the light of this fact. Following upon her pledge
to Orgilus, Penthea had been enforced into marriage with
Bassanes. It was not Penthea who, insidiously or otherwise,
questioned the 'laws of conscience and of civil use' but Ithocles
who had sacrilegiously broken them, 'by cunning partly, / Partly
by threats'. Enforced or unduly 'arranged' marriages were a
feature of the time, and were recognized by the makers of
conduct books as a primary cause of matrimonial unhappiness;[1]
the marriage of ill-assorted couples, too, was condemned and
warning *exempla* provided.[2] The marriage of Penthea and Bassanes falls under all these bans and is a denial of the rights of
precontract.

Penthea's despairs need to be set against this background.
The Broken Heart is not the first play to deal with the theme of the
broken precontract.[3] But a glance at the regular domestic drama
alone will indicate the continuity between it and the domestic
theme that lies, overlaid with sophisticated cruelties and a more
penetrating and scientific characterization, in the very core of
Ford's play. William Sampson's *The Vow-Breaker, or the Faire
Maide of Clifton* opens with a spousals *de praesenti* between Anne
and Young Bateman: to Bateman's father Anne is now his
son's lawful wife.[4] But Anne, urged by her own father, breaks
the contract and marries another. Young Bateman's despair is
terrible: he tells Anne, 'German / Is not thy husband: 'tis
Bateman is the best' (1.ii.149–72) and, finally, in a paroxysm of
love-melancholy, he hangs himself (1.iv.1–41)—'that ever poore
young gentleman should die like a bird on a Tree, for the love
to a woman!' Anne is haunted by her lover's ghost and finally
carried off to Hell. In a more famous play, George Wilkins's
The Miseries of Enforced Marriage, Clare and Scarborow plight
their troth with the consent of Clare's father; but Scarborow is
then forced by *his* father into a marriage with Katherine. Clare

1. Powell, p. 124.

2. As in *The Passionate Morrice*, one of the most entertaining of the marriage treatises. Reprinted by the New Shakspere Society (London, 1876). I am grateful to Mr
L. G. Salingar for drawing my attention to this work.

3. The Mariana story in *Measure for Measure*, on which see R. W. Chambers in
Man's Unconquerable Mind (London, 1939), pp. 283–4, and Middleton's *The Change-
ling*, are leading examples.

4. *The Vow-Breaker*, 1.i.82 (ed. Wallrath, in *Materialien*, xlii, Louvain, 1914).

kills herself with a knife, and Scarborow and Katherine live a wretched life until they are finally reconciled. In this play the notion that marriage with one partner after a precontract with another is simply adultery receives continual emphasis. Scarborow objects to his father that the enforced marriage makes him an adulterer, his wife a whore, and their children bastards.[5] Clare cries:

> He was contracted mine, yet he unjust
> Hath married to another; what's my estate then?
> A wretched maid, not fit for any man;
> For being united his with plighted faiths,
> Whoever sues to me commits a sin,
> Besiegeth me; and who shall marry me,
> Is like myself, lives in adultery . . .
> Than live a strumpet, better be unborn.[6]

So, too, Penthea thinks of herself as a 'spotted whore' (1197), 'widow'd by lawlesse marriage', and 'strumpeted' (1954–5). Clare's father tells Scarborow, later in Wilkins's play, that his wife Katherine

> . . . is but a strumpet, thy children bastards,
> Thyself a murderer, thy wife accessory,
> Thy bed a stews, thy house a brothel.[7]

Penthea's despair, then, is rooted in the same conditions of domestic crisis as Bateman's, Clare's, and Scarborow's. Her end, too, must be seen in a like perspective. She dies, like Clare, like Bateman, and, be it said, like Mistress Frankford and Wincott's wife in *The English Traveller*, not only because she is deprived of her chosen love but also because her conscience has been violated. It is in his handling of the theme of conscience that Ford's genuine originality is seen in striking detail. Mistress Frankford starves herself to death as a punishment for her betrayal of her husband; Wincott's wife dies because she had betrayed doubly— her husband and the lover precontracted to her in a spousals *de futuro*. Penthea, too, starves for such a betrayal but the 'husband' whom she has betrayed is not her legal husband, but her legally contracted lover. Ford thus cleverly combines the theme

5. Hazlitt's Dodsley, ix.486. Cf. Penthea's bastardizing of her 'little ones' (iv.i. 1899).
6. Hazlitt's Dodsley, ix.500–1.   7. Ibid., p. 506.

of the false wife stricken by conscience, the subject of many homilies and many plays, and the theme of the enforced marriage. But this cleverness is a matter of dramaturgical plenitude rather than of a subversive and decadent immoralism. Ford's questioning of the enforced marriage, and his demonstration of the disasters that follow it, is not a turning of morality upside down, as Sherman would have it,[8] in order to undermine the institution of matrimony. Enforced marriages of so gross a kind were generally censured. Penthea might rather be thought, even for the taste of those who approved the deaths of Mistress Frankford and Wincott's wife, to have too nice a conscience if she worries about her falsèd faith to a lover betrayed through no fault of her own. But it is a conscience operating well within the framework of the matrimonial sanctions of the time that induces her to starve herself to death; nor must Burtonian frustration of the blood, however analogous to Freudian syndromes, be allowed to have too much weight in explaining why she dies. Her last speech makes it clear that she is punishing herself, like Mistress Frankford, for what she considers a wanton fulness of the blood indulged by her 'adultery' with Bassanes; she sentences herself:

> But since her blood was season'd by the forfeit
> Of noble shame, with mixture of pollution,
> Her blood ('tis iust) be henceforth neuer heightned
> With tast of sustenance. Starue; let that fulnesse
> Whose plurisie hath feuer'd faith and modesty,
> Forgiue me: ô I faint. (IV.i.1956–61)

This passage, and others, show that there are no grounds for Sensabaugh's theory that Bassanes is, in any sense, sexually impotent.[9] Penthea's trouble is not modernism, but a conscience, a too literal adherence to Henry Swinburne's dictum that a partner to a spousals may not 'with safe Conscience' marry elsewhere, and she is therefore represented as a pathetic, though admirable, creature.

---

8. *John Fordes Dramatische Werke*, p. xviii. Cf. Sensabaugh, p. 180.

9. The marriage was certainly consummated (as witness Penthea's remark, 975–6); there may even have been children—Penthea, in her distracted mood, thinks she is 'past child bearing' and refers to her suppositious little ones as 'bastards': the whole point is that in this state she would not consider any of Bassanes' children as true children—they are merely fruits of her 'adultery'.

Yet her tragedy is of a kind we are already familiar with. In the distresses of Orgilus and Penthea we perceive once again the theme of the broken marriage—in this play, the broken spousals —and it is one played upon in other parts of the drama. Calantha's troth-plighting with Ithocles is, in miniature, a marriage drama which follows the lines of Heywood's: Ithocles accepts her ring, and, later, when he has been murdered, the lovers are reunited in death as the Princess puts the ring back on the finger of the corpse with the words: 'Thus I new marry him whose wife I am; / Death shall not separate vs' (v.ii.2585–6). The immense difference between Ford's manner of writing and Heywood's effectually obscures the fundamental similarity of their themes. This is, indeed, a difference which cuts very deep. It is idle to suggest that the two dramatists are akin in more than common assumptions derived from contemporary marriage customs. Yet the light shed by these assumptions on both is broad enough to bring them together for a shared illumination. And, in a final count, Penthea's tragedy can be defined in some relation to Mistress Frankford's. Her contract with Orgilus was binding before law and before God; so, too, was her marriage with Bassanes. It was a dilemma inescapable in a world where matrimony was controlled by practices that concealed a hidden rivalry, where, as between Calvin and the Catholics, custom might well be confused about the relative importance of a civil contract and solemnization in church. Penthea's tragedy, then, is written, like Mistress Frankford's, not in the stars but in the social habits of a particular period. It is the closest link between Ford and Heywood, and the one that most cogently demonstrates the extent of Ford's allegiance to the domestic theme.

IO

Chapman's tragedies

'Tis greatest now, and to destruction
Nearest; There's no pause at perfection;
Greatnesse a period hath, but hath no station.
JOHN DONNE, *The Progresse of the Soule*

At the beginning of *The Tragedy of Bussy d'Ambois* the soldier Bussy, reduced by poverty and unemployment to retired walks and solitary meditations, comes alone upon the stage and speaks about the contrariness of a world where Honour goes with its legs in the air and Reward turns its back on its pursuer. In a world where men flourish and come to be called 'great' by building themselves up into colossi; inside, though, they are full of rubbish. Lear, when he saw man stripped of his lendings, called him a poor, bare, forked animal; for Bussy unaccommodated man is the most tenuous, evanescent thing that can be: Pindar's dream of a shadow, Petrarch's torch carried in the wind, Jeremy Taylor's Man 'for which you cannot have a word can signify a verier nothing . . . forgotten like the dream of a distracted person'. Bussy's moral resembles Taylor's, too; no matter how elaborately a man dresses up, Time will preach his funeral sermon; he must resign himself to unaccommodation. He is like a tall ship sailing the high seas, 'ribb'd with brass', 'topt with all titles', but when the voyage draws to an end the great ship is dependent upon the pilot. This pilot is Virtue, and ends the soliloquy:

> We must to Virtue for her guide resort,
> Or we shall shipwrack in our safest port.

There can be little doubt, because of the character of the metaphor with which it is described, that this Virtue is not power,

First published in *Stratford-upon-Avon Studies*, vol. i, *Jacobean Theatre* (ed. J. R. Brown and B. Harris, London 1960), pp. 227-47.

virtù, the Achillean 'High birth, vigour of bone, desert in service' (as Ulysses describes it in Shakespeare's play), but moral
virtue, spiced with humility and self-knowledge; for the richly
adventuring and brass-ribbed ship is guided by

> A poor, staid fisherman, that never pass'd
> His country's sight.

Only this man knows the dangerous reaches where *virtù* may be
wrecked for want of Virtue.

The speech seems to have, then, a clear and unexceptionable
moral. It is less easy to determine its relation to its speaker and
his subsequent actions. It may sound like making difficulties, in
a play, to doubt whether what a character says does not also tell
us what he is, either directly or by its ironic contrast with his
other deeds and words. But this is a genuine and recurring problem in all Chapman's tragedies. If we are to read this speech
simply as an index of Bussy's state of mind when his story begins,
then most of that story is, by the standard of the as yet unfallen
Bussy, an increasingly rapid process of moral declination and
self-betrayal. 'Who is not poor, is monstrous', Bussy says in the
third line; but by the end of the scene he has accepted a thousand
crowns from Monsieur, King Henry III's brother, well knowing
that this gift, which is conveyed to him out of Monsieur's ambitious desire to gather about him a party of bold but obedient
spirits for a possible design upon the crown, entails dressing
himself in the 'enchanted glass' of the court—a glass which
reflects no amiable images, only demonic ones, sights that will
make a man's eyes 'as hollow as his mistress' heart'. The very
money itself is planted in blood, for when Monsieur's steward
brings it to him Bussy answers his patronizing impertinence with
a blow in the face. By the end of the act he is responding in the
same way on the stage of the court itself. The courtiers who mock
him for his self-confidence and his new clothes become the victims of a vengeance during which Bussy's anger assumes the
aspect of some terrible natural phenomenon, smashing men as
though they were trees in a storm (II.ii.77–104). All this, conducted in the open day of court, is only a prelude to a darker and
more labyrinthine business. Bussy's adulterous love affair with
Tamyra, wife of Count Montsurry, is involved from the first in

deceit and darkness and emerges into horror. The noble politician who so unthinkingly introduced him to greatness and now finds him too fiery to handle sees his chance to destroy him. Bussy himself loses control of his destiny, blinded by the juggling fiend whom he summons to his aid and in whom he trusts as rashly as Macbeth. If we wish to measure how far he has fallen from the grace of his first speech, we need only look at another speech at the end of the fourth act where he stakes everything on the game of politic murder and on the terrible image of the smiler with the knife:

> I'll bind his arm in silk, and rub his flesh,
> To make the vein swell, that his soul may gush
> Into some kennel where it longs to lie,
> And policy shall be flank'd with policy.

But outflanking the politicians is not within Bussy's competence; his 'cannibal valour' (Monsieur's phrase) resembles the tree-uprooting tempest, not the politic lightning that should melt 'the very marrow, and not taint the skin'. Poor and distorted instruments—a cowardly and jealous husband, a mistress tortured to yield her secret, a corrupted maid of honour—effect the end of the great Bussy, shot to death by gunmen from behind the arras. And when he dies, his eyes are fixed upon a futurity which has nothing in common with the haven-heaven of the 'poor fisherman'. Man, he confirms in his dying moments, is indeed 'a dream but of a shade', but the Bussy of the first act, who was to 'rise in court by virtue', blazed like a 'pointed comet' in Act II, and became by turns 'eagle' and 'snake' in the main business of the play, is now a 'falling star', quenched and silent.

If we read Bussy's story in this way, as one of moral declination, the feeling that a 'great' man has been wasted is substantially qualified by the reflection that he threw himself away upon objects that Virtue would have despised. He exemplifies the Achillean 'wrath', 'Predominant Perturbation . . . the Bodie's fervour and fashion of outward Fortitude',[1] and he is shown to us only that he may be shunned, in accordance with Chapman's other famous principle that 'material instruction, elegant and sententious excitation to virtue, and deflection from her contrary [are] the soul, limbs, and limits of an autentical tragedy.'[2]

---

1. *Chapman's Homer* (ed. A. Nicoll, London, 1957), ii.4.   2. *Tragedies*, p. 77.

This is a reading which agrees with what we may presume to have been Chapman's general intention as a dramatist. It has the immense convenience of reducing a play which at first sight seems to have burst rather raggedly out of the cerements of moralized drama to its compass and to coherence again.

But with many readers of *The Tragedy of Bussy d'Ambois* the suspicion will persist that this coherence is indeed gained at the cost of a reduction—a reduction of the size, the 'feel', the splendours of the play and its hero. Most commentators certainly, while showing a bewilderment that may be generated by a measure of incoherence in the play, have implied that there is more in it than a firmly regulated moral assisted by an ironic showing-forth of the hero's defects. It was Edwin Muir who summed up most exactly the general direction of criticism: 'Chapman', he wrote, 'is not interested in human nature, or in practical morality, or in evil, but in the man of excessive virtue or spirit or pride', and again: 'His judgements of conduct are sometimes strange and almost incomprehensible ... We do not come to know Bussy or Byron morally, as we know Macbeth and Hamlet, for the action has no real effect on them, since they live in a different world from the other characters, and are a law unto themselves.'[3] And there are other reasons, besides this sense of something strange and incomprehensible, for supposing that there is more in the play than meets the eye of the moralist and ironist.

What, for example, is the moralist to make of the poetic and elegiac excitement that Bussy's death calls forth? 'Chapman', answers Ennis Rees, 'is ... following the convention that a tragic hero must die nobly and is here attempting to gain a little more sympathy for his protagonist than some of the spectators are likely to have at this point.'[4] But what if Chapman —as some spectators at least will be ready to testify—succeeds in his attempt? succeeds all too well for the reader to be able to keep his moral wits about him? Although sympathy with the protagonist is not the exact phrase one would have selected to describe the feelings generated by this remarkable scene, subtly sustained and majestically evocative as any Elizabethan play can show, we are at least in our amazement quite proof against the

3. *Essays on Literature and Society* (London, 1949), pp. 20, 22–23.
4. *The Tragedies of George Chapman* (Cambridge, Mass., 1954), p. 47.

dry detachment from it all that might, had not Chapman so triumphantly drawn us in, preserve the proper distance between the moralist and the object of his reproof. We readily call objects sublime, Kant remarked, 'because they raise the energies of the soul above their accustomed height'; the title cannot easily be refused to this scene. The price we—and Chapman too —pay for this amazement is some loss of coherence, some sense of the strange and the incomprehensible in Bussy's fate which disables us for too tidy and detached a condemnation of him. If we wish to describe what Chapman is doing here, Muir's account seems truer to experience than that of Rees: 'We can feel', Muir writes, Chapman's 'impatience to arrive at those places where the souls of his heroes can expand to their full range, places on the frontier-line between life and death, time and eternity, where all terms seem to become absolute' (p. 22).

Throughout the play there are many places where Chapman fails to reprove and seems to admire. One way out of the incoherence that this causes is to suppose that such passages must be read ironically; that the spectator is required to measure what appears to be intended to arouse our admiration and amazement at Bussy, our sense that he lives 'in a different world from the other characters', by the altogether more base and commonplace actualities of Bussy's story as those have been set out, for example, in the first paragraphs of this essay. There are two objections to this view, which may be stated in the order of their increasing gravity. First, these summations of Bussy's character and status in the catalogue of men, made by other speakers from time to time in the course of the piece, invariably enlarge and elevate him. In the second scene, where Bussy, brawling with the Guise over a comparatively trivial matter of court behaviour, conducts himself like the proverbial bad-tempered schoolboy, Monsieur turns aside to comment thus:

> His great heart will not drown, 'tis like the sea,
> That partly by his own internal heat,
> Partly the stars' daily and nightly motion,
> Their heat and light, and partly of the place
> The divers frames, but chiefly by the moon,
> Bristled with surges, never will be won,
> (No, not when th' hearts of all those powers are burst)

To make retreat into his settled home,
Till he be crown'd with his own quiet foam. (I.ii.157)

If this is irony, it is of a singularly barren kind which hurts no one
but itself; for we do not, in order to diminish a figure, gaze at it
through a pair of binoculars. The spectator can see for himself
how Bussy is behaving, and Monsieur's attempt to assist his
vision must either be accepted at its face value as a genuine
attempt to enlarge the dimensions of what he sees or it must be
dismissed as simply wrong: 'Your instrument is telling lies:
we can judge that by our own unaided sight.' The speech then
becomes exclusively a ground for inferences about Monsieur,
not about Bussy at all. A major difficulty in interpreting Chapman's plays derives from a continual uncertainty about whether
the things said by the lesser characters about the protagonist, in
speeches which, as in this play, are remarkable for length, force,
and elaboration of metaphor, are meant to be evidence about
the speakers' own characters as well. But it is pretty certain that
they are rarely if ever *exclusively* directed to that end, that they
do give us information about the hero that must be taken into
account. So it is that Monsieur later on in the play, when Bussy's
fate is almost decided, offers us his binoculars again. The passage
in which he does so may conveniently be used to advance the
second of the graver objections to the attempt to reduce the
play to coherence by the discovery of ironies.

At this point the jaws of the trap devised by Monsieur, Montsurry, and the Guise are just about to snap shut on Bussy.
Tamyra, tortured on the rack by her frantic husband, has been
forced to write a message to Bussy summoning him to her
chamber by the secret passage. The Friar, the go-between of
the adulterous pair, has died of shock at the brutalities inflicted
on Tamyra, and Montsurry has disguised himself in the Friar's
robe in order to act as the bearer of her message. Meanwhile
Monsieur and the Guise are waiting near the secret passage for
the arrival of Bussy. Monsieur is now about to witness the triumph of his scheme; as far as he is concerned, Bussy is already a
dead man. It is at this crisis that he turns aside to moralize on his
victim's fate, assuming a role and a tone which suit oddly with
that of a politician waiting with his band of gunmen to eliminate a rival. Blake's words in *The Book of Thel* might be adapted
to his purposes, for his argument is that 'without a use this

shining man lived'. Nature, he says, in creating men like Bussy,
works at random:

> here will be one
> Young, learned, valiant, virtuous, and full mann'd;
> One on whom Nature spent so rich a hand
> That with an ominous eye she wept to see
> So much consum'd her virtuous treasury.
> Yet as the winds sing through a hollow tree
> And (since it lets them pass through) let it stand;
> But a tree solid (since it gives no way
> To their wild rage) they rend up by the root:
> So this whole man
> (That will not wind with every crooked way,
> Trod by the servile world) shall reel and fall
> Before the frantic puffs of blind-born chance,
> That pipes through empty men, and makes them dance.
> Not so the sea raves on the Lybian sands,
> Tumbling her billows in each others' neck;
> Not so the surges of the Euxine sea
> (Near to the frosty pole, where free Boötes
> From those dark deep waves turns his radiant team)
> Swell, being enrag'd, even from their inmost drop,
> As Fortune swings about the restless state
> Of virtue, now thrown into all men's hate. (v.ii.32–53)

There is of course a contrast between the baser actuality of
Bussy's self-exposure to Fortune's storms by his commitment
to an adulterous affair and how Monsieur sees his situation in
this passage. But it is not one which diminishes Bussy, but gives
us a nobler prospect of his ruin, linking him by means of those
natural images, the falling tree and the turbulent ocean, with a
region where reproof becomes irrelevant and the poet can at last
indulge his secret and irrational love affair with his hero, whom
he values because he is astonishing, wasteful, and altogether
unlike ordinary man. Tragedy is, as Yeats remarked, a drowner
of dykes. The objection to reading such a passage as this as irony
derives from the critic's sense of diction, rhythm, and metaphor,
and he can only in the last resort turn round on the ironist and
beg him to unstop his ears. This is not a comfortable thing to be
obliged to do, for it makes it apparent that Chapman in this play
is working with two substances: stirring the waters to make a
foamy spectacle, but mixing the mud with the foam. The mud is

all that part of the play which is a story of moral declination; left to itself it could sink to the bottom and be seen clear.

We shall also have to ask, in connection with Monsieur's speech and with others which enlarge our view of Bussy, *who*, in the fullest sense, is speaking them. The tone and substance of these characterizations of the hero do not accord well with the speakers' role in the muddy part of the story; they seem to draw upon a stock of evidence which is nowhere directly yielded by that story itself. It is not simply that King Henry is deceived about Bussy and out of his own weakness glorifies him (III.ii. 90–107), but that there is in Bussy, imperfectly conveyed to the audience by the story alone, some spring of being which touches off a response that does violence to the decorum of Henry's character. So also when Bussy speaks about himself, after the duel scene (II.i.194–204), in the scene where he proffers himself as the king's 'eagle' (III.ii), and in the death scene (v.iv.) his speeches have a rightness and power, savage or elegiac, which strains the contextual link with story and person. They no more sound like boasting, for example, or hypocrisy, than Monsieur sounds like an ironist. The inner truth of their gesture is unaffected by its ostensible source in the character, because the ultimate source lies beyond that in Chapman's own response to the idea of the Achillean man, labouring in 'wrath':

> the strong
> Iron-hearted man-slaying Achilles
> Who would not live long.

We may have suspected, indeed, from the first lines of the play, from the soliloquy with which we began, that not every word in it would proceed from a perfectly coherent moral scheme and from fully objectified characters. For that speech contains two metaphors in implicit and troubling opposition to one another. Both describe great men, the first using the Plutarchian metaphor of the colossi:

> [They] differ not from those colossic statues,
> Which, with heroic forms without o'er-spread,
> Within are nought but mortar, flint, and lead;

The second is that of the ship and its captain:

> great seamen, using all their wealth
> And skills in Neptune's deep invisible paths,
> In tall ships richly built and ribb'd with brass,
> To put a girdle round about the world.

The 'great seaman' is a figure from the heroic age of Elizabethan adventure, active, vigilant, and wealthy; but he is as much a metaphor for the suspect 'greatness' as the neo-Stoic one of the straddling giant filled with rubbish. The play itself beats out these converging paths so that this dichotomy is never resolved, and we cannot feel at the end of it that we have simply been shown how empty and rubbishy-hearted is the Achillean man. It is, rather, suggested that death itself is an artificer and completes the work of those 'unskilful statuaries' who build colossi: the wounded Bussy props himself on his sword, determined to die on his feet like Vespasian, and cries:

> Here like a Roman statue I will stand
> Till death hath made me marble.
>
> (v.iv.97)

And so Bussy is transformed into what Yeats called an 'uncommitted energy'.[5]

It would be wrong to exaggerate the degree of incoherence introduced into the play's structure by this double vision of its hero. Bussy has been, and is always likely to be, a rallying-point for critics because of the problematical manner of his presentation. But it would be untrue to theatrical experience of *Bussy d'Ambois* to accept all the implications of T. M. Parrott's view that 'the true theme [is] . . . not the hero's passion for Tamyra . . . for the amour is plainly enough only an incident in Bussy's career' (p. 546). To agree with this would be to increase the risk, which has already been incurred, of abstracting Bussy too much from his context and turning the play into an anthology of poems about him. The intrigue takes up more than three acts and is worked out with great coherence. One moral theme, for example (that Fortune is the natural victor over the man who exposes himself to her black storms), is neatly and theatrically enforced by an accident placed in its very centre (iii.ii.210): Monsieur, who is already actively casting around for the means to Bussy's destruction, happens to hear from the waiting-maid

5. *A Vision* (London, 1925), p. 188; the whole passage is relevant.

Pero, in the midst of some casual raillery, that she has seen
Tamyra and Bussy together—for the prince a tonic discovery,
for Bussy a deadly mischance. Tamyra, the only woman of any
stature or importance in all Chapman's tragedies, except the
Queen in *Chabot*, makes as vivid a demand for our attention in
the theatre as the hero himself. But both Tamyra and her story
strengthen the feeling that Chapman was as much absorbed in
the fascination of 'greatness' as with working out a moral
paradigm. This adulterous union is marked by a great display of
crooked audacity on the part of both lovers, and this element
received further emphasis in Chapman's revision of his play. But
it is also marked by conduct on the part of the wronged husband
Montsurry (his torture of his wife) which puts him beyond the
range of a sympathy which wholly includes Tamyra and her
brave resistance to his breach of 'manhood, noblesse, and
religion' (v.i.127). This is 'her other excellence' which sets off
her offence. By it, as by much in the lovers' response to their
danger (iii.i), we are given the sense that their coming together
is a dark but deep compulsion far removed from the ordinary
life of the shallow or beastly courtiers who surround them.
These elements in the intrigue—deceit and exaltation, strong
currents of exceptional life, enemies whose viciousness ennobles
their victims—aptly correspond in their mixed nature to a view of
the hero which constantly shifts its perspective. We remember
Chapman's interest in those Renaissance toys of canvas or pleated
paper:

> a cozening picture, which one way
> Shows like a crow, another like a swan.[6]

By this judgement, the amour, so far from being an incident in
Bussy's career, does more than put the ironist's view of the play
out of court; it helps us to discern the lineaments of a puzzling
hero and by that much increases the coherence of his tragedy.

It was of course against Chapman's principles as a moralist,
which are plainly stated in his poems and elsewhere, to excite in
us anything approaching admiration or suspense of judgement
towards the man of wrath or the body's fervour. But it is not
wholly surprising that he did so in this play. The very bitter
satirical passages in his poems, the pugnacity of his comments

---

6. *All Fools*, i.i.47–48, in *Comedies* (ed. T. M. Parrott, London, 1914).

on the commentators on Homer, the invective against Ben Jonson, and his general habit of dissenting from a 'manless' age and allotting himself an exceptional role in it, are some evidence about his own temperament. Chapman would not be the first naturally 'wrathful' man whose encomia of calm and attempts to draw the lines of moral conduct derived their rigour from his knowledge of proneness to disorder within. The evidence suggests that in *Bussy d'Ambois* something not perfectly within the moralist's control came up from below the threshold of his mind, and that it was this that transformed a moral spectacle into a piece of tragic theatre.

This was not an event which Chapman permitted to occur again, to his satisfaction perhaps, but to our loss certainly, for none of his other tragedies equals *Bussy d'Ambois* in merit. This is not to assert that the more clearly defined moral structure of the later plays precludes a fiery apprehension of his heroes' natures, whether they are transgressors and men of wrath as Byron is or exemplars of calm and of the 'mind's constant and unconquered Empire' as Clermont (in *The Revenge of Bussy d'Ambois*) and Chabot are. What *Bussy d'Ambois* lacked was an unquestioned source of moral authority, of 'over-ruling Wisdom', able to measure 'greatness' and answer to its own name; but Chapman sets such an authority in each of his other plays: Clermont, Cato (in *Caesar and Pompey*), Chabot, and King Henry IV of France in the two-part play called *The Conspiracy and the Tragedy of Charles Duke of Byron*.

In the Byron plays Chapman adheres to the main lines of his source, which is to be found in his cousin Edward Grimeston's *General Inventory of the History of France*. The ground of the plays is the character of Byron as sketched by Grimeston, 'adventurous in war, ambitious beyond all measure':

This Marshall had goodly parts, communicable to fewe, his Valour was admirable, and happy in all his incounters; of an invincible Courage, infatigable and never tired with any toyle, continuing ordinarily fifteene dayes together on Horse-backe. He was not inclined to Voluptousnesse, nor much to the love of Women, sober ynough, the which began to quench that furious humour, as Intemperancy & greatnesse increased, or that Rest did moderate his boyling passions. He was extremely Vaine-glorious, yea sometimes he would refuse his meate, and content himselfe with little to feede his Fantasie with Glory and Vanity . . . The excesse of his Ambition made him to brave it without judgement. He became so presumptuous, as he thought that the King, nor *France* could not subsist without him. He was become ill-tounged, speaking ill of all the Princes, threatning the Parliaments, and the Officers of Justice, some with death, and to dispossesse others of their places.[7]

In Chapman's play this man has no source of inner authority, but builds himself up into a colossus by generating from thoughts of his past valour and services to France a series of fantastic images of his own splendour, so that he constantly ranges himself with the classical heroes, with Alexander who triumphed over Fortune, Hercules who adventured into Hell, Curtius who saved Rome, Orpheus who intoxicated his judges with his music. ('He flattred himself in his Vanity', writes Grimestone, 'and pleased himselfe as Pigmalion did in his Image, and Narcissus in his shadowe . . .') On this airy projection of his own worth he relies, so that in *The Conspiracy* certain enemies of the King of France find it easy to blind him by flattery and gradually ripen him for the mischief of treason. The play ends with his act of submission to the King, but by the beginning of *The Tragedy* he has revolted from his allegiance again. This time the King takes decisive measures. Byron, who remains oblivious to the fact that a monstrous crime will cancel a mighty merit (*Tragedy*, v.ii.277), is trapped, brought to trial, and executed.

Byron is, therefore, like Bussy, a victim, but not of a Montsurry or a Monsieur, but of the King. Henry IV is the standard-bearer of moral authority in these plays, their true Alexander, owing his power to Virtue (under God) and not to Fortune. In *The Conspiracy*, although he is angry when Byron arrogates to himself all the glory for victory at the battle of Fontaine Française some years before (ii.ii.93–241), he at first tempers the wind against him (ii.ii.25–57), solemnly warns Byron against his sycophantic friends (iii.ii.244–72), and even, as a curative measure, sends him on an embassy to the court of Queen Elizabeth, which Chapman pardonably represents (iv.i) as a way of correcting Byron's false image of the state by exposing him to a true

7. *A General Inventory* . . . (London, 1607), p. 992.

one. But when in *The Tragedy* these mercies prove ineffectual,
Chapman is careful to show, by means of Henry's prayer over
the newly born Dauphin (I.i.109–49), his resolve if possible to
pardon Byron (I.iii.29–38, a passage very close to Grimeston),
the Masque of Cupid, an emblem of discord resolved, which
is performed at court (II.i) and by other appeals to Byron
through his ministers D'Escures and Janin (III.i), that what is
at stake is the peace of an ordered and fruitful kingdom. This
is the plenitude and forbearance by which we judge Byron's
resolve to imitate Jehovah, and from the Chaos made by his
intended revolution to 'sit brooding up another world', to
ruin his country in order to re-advance it (I.ii.30–35):

> If they bring me out, they shall see I'll hatch
> Like to the blackthorn, that puts forth his leaf,
> Not with the golden fawnings of the sun,
> But sharpest showers of hail, and blackest frosts.
>   (*Tragedy*, III.i.126)

It is after this issue has been thoroughly exposed that the King
finally sends the spy La Fin, whom Byron trusts, to bring him
back to court. Even after he has Byron in his power, Henry still
hesitates, consults his ministers, prays that his judgement in the
matter may be guided by God (IV.ii). The final resolve to bring
Byron to trial is taken against the advice of the ministers, who
recommend summary execution. But Chapman had read in
Grimeston about this aspect of the affair. The discriminations
made by Grimeston are of fundamental importance to that
aspect of the play that has earned it the title of Chapman's
'political testament':

Many thought it was to shorten the course of Justice, in so apparent a
crime, and begin with the execution, dealing with the Duke of *Biron*
as *Alexander* did with *Parmenio*, for Princes are Masters of the Lawes,
they have one form of Justice for great men, and another for those
whose quality requires not so great respect. In these accidents there is
no difference whether bloud be drawn before or after dinner; Necessity
teacheth the disorder, and the Profit doth recompence the example, so
as the Estate be preserved by the death of him that is prevented. But
the King will none of that. He proceeds with more Courage and Generosity: These examples of Execution had beene blamed in his Predecessors, he will have his Subjects, and all the World to know, that he
hath power and authority sufficient to roote out by the forme of Justice,

not the Authors of such a Conspiracie, for they be Devils, but the Com-
plices and the instruments how terrible soever. He will have the Sol-
emnities and lawfull Ceremonies observed, and that they be judged
by the rigour of the Lawes.[8]

To Henry's insistence on the sanctions embodied in outward
human institutions such as the law, with its manifest working,
there are cross-references in Byron's contempt of them. The
King resists the persuasions of his minister; but Byron in *The
Conspiracy* owed his first fall to the analogous arguments advanced by La Fin and by the Spanish agent Picoté, who urges that

> simple loyalty,
> Faith, love, sincerity, are but words, no things,
> Merely devis'd for form, (*Conspiracy*, I.ii.116–18)

and retails a bit of international conference gossip to support his
point. Later, La Fin takes up the theme: for other laws than that
of friendship (which La Fin has an obvious motive for excepting
at this juncture),

> He is a fool that keeps them with more care
> Than they keep him safe, rich, and popular.
> (*Conspiracy*, II.i.138–9)

Love, reputation, loyalty are 'mere politic terms' which
dissolve 'the free-born powers of royal man' (III.i.31). Solicita-
tions of this kind, combined with the sense of injured merit
and vainglory blazing with the oil of flattery, convince Byron
that he owes nothing to any authority outside himself. As he
boasts to Henry:

> men in themselves entire
> March safe with naked feet on coals of fire:
> I build not outward, nor depend on props,
> Nor choose my consort by the common ear,
> Nor by the moonshine in the grace of kings.
> (*Conspiracy*, III.ii.227–31)

With all its radical suspicion of kings and outward forms this
was a doctrine which in another context (that of Clermont
d'Ambois, for example) Chapman held very dear. That is why,
here and elsewhere, Byron expresses it with such rich and cogent
metaphor. Chapman's imagination and poetic power is fired by
the idea itself; the eloquence with which this endows Byron,

8. Grimeston, p. 968. Cf. *Tragedy of Byron*, IV.ii.29–47.

perhaps somewhat adventitiously, is the chief means for astonishing us with him, for maintaining always the sight of his active
imperious presence alive before the mind's eye. His eloquence is
due to Chapman's response to martial valour and the Achillean
virtù, the body's fervour, of which his hero is an undoubted
exemplar, and which, as we have seen in the case of Bussy, released Chapman's tongue to speak of wonders. But, in the Byron
plays, the dramatist has so firmly grounded his moral scheme
and embodied it so successfully in the continued contrast between the righteous Henry and the errant Byron that we are not
likely to misunderstand where true order lies. For Byron is a
wildfire without a centre; the context shows that his is a perversion of the sacred doctrine. His turbulence had its first rise in
outward-going pride with its claims for excessive recognition of
its worth by other men. Very early in his story, before he has
yielded to the conspirators, he shows his awareness of the direction in which he may be going. It is a dangerous and a dreadful
thing, he says,

> To trust our blood in others' veins, and hang
> 'Twixt heaven and earth in vapours of their breaths;
> To leave a sure pace on continuate earth,
> And force a gate in jumps from tower to tower.

Such men forsake

> all the sure force in themselves
> To seek without them that which is not theirs.
> (*Conspiracy*, I.ii.40–43, 157–8)

And later he is troubled because he has 'cast [himself] into
the arms of others' (III.iii.33–34). At first dependent upon the
nourishment which he greedily draws from the outward flat-
teries of La Fin and the conspirators, he is in the end even more
critically dependent upon the King and his judges. The paradox of his fall is that his theory of self-sufficiency, which helped
him to cut loose from the 'natural clime' of his society and to
try to become a 'lonely dragon' like Shakespeare's Coriolanus,
blinds him to the extent to which he has in reality given hostages
to that society and put himself wholly in its power.

If Chapman, faced with the political world of the Byron plays,
asked, 'Where is the source of moral authority?', he answered
'in the just king', but at the same time hinted that in other cir-

cumstances the answer might be 'in the just man'. This is the answer given in *The Revenge of Bussy d'Ambois*, a play which explores, as do all Chapman's remaining tragedies, what happens when political power and moral authority are not coincident (as they are in the Byron plays) but at odds. We are back in the France of Henry III, where the central personage is now Bussy's brother Clermont. His friendship with the Guise, the suspicion it arouses in Henry (whipped on by the politic Baligny, a counterpart of La Fin), the eventual fall of the Guise and Clermont's consequent suicide are one main part of the story, dominating the first four acts. The other is revenge for the murder of Bussy, which Tamyra and Bussy's sister Charlotte (a new character) urge Clermont to execute upon Montsurry. The delay classically demanded by the revenge plot is caused partly by the cowardice of Montsurry, hardly at all by the revenger's reluctance, and very considerably by the inartificial fact that Clermont and his author are too occupied in other matters. But Bussy's ghost rises in the fifth act to tell Clermont that God demands Montsurry's punishment, and Clermont at last persuades his terrified victim to fight and die.

Commentators have explained that Chapman was contriving a variation on the mode that he inherited from Kyd, Shakespeare, and Marston, and there can be no appeal from their verdict that his contrivance was a failure.[9] Clermont is the perfect 'Senecal man', an exemplar of calm and inward peace; burdening him with the revenger's bloody duty led Chapman into awkwardnesses which he could not surmount, although they are not so essentially disabling that they could not have been turned to positive advantages if the attempt had been made. Although there is some theatrical liveliness in the play (in the scenes with Montsurry and in the long series showing Clermont's arrest), its interest is chiefly historical: it is the most complete and whole-hearted of a number of attempts by previous dramatists to show us the Stoic Wise Man in a world of Neronian equivocation. Clermont endlessly manipulates the contrast between inward authority in the 'full' man and the outward blaze and glory of the 'empty' man, the rubbish-choked colossus.

9. See especially F. T. Bowers, *Elizabethan Revenge Tragedy* (Princeton, 1940), pp. 144–9, and J. W. Wieler, *George Chapman—The Effect of Stoicism upon his Tragedies* (New York, 1949), pp. 179–212.

He himself, being inwardly solid with virtue and soul, needs no
other authority but himself by which to live, and he may even
choose his own time to die. Although he is fierily valorous, his
'inward guards' are his real surety against the storms of Fortune.
After he has—somewhat casually, it is true—renounced revenge
(III.ii.109–16), it is incongruous that this inner-directed man
should in the end have to obey the external authority of the
Ghost. The Ghost claims to proceed from God, of course, but we
suspect that his appearance is really determined by the needs
of the revenge-play mode. If so, the chosen genre has here
curiously disrupted the moral scheme of the work of art.

Of Chapman's last two plays, there are several reasons why
Caesar and Pompey could have been the most interesting. It is
Chapman's only attempt to write a play about those characters
of ancient history whose world had long fed his imagination
through the writings of the Stoic moralists Plutarch and Epictetus; in devising the character of Pompey he tried to show a man
educating himself to 'live with little' after the Stoic precept, so
that a change has to be wrought in him before our eyes as
Pompey endeavours to move from 'wrath' to peace; and the
play is also a fresh venture because it is equally concerned with
two other men as well: the Byron plays had an antagonist and a
protagonist, *The Revenge of Bussy* a master and a disciple, but
Caesar and Pompey develops both these kinds of relationship:
Caesar is Pompey's mighty enemy, and Pompey is the pupil and
ally of Cato. Yet despite all this, it seems the dullest of his
tragedies. Its historical hurly-burly never achieves full form or
meaning; it is ill-related to the three major characters and
allows them little room and not much life. This is by no means
an opinion which all the commentators, or even a majority of
them, have shared. J. Jacquot, for example, discerned epic
fullness and grandeur in the play, and Parrott has praised it for
putting into Pompey's mouth 'words that we can only interpret
as the poet's own utterances on the deepest mysteries of life and
death'. But it will probably be agreed that, whatever its merits,
Chapman's only Roman play is a branch that takes us away from
the main body of his work. Therefore it seems more profitable
here to spend time upon *The Tragedy of Chabot Admiral of France*.

This play was probably revised by Shirley after Chapman's
death but there is not much doubt that its design and essential

virtues are Chapman's, however much they have been cropped and conventionalized by the younger dramatist. Its hero is closely related to Clermont, but this time Chapman has gone within his protagonist rather than set him up as our mentor. Chabot is a spotlessly honest judge whom a jealous chancellor persuades King Francis I to investigate, on the assumption, shared by both king and minister, that there is always *something* of which a man must needs be ashamed. Nothing is found, but Chabot's judges are bullied into delivering an adverse verdict. The easy conscience of king and court is startled into reappraisal when Chabot refuses the pardon that is then offered to him. But the damage has been done; the pain and poison of mistrust and 'unkindness' kill Chabot. He is like the healthy victim of an exploratory operation who dies under the knife because of the surgeon's careless over-confidence.

There is an excellent account of this play by Miss K. M. Burton,[1] in which she points out that in it 'a debate has a direct effect on the course of the action; it does not merely demonstrate the position which this or that character has taken up'. Two features especially deserve attention as contributing to the impression of tight and dramatic organization throughout: there is the character of Montmorency the High Constable, at first hunting with the pack and then withdrawing; he acts as the visible pivot to a structure which shifts over a large space of ground, much as Pompey was intended but failed to do in *Caesar and Pompey*. Secondly, there is the moment where Chabot refuses his pardon (IV.i.235)—'You cannot pardon me, sir'—an effect not so much of surprise as of *peripeteia*. After that nothing can be the same again for anybody. This is an unusual effect for Chapman, whose plays normally develop rather ponderously, the ground for action well prepared before the armoured vehicle rolls forward. Above all, the play is interesting because its major theme and that which controls its metaphors is an inner violence, a wrong done to the soul. Chabot's inner nature is delicate as a needle, trembling in its tender posture upon the sundial (I.i.49 ff.), and his death is consistent with this temper. The play depicts a tragic assault upon the invasion of a man's inward authority, created by the envy and innovating spirit of power. In stretching his exemplar of calm upon this

1. *Essays in Criticism*, ii, 1952, 408–9.

rack, Chapman recognizes the human weakness which is the subject of tragedy, a recognition obscured by didactic pressures in *The Revenge of Bussy*.

The relative merits of Chapman's different tragedies have been sufficiently indicated by the proportions of this chapter, and the effect as of a long *decrescendo* cannot be overcome. The body of his work separates itself from the rest of Jacobean tragedy. If there is a relationship to be discerned, it is with the Roman tragedies of Jonson and Samuel Daniel, who share his interest in 'greatness' and its bearing on political order, and with the academic French Senecan work of Fulke Greville, who adds the interest in the consonance between the inward and the outward man, how one betrays the other, and how both struggle against enemies in society and demons in the soul. Also, the forms chosen by these neoclassic writers have something to tell us about Chapman's. What distinguishes Chapman and what made it possible for him to write his masterpiece in tragedy is a fiery and imaginative response to 'greatness' and its role among men. The story of his work is in part the story of how this response generated an antithetical rigour, binding some of his work with frost, but permitting some of it to rise to the level of elegy. So that if in some respects Chapman is second cousin to the mild, sad, and too well-mannered Daniel, he still remains in others the heir of Marlowe.

The structure of his plays is not specially adventurous, making competent use of the threefold division of the neoclassic theorists (protasis, epitasis, and catastrophe, terms of which the learned Jonson was fond). The natural unit of his composition and the one with which he operates most eloquently is the long speech, highly charged with metaphor, and often a complete 'poem' in itself. But it does Chapman violence to detach these from their contexts, for they are often carefully wrought into the dramatic fabric. His fondness for literary allusions, resembling that of such poets as Pope or T. S. Eliot, for borrowing chunks of matter from Epictetus, Plutarch, Ficino, and his other favourite sources of wisdom, has been much studied. Sometimes these remain far-fetched and inert, but often, as in the references to Seneca's *Hercules Oetaeus* in the last scene of *Bussy d'Ambois*, they nourish and deepen their contexts.[2] His speeches are not empty,

2. I owe this point to B. A. Harris.

repetitive, and formal, after the manner of the weaker neo-Senecans, but frequently make some genuine discrimination concerning the business of the play and the varying states of mind; they enforce or qualify a sequence, and do not run round in circles like the lamentations of Videna (in *Gorboduc*). One of the difficulties of grasping the whole of a Chapman play on first experience of it comes from our being told so much. His stories are initially rather simple and familiar, and the underplot is largely absent from them. With very many Jacobean tragedies from Fletcher to Ford and nearly all neoclassic comedies, the bare bones of the tale itself can form a pleasingly ingenious network of scaffolding. But Chapman has at least this in common with Henry James: it would be useless to extrapolate his stories without the moral and characterological ado that is organized about them.

The final impression left by these tragedies might be that they are the work of a man who grew to be one of nature's academicians, resisting his age more than he explored it; and it is true that Chapman, although unusually learned, did not resemble Donne or Bacon in being unusually intelligent as well. This impression would need a good deal of correction from his other works, and on other grounds could not be accounted a wholly truthful one. For Chapman, by devising a drama that is controlled by an idea of heroic worth held up to us for our wonder, was exploring a new way in tragedy. The basis is beginning to shift, though only slightly, from the Shakespearian emphasis on personality towards a new stress on heroic ideals; the design is affected by the concern with those moments or periods of intense emotion, such as the death of Bussy, the trial and death of Byron, or the contemplative *furor* of Clermont, by which it is not the man, as a coherent human being, who is brought nearest to us so much as the emotion itself—that passion which Yeats praised as the subject of all art and which 'can only be contemplated when separated by itself, purified of all but itself, and aroused into perfect intensity by opposition with some other passion, or it may be with the law'. It is this 'emptying' of the drama, as Yeats called it, of human character and its replacement by heroic energies which helps to differentiate the plays of such workers in the heroic mode as Fletcher and his successor Dryden from those of Shakespeare. Dryden was to declare that in a heroic play all things ought to be 'as far above the ordinary proportion of the stage, as that is beyond the common words and actions of human life'. His contemporary Thomas Rymer, in his notorious attack on Shakespeare in 1692, chose as his main target *Othello*, that supreme masterpiece of characterization in which the dramatist leads us to meditate not upon the passions of love and jealousy but upon the man and woman who love and suffer. For Rymer, this was to confuse Poetry, which is led by Philosophy, and is general and abstracted, with History 'which only records things higlety, piglety, right or wrong as they happen . . . history and *fact* in particular cases . . . are no warrant or direction for a Poet'.[3] Chapman, although faintly and far off, anticipates both the magnification of life with which Dryden amazes us, and the neoclassical critic's advocacy of philosophy as a guide. In portraying Byron and Bussy and Clermont he seems on occasion not as much concerned with the particular case as with manoeuvring his heroes into situations where they become almost catalytic exemplars of heroic vigour or virtue. 'What can remain with the Audience', Rymer asked indignantly about *Othello*, 'to carry home with them from this sort of Poetry, for their use and edification?'[4] Chapman could have sustained such an inquisition with some confidence. He participates in however slight a degree in the movement which thirty years after his death was to flood the stages of England and France with God-defying Maximins and Rival Queens. The movement is important still. Although no one nowadays is on Rymer's side, perhaps his legatee is all that cultivated European distrust of Shakespeare's undignified concern with the particular case which has found expression, for example, in T. S. Eliot's plays, or in his remark that he had never seen 'a cogent refutation of Thomas Rymer's objections'. Rymer would have found most of Chapman as monstrous and unnatural as Shakespeare himself, but he might have had a kind word for his soldierly soldiers and his kingly kings, and for the dignity with which they are exalted in death. Chapman was, after all, contriving something more philosophical than history when he measured 'greatness' by refining Stoic precepts from the turmoil of the court of France.

3. *The Critical Works of Thomas Rymer* (ed. C. A. Zimansky, New Haven and London, 1956), p. 163.   4. Ibid., p. 164.

II

Patient Madman and Honest Whore: the Middleton–Dekker oxymoron

I

Most Elizabethan and Jacobean plays of the second rank get tied together in bunches and are used for making generalizations with. Perhaps this is all they are worth. This paper is an attempt to come to a decision about one of the most sizeable of them *The Honest Whore, Parts I* and *II*, and therefore has to be chiefly about two elements in it: those which centre on Candido the patient man and Bellafront the converted courtesan. The ways in which the reputation of Elizabethan drama is sustained are sometimes obscure: there are, for example, the four superb textually new-minted volumes of Dekker's plays. What is the point of it all when we get down to Dekker's level, and away from those few mysteriously self-selecting plays which are always being written about, such as *The Revenger's Tragedy*? Is Dekker only a stalking-horse? Greg called *The Honest Whore* Dekker's finest achievement. How fine is that?

The playhouses started again in April 1604 after an inhibition of more than a year caused by the plague. A number of plays of a rather new fashion—problematical, urban, sexy—appeared during the next few years. It is the time of *Measure for Measure* (performed at court in December 1604). The playwrights—Dekker, Middleton, Webster, Jonson, Marston, Chapman—had all started their careers before the theatres were shut down; and all of them (with the exception of Webster, who was still too much of a novice) had shown in their earlier work an increasing interest in what Yeats called the 'emotions of cities'. The theatre of the city was, to use Yeats's terminology, forgetting the 'emotions of sailors and husbandmen and shepherds and users of the

First published in *Essays and Studies 1966* (ed. R. M. Wilson, London, 1966), pp. 18–40.

spear and bow' and replacing them with the present realities of huckster and bawd. In Yeats's view, therefore, it was preparing for the end of its brief day; when the city has forgotten or mocks everything but itself, then everything must end in irreconcilable opposites, romantic pantomime, or tedious mimicry of the surface of life.

It is difficult to arrange the city plays of 1604 in a satisfactory order. Accounts have varied accordingly. One version would seem to cast Middleton for a kind of villain of the piece. Before he came Dekker had written about the city in a kindly and wholesome manner; *The Shoemaker's Holiday* (1602) is still one of the few universally prescribed and tolerated Elizabethan plays; then, under the malign influence of Middleton, Dekker developed what T. M. Parrott described as 'a partiality for questionable scenes and characters [ie brothels, bawds, and whores] and a general moral laxness, happily absent in the earlier plays'.[1] Parrott was certainly thinking of *The Honest Whore*, which may or may not be a Dekker–Middleton collaboration. This infective Middleton was the author of city comedies during these years (1602–6). They signalize a change in taste and subject matter, but the confusion about exact dating makes it extra difficult to say who infected whom. It may well have been Dekker who started courtesan scenes, 'questionable' scenes in which courtesans are depicted, with a certain bravura and loving concentration, running their households and clients. For the consensus now is that *Blurt, Master Constable*, one of the earliest plays to contain such a scene (Quarto in 1602) and formerly given to Middleton, is probably by Dekker.[2] If this is so, Dekker ought to get the blame for lowering the moral tone and Louis B. Wright's strictures in his great and influential book ought to be rewritten to apply to Dekker.[3] The Imperia scenes of 1601 or 1602 in *Blurt, Master Constable* are at any rate the genesis of the still more brilliant courtesan scene of *The Honest Whore, Part I*

1. *Comedies of George Chapman* (London, 1914), p. 839.

2. See D. B. Dodson in *Notes and Queries*, cciv, 1959, 61–65. Mark Eccles, E. H. C. Oliphant (cited by Dodson), and Mary L. Hunt (in her *Thomas Dekker*, New York, 1911) were others who held Dekker to be the author of this play (as against Chambers, *Elizabethan Stage*, vol. ii, p. 439). I am not convinced by either Dodson's arguments (which depend partly on suppositions about Middleton's 'mordant bestiality') or those of W. J. Lawrence in *Speeding up Shakespeare* (London, 1937), pp. 114–19.

3. *Middle-Class Culture in Elizabethan England* (Chapel Hill, 1935), p. 630.

(1604). Living on her nerves, the volatile Imperia fusses away with her maids, the perfect exemplar of the citified Cleopatra, 'a most triumphant lady':

Fie, fie, fie, fie, by the light oath of my fan, the weather is exceeding tedious and faint. Trivia, Simperina, stir, stir, stir: one of you open the casements, t'other take a ventoy and gently cool my face. Fie, I ha' such an exceeding high colour, I so sweat! Simperina, dost hear? prithee be more compendious; why, Simperina! (II.ii)

She gets ready for Lazarillo's lecture to the ladies on how 'to carry their white bodies, either before their husbands or before their lovers'; an unwelcome customer ('an old rotten aquavitae bottle') is sent away; the class settles itself:

No, no, no, no. Stools and cushions; low stools, low stools; sit, sit, sit, round ladies, round . . . So, so, so, so; let your sweet beauties be spread to the full and most moving advantage; for we are fallen into his hands, who, they say, has an ABC for the sticking in of the least white pin in any part of the body (III.iii)[4]

Such writing and such plays have been severely censured: by Wright, because they sentimentalize vice and mock the virtues of respectable citizens; by L. C. Knights, because they are examples of 'completely generalized conventionality'.[5] Knights was referring to the brothel scenes in another play of this group, *Your Five Gallants* (?1605), probably another Paul's Boys private theatre play, the unaided work of Middleton; other Middleton Paul's examples are *Michaelmas Term* and *A Mad World My Masters* (both about 1604). From *Blurt, Master Constable* the fashion had certainly spread; *The Honest Whore* is right in the middle of this spread. Henslowe's diary records between January and March 1604 an advance of £5 to Dekker *and* Middleton for 'the pasyent man & the onest hore'. The first part was performed by the Henslowe/Alleyn company, Prince Henry's Men (formerly the Admiral's), at (presumably) the Fortune playhouse later in 1604; the second part followed hard upon the success of the first, presumably in 1605.[6] *The Honest*

---

4. *Works of T. Middleton* (ed. A. H. Bullen, London, 1885), vol. i, pp. 33, 60–61.
5. *Drama and Society in the Age of Jonson* (London, 1937), p. 258.
6. For the latest summary of the facts and inferences on which this is based, see M. T. Jones-Davies, *Un Peintre de la vie Londonienne : Thomas Dekker* (Paris, 1958), vol. ii, pp. 369–70; also Chambers, *Elizabethan Stage* (Oxford, 1924), vol. iii, pp. 294–5; Bowers, *Dramatic Works of Thomas Dekker*, vol. ii (Cambridge, 1955), pp. 3, 133.
I have used Bowers's text for all quotations from *The Honest Whore*.

Whore is therefore one of the first plays to transmit something of the new mode by means of an adult company and a public playhouse. We should expect some softening.

It is also caught in other complexities, for there is the *pasyent man* to be accounted for, too. His is perhaps the part of the play that Wright and Parrott would have thought of as mocking the virtues of respectable citizens. Candido the wonderful linen-draper also has his likely counterparts in other Middleton plays, just as the courtesan has. There is Quieto in *The Phoenix*, which may be as early as 1602 but is not likely to be later than 1604.[7] He is a reasonably instructive analogue, although he is, unlike Candido, both a very minor character and also a kind of *deus ex machina*. His love of quiet leads him to believe that people should not litigate; at the end of the play he binds a litigious person with a silken band and rubs him with a wondrous balsam or oil of patience. This causes him to vomit up some indigestible things:

O, an extent, a proclamation, a summons, a recognisance, a tachment, and injunction! a writ, a seizure, a writ of 'praisement, an absolution, a *quietus est!* (v.i.309–11)

I do not know that anyone has pointed out that this Lucianic episode must be a direct reflection of the famous scene in Jonson's *Poetaster* (1601) where Marston vomits up his pretentious vocabulary.* This may suggest that *The Phoenix* belongs to the earlier date (1602) rather than the later, and that Quieto is a genuine predecessor of Candido. He and his patient end the play extolling patience just like Candido and his cured shrew at the end of *The Honest Whore, Part I*; the *pasyent man* has a patient whose state he amends. Far on the other side, in point of date, stands *Anything for a Quiet Life* (1621). In the story and person of Mr Water Chamlet, citizen and linen-draper, we have much the completest analogue to Candido. *Anything for a Quiet Life* is

---

* This is in fact noted by R. H. Barker, *Thomas Middleton* (New York and London, 1958), p. 33.

---

7. The fullest discussion of the date of this play is by Baldwin Maxwell in *J. Q. Adams Memorial Studies* (Washington, 1948), pp. 743–53. Maxwell argues for composition between June and December 1603.

probably an unaided Middleton play.[8] Although one commentator has asked us to believe that Middleton had nothing to do with either part of *The Honest Whore* and that it is all Dekker's work,[9] the sequence Quieto/Candido/Chamlet makes out a very strong prima facie case for a Middleton share. There is other evidence for his participation, as we shall see. So the Candido part of our play is right in the middle of a spread of fashion too. The history of mockery of the respectable citizen has its own interest and uncertainties also; I have put some discussion of this history and its relevance to *The Honest Whore* in an appendix at the end of this paper.

II

The brilliant success of the Candido scenes in the first part assuredly owes a lot to the decorum by which everything is referred to his status as a shopkeeper and linen-draper and firmly related to the shop itself. It is not just any botheration that his wife (and her brother Fustigo) and the three men-about-town—the two sets working quite independently—try to afflict him with. Fustigo's blundering ideas right at the beginning—why not make Candido a cuckold or why not 'make him drunke and cut off his beard'—are rejected for the subtler vexations deployed in the two major Candido scenes (i.v and iii.i), and these are plotted in strict relations to the particular trade. One finds Satan exercising the same principle in *Paradise Regained*.

The first of these scenes is beautifully done. The time spent upon George the journeyman is purposefully spent. We need to get to know this notable 'head man' because the attitude that he and his fellows take towards Candido helps to validate Candido. George's talk is done with an element of comic exaggeration that signalizes his awareness of the range and shapeliness of his own speech. These techniques are consciously directed to the buyer, drawing seller and buyer together into an ironic conspiracy, after the manner of some modern advertisements. Candido, says

---

8. H. D. Sykes in 1921 suggested that it was a collaboration between Webster and Middleton, and F. L. Lucas accepted and enlarged upon this theory (*Works of John Webster*, London, 1927, vol. iii, pp. 66–68). It was very decisively rejected by G. E. Bentley, *Jacobean and Caroline Stage* (Oxford, 1956), vol. iv, p. 860.

9. S. Schoenbaum, 'Middleton's share in *The Honest Whore*', *Notes and Queries*, cxcvii, 1952, 3–4.

George, is 'a little negotiated':[1] this is George's idea of how to
put things (he owes it to himself), and so is his description of the
calicoes: 'a meeke gentle calico, cut upon two double affable
taffataes, ah, most neate, feate, and unmatchable'. The gentlemen are taken aback by George's mastery of a situation in which
they had intended to domineer. This sets the pattern for the
whole scene. Unable, subsequently, to make Candido lose his
temper, they dwindle helplessly, frustrated lilliputians. Part of
the fun of the scene is an alteration in the respective scales of
Candido and the three jesters. They enter as bullies with the
rights of customers; they are transformed into guests abashed
in the presence of a host. Nothing shows the majestic scale and
deliberate speed of Candido better than the second episode just
after the three men have made off with the best wine-cup:

> *Wife:* Why foole, why husband, why madman, I hope you will
>   not let 'em sneake away so with a siluer and gilt beaker, the best in
>   the house too: goe fellowes make hue and cry after them.
> *Candido:* Pray let your tongue lye still, all wil be well:
>   Come hither *George*, hye to the Constable,
>   And in calme order wish him to attach them,
>   Make no great stirre, because they're gentlemen,
>   And a thing partly done in meriment,
>   Tis but a size abou a iest thou knowst.
>   Therefore pursue it mildly, goe be gone,
>   The Constabl's hard by, bring him along,—
>   Make hast againe. (I.v.178–89)

In this first scene, as we take the measure of the playwrights'
conception of Candido, we begin to see that he is more than the
series of comic turns foreshadowed by the Quarto sub-title ('The
Humours of the Patient Man, and the Longing Wife'). It is
because they think that he will be provoked into some such series
that the gentlemen first approach him: 'Do but thinke what
sport it will be to make this fellow (the mirror of patience) as
angry, as vext, and as madde as an English cuckolde.' This is
indeed the Devil's voice. Some of the pleasure of the scenes
comes from watching the various ways in which the tables are

---

1. This is the first and only citation of the word *negotiated* in the sense of 'busy',
'engaged' in *OED*. Dekker's use of words remains to be examined at a level more
exacting than that implied by traditional approval for his 'Elizabethan' vigour and
savour.

turned on the tempters. The comic dynamism springs not from the moving and stirring of the gullers but out of the patience and passivity of the gulled. That the tables are being turned, at least, is plain enough in the slapstick episodes, because those who intended to beat do get beaten themselves: Fustigo is thrummed by George and the others for trying to make a fool of their master (III.i), and when he hires Crambo and Poh to beat up George for him, the two bravoes are worsted by the prentices (IV.iii). But this compromise with violence in what is represented as the humours of the patient man requires explanation. It happens in a roundabout way, so that Candido himself is peculiarly implicated. The shrewish wife persuades George (much against his better judgement) to dress up as his own master in the hope that this will at last make Candido angry; but Candido, exemplary and literal as always, in reply assumes the garb of humility—a journeyman's dress. Consequently, Crambo and Poh mistake the master for the journeyman and attack Candido instead of George. George and his fellows are horrified ('strike a Citizen in's shop!') and deal promptly and decisively with the two bravoes.

To insist upon detecting overtones of solemn parable in these episodes would not be very wise, but that something parabolical is present in the atmosphere need not be denied. Certainly, two quite positive accessions to our conception of Candido arise from these incidents. Candido himself is not compromised. He does not directly incite to violence; the single blow that he receives from Crambo allows him to practise his special virtue:

> Let them alone pray, this did me no harme,
> Troth I was cold, and the blow made me warme,
> I thanke em for't. (Part I, IV.iii.103–5)

But Candido's literal enactment of parable—his garb of humility, his turning the other cheek—exemplifies that very strange brand of passivity which is both ethically and also dramaturgically a source of dynamic action. In thinking about Candido it seems necessary to keep in mind both the transforming power of his ethic—its capacity to change lives—and also the role of the dramatic character in what is advertised as a comedy of 'the *humours* of the patient man'.

Even at a superficial level we can observe, from the episodes just mentioned, that what was expected to be passive and easy to bully (because 'pasyent') turns out quite unexpectedly to be the means of humiliation for the bullies. Candido remains true to his humour; but unruly, violent stage-fun proceeds even from the triumph of the peculiar virtue to which he is so humorously true. The event cunningly reconciles the official Christian ethic (as expressed through Candido's actual behaviour) with the lusts of the unregenerate playgoer. That playgoer wants to see the bullies downed and at the same time wants to keep his cake (both the dramatic and the ethical slices) by *not* seeing the patient man's humour unhumorously flawed or his virtue unethically betrayed. The device somewhat resembles the one with which Shaw saves the Christians without compromising them in *Androcles and the Lion* (when Ferrovius breaks out in the arena). Candido's person is strengthened, too: the degree to which the fierce loyalty of his pleasant servants towards him helps to make him positively likeable (as well as funny and virtuous) ought not to be overlooked.

Nor ought it to be overlooked that a humour in Jacobean drama is not normally a virtue. The ordinary perspectives of humour comedy seem likely to shift about a bit when we find such an abnormality at the heart of the manner. (The importance of Quieto in *The Phoenix* as a forerunner is stressed, too.) Patience is a favourite theme of Dekker's, and he doubtless has nothing very fresh or illuminating to *say* about it. But embodied in the action of this play the treatment becomes more original. Morose in *The Silent Woman* wants to live a noiseless life and as a consequence finds himself plunged into a continual racket. That is a characteristic humour comedy device. It achieves its effect by repetition, by a continuous reversal of the victim's expectations: possessed by what is shown to be a silly and selfish affectation for quiet and solitude he is continually tormented by company and din. Northrop Frye writes:

The humour's dramatic function is to express a state of what might be called ritual bondage. He is obsessed by his humour, and his function in the play is primarily to repeat his obsession.[2]

Candido's situation—and this perhaps is why, like Morose's, it is

2. *Anatomy of Criticism* (Princeton, 1957), p. 168.

funny/cruel—does superficially resemble that of Jonson's cur-
mudgeon, and could therefore be fairly advertised on the title-
page as a display of humours. He is a man who wants 'calm
order', and gets instead a succession of discords, affrays in his
shop, a termagant wife, and so on. This might be the laughter-
arousing principle of unincremental repetition that Frye is
talking about. But to practise patience in the face of trouble and
adversity (a thing which Morose notably fails to do) is not, in any
ordinary interpretation of words, to be obsessed by a humour.
It is to persist in righteousness. And patience, in particular, is a
virtue of such a kind that the more you practise it the grander
and the more exemplary and admirable you become. It suffer-
eth long. This is incremental repetition, perhaps. Candido's
humour, in fact, makes him seem ridiculous and touchingly
good at one and the same time; we look upon him with one aus-
picious and one dropping eye. In iii.i, for example, when his wife
perversely refuses to let him unlock the gown in which he must
attend the Senate, dressed in a carpet he enacts the fool for
Christ's sake:

> Go, step vp, fetch me downe one of the Carpets,
> The saddest colour Carpet, honest *George*,
> Cut thou a hole ith middle for my necke,
> Two for mine armes, nay prithee looke not strange.

At the same time, there is nice calculation in the episode suitable to the decorum of his character as city merchant when he
reflects that the damaged carpet will mulct him in far less than
will the fine for appearing in the Senate without his gown.
Candido's righteousness is not of the kind that makes him either
depersonalized or stiffly and strainedly unsympathetic.

Yet his virtue was, in Dekker's and Middleton's ethical milieu,
an extraordinarily important one. It is not an accident that we
have at the very end of the play, in Candido's panegyric on
patience that concludes it, that startling reference to

>   the best of men
> That ere wore earth about him, was a sufferer,
> A soft, meeke, patient, humble, tranquill spirit,
> The first true Gentle-man that euer breathd.
>   (v.ii.491–4)

It would be too much to say that Candido is a figure of Jesus; but the meek shall inherit the earth, and Candido, supposing that he (as, technically, a humour character) can be described at all as being in ritual bondage to his *virtuous* humour, has a wider function. By being, after the fashion of the humour, consistently what he is, he transforms what is around him. Shadowly behind him is the exemplary question: Was ever Patience like Mine? Because it *is* a virtue and not just a humour (though it may be that as well), patience when embodied in an exemplary human figure has the power to change lives, indeed to *convert*. Any argument about the thematic unity of *The Honest Whore, Part I*, would need to take account of the way in which the converted shrew of the Candido scenes matches the converted courtesan of the Bellafront scenes. In all its stories, indeed, not least in the Hippolito/Infelice one, the play echoes and re-echoes to the theme of transformation, or rebirth, of starting to live again. Some modern commentators, doubtless, could without difficulty call forth from the plays a ghostly pageant of such elements, but they might in so doing be unnaturally gilding the rough edges of Middleton's and Dekker's art. That art wears earth about it and keeps its feet on the ground, even if the feeling that we can live for a time in the world of the plays as a whole may be attributed to a vague awareness that the same sky stretches over everything that happens in them.

Candido, at any rate, turns out to be thoroughly aware of the responsibilities of his virtue. That virtue is, unlike a humour, an active thing. It works upon his nearest object, Viola, the shrewish wife; but not for a long time. It is because Candido permits Viola to overreach herself that the example of Patience which he sets her finally takes hold. The outrage of Bedlam tips the scale. If this seems untrue to life, the playwrights were being sufficiently uncynical to save the ethic, which presumably holds that if you endure long and suffer even the worst wrongs meekly your persecutors will turn from their wickedness and permit you to live. In the prevailing comic context, the conversion of Viola is rendered neither with these heavy overtones nor in any explicitly didactic way. It is done with touching delicacy in one of the best fleeting moments of the play when she appears with George outside the gates of Bedlam (to which she has committed Candido in a last attempt to make him angry):

Wife: How does he talke *George*! ha! good *George* tell me.
George: Why youre best go see.
Wife: Alas I am afraid.
George: Afraid! you had more need be ashamd: he may rather be afraid of you. (v.i.19–22)

The delicacy here, the reliance upon the actor's ability to put across Viola's transformed condition, suggests something of the resources that lay ready to the playwrights' hands amongst Prince Henry's Men in 1604. Miss Bradbrook is surely right in claiming that Candido is far from guileless. He uses his virtue in order to teach and to tame. The part can be played in order to give expression to the varying degrees of self-consciousness with which he does this. In the scene with the carpet Candido makes us laugh at him and at the same time instructs by his very willingness to be made fun of rather than compromise his peculiar humour/virtue. It is no small thing for a grave linen-draper to do. There are strata in his final speech in Act v. It lays together comedy and ethic, humour and virtue, the exemplariness of the patient man and his role in the story of linen-draper and shrew:

> O my dread liege! It [Patience] is the sap of blisse,
> Reares vs aloft; makes men and Angels kisse,
> And (last of all) to end a houshould strife,
> It is the hunny gainst a waspish wife.

The anti-climactic casualness with which that last couplet is placed might be clumsiness; but it is more likely to be the playwrights' reminder that they were after all not creators of a ghostly pageant but (in the circumstances a prouder claim) of a domestic comedy.

In these Bedlam scenes Candido embodies also an ironic contradiction resembling that of the main title. *Onest hore*, like *woman killed with kindness*, would appear to be a turn of phrase that impudently calls attention to its wares by means of a small outrage upon our ordinary expectations. Its Candido counterpart would be *patient madman*, a contradiction in terms that matches aptly enough with the representation of a humour as a virtue, an exemplary man as a comic butt, and, of course, a courtesan as chaste. The mirror of patience finds himself temporarily in Bedlam, the mirror of all impatience. From their positions in the oxymoron Candido and Bellafront severally instruct us in the straightforwardness of virtue.

The implications of this for thematic unity need to be followed up. But what has been said about Candido's role in *The Honest Whore, Part I* does enforce some speculation about the Candido of the second play, and about authorship. Surely no part, not even Jeremy Face's, ever fell like this one. It is not simply a case of vanished inspiration, but also of a profound misunderstanding of the Candido we have hitherto recognized. His marriage to another shrew can be accepted as a perfectly excusable attempt to get him going again; that he should tame her by threatening to beat her with his yard-measure is an outrage on the whole earlier conception of the paradoxes of patience. The shrew's story is then dropped. Apart from a brief and pointless sketch for a shop scene (III.iii.88 ff.) in the manner of *Part I*, Candido has little to do until by a mere accident he ends up in Bridewell falsely accused as a receiver of stolen goods. This is another meaningless outrage. Candido the patient madman makes an ironic point; Candido the patient thief makes none at all. When we take into account the Henslowe payment to Dekker and Middleton for *The Honest Whore, Part I*—an entry that can hardly be regarded except as clear evidence that the text we have contains work by Middleton[3]—and the absence of any evidence for Middleton's participation in *The Honest Whore, Part II*, it looks as though Dekker in the second part must have been botching the continuation of what was originally a Middleton idea. Add to this the fact that Water Chamlet in Middleton's *Anything for a Quiet Life* is much the closest analogue to the Candido of *Part I*, and one is content to ascribe the best of Candido to the younger playwright.

III

Northrop Frye's observation that a humour-character 'can never do anything inconsistent with the role that he has prescribed for himself' might also apply to an allegorical character. Perhaps, since Candido's humour happens to be a virtue, he ought to be described as an allegory of patience—except that the 'unnatural' consistency which he shares with Patience is in his case thoroughly integrated with the realistic scenes and actions that ordinarily accompany Jacobean humour-characterization.

3. I remain unpersuaded by Schoenbaum's assertions to the contrary, *Notes and Queries*, cxcvii, 1952, 3–4.

At any particular moment—when the pennyworth of lawn is bought, the beaker stolen, or the gown locked away—Candido's reactions seem entirely proper to the kind of patient-tempered soul which he has been established as being. He is not saintly; he is a trifle ridiculous, almost at times a fool, a Milanese linen-draper. His patience seems believable because it is a gift of nature not of will, like Falstaff's girth. But inner consistency, the bracing skeleton of the moral idea, is just as important to his construction as the free naturalness of his outward behaviour. When the Candido of the second part threatens to beat his wife, that consistency is betrayed and the character collapses. Candido, therefore, can be taken as a successful example of what T. S. Eliot called the 'impure art' of the Elizabethans:

The aim of the Elizabethans was to attain complete realism without surrendering any of the advantages which as artists they observed in unrealistic conventions.[4]

Candido fuses an element of convention, the humour/virtue or allegory of Patience, with an element of realism, the moment-by-moment circumstantiality of dialogue, settings, and action. Dekker's art, says Mme Jones-Davies, 'semble osciller entre l'adoption de formes conventionelles et le choix de principes naturalistes'.[5] What balance between the two is achieved in the Bellafront scenes?

The element of convention in the Bellafront/Hippolito confrontation was clearly identified long ago by Hardin Craig. She exemplifies the theory that 'one emotion or passion drives out another, and that the substitution is immediately operative'; she is 'a victim both of the psychological theory that woman's substance is weak and changeable and of that which makes conversion a matter of the access of spirits to the heart and renders hesitation and deliberation impossible'. Once Hippolito's rhetoric of persuasion has been worked upon her, 'her conversion follows as a matter of necessity'.[6]

From what the playwrights actually made, they seem to have been trying to surprise some sort of circumstantiality out of these dry bones.

4. *Selected Essays* (London, 1934), p. 116; cf. I-S. Ekeblad, 'The "impure art" of John Webster', *RES*, ns, ix, 1958, 253.
5. Jones-Davies, vol. ii, p. 209.
6. *The Enchanted Glass* (New York, 1936), pp. 124, 175, 176.

The first of the Bellafront scenes, comprising all Act II of *The Honest Whore, Part I*, is an admirable one; but it may appear designed only to make the sharpest of contrasts between juxtaposed elements. The first half of the great act, in prose, is fresh in every detail, intimate, 'Dutch', and beautifully relaxed. As theatrical journalism, the playhouse equivalent of the pamphlets about underworld behaviour, it would be hard to overrate the episode during which Bellafront and her servant Roger combine to extract extra cash out of clients by pretending that the first bottle of wine paid for by the gentlemen has been spilled. Bellafront at her dressing-table is a Jacobean Belinda, coarse and vital. The second half of the scene, in verse, removes us to realms where one passion drives out another and all is high-toned and schematic. Yet the 450 lines of this act, when read or acted, may seem plausible as a way of rendering a conversion on the stage. The act's shape and the journey it conducts us on—from Bellafront murmuring over her rouge-pot to Bellafront hysterically threatening herself with Hippolito's dagger— objectify a massive psychical revolution. It is not more difficult to lend credence to because it all happens in one theatrical movement, for theatrical time is not to be measured like ordinary time. The writers are involving us in the *radical* character of the change in Bellafront, not its speed. This seems closer to their minds than a theory about the weakness of woman's substance.

The impression that Hippolito converts Bellafront by 'one parlee' only is sustained by his later reference to the episode (*Part II*, IV.i.245). What he there calls 'the power of Argument' is of course no less important than Craig and others claim. The rhetoric of persuasion is very formally deployed. Soul and body, the courtesan is lost (*Part I*, II.i.322–34), in her beastlike existence all ordinary human discriminations are lost or muddled (335–51); thwarted and exploited and doomed to poverty in the end, she is trapped in 'her fatall-circled life' (360–97) and even her pleasures are curdled with fear (400–20). There is an effective absence of self-righteousness on Hippolito's part. It is not the harlot's wickedness but her disappointments that are stressed. The direction is social, secular, factual: 'And mildly too: not without sense or reason' (317). If we are to identify this practical-minded homiletic with some conventional assumptions about rhetoric and psychology, it would be wrong to regard it as being enacted here in an impersonal and undramatic way. Hippolito is not just any young man with the right set of principles; he is the man whom Bellafront suddenly falls in love with. The depiction of the gradual awakening of his interest in her and of her (very different) interest in him, from her first notice of Hippolito (192) to her abashed and hesitant 'Shall I sweare? / Will you beleeue me then?' (291–2), is itself a finely paced example of complete realism in language and attitude. It is sensible to infer that his words work strongly upon her at least in part because of this relationship, just as Hamlet's words work upon Gertrude partly because he is her son.

It is not entirely accurate to say that Bellafront is converted by 'one parlee'. Her second scene with Hippolito (iv.i) is a completion of the process. But it is here overlaid with some Jacobean theatrical modes that may hide its actuality. Hippolito meditates on the picture of Infelice, on the skull and the book; Bellafront wins her way into his presence disguised as a page. The dramatist, though, is still interested in showing the ways in which her passions have focused themselves on Hippolito. It is not rhetoric of persuasion alone that works the change in her but also the growth of a passion for the one man whom she cannot have so extravagant that it drives her to the hysterical supplications of this scene. The Bellafront story here borrows tones and colours from its nearness to the Infelice story, moving from the 'Dutch' realism of the first half of Act ii a long way into Fletcherian tragi-comedy. Love-melancholy as well as homily combine to alter Bellafront for ever.

The rest of the scene, however, is not worked out in terms of her inner development. She says that she fears being forced back to her trade if Hippolito rejects her:

> Be greater then a king, saue not a body,
> But from eternall shipwracke keepe a soule,
> If not, and that againe, sinnes path I tread,
> The griefe be mine, the guilt fall on thy head.
>
> (iv.i.168–71)

But when he does reject her, she says that she will leave 'this vndoing Cittie' and go back to her father rather than relapse. The playwright has not troubled himself to demonstrate that these cross-currents and contrary decisions arise from any inward compulsions. That she can decide after all to flee from the city means that it is within her powers to remain honest although unsustained by his love; perhaps, therefore, her plea to him must be regarded as purely an argument (or a bit of moral blackmail) and not also as the index of a genuine self-knowledge. It does not imply a real awareness on her part of how frustrate love-melancholy might drive her to whoredom again in despair. The playwright is unlikely to have considered so curiously, nor will this thin crust bear the weight of these speculations. It is a pretty fair indication that he is working from the surface that he should devise a third and totally unexplained course of action for his heroine and surprise his audience in the last scene (v.ii) with her appearance in Bedlam and her consequential marriage to Matheo. As so often, a Jacobean dramatist contrives a *coup de théâtre* but relinquishes his grip on inner truths which elsewhere he had shown a growing disposition to explore and cultivate. Finally, Bellafront's exceptional, outsider's role as the strumpet who turns chaste ('that woman hardly found', iv.i.199) vaguely fits her for her appearance amongst the wonders of nature in Bedlam; her presence there does not, as Candido's does, lend special point to the paradox which she embodies.

In the second part Bellafront's story has been thought out afresh, as Candido's has not. Madeleine Doran has detected in it a 'serious emphasis on a moral problem'.[7] Bellafront certainly carries what is artistically and ethically serious in the links that exist between the two parts. The chief male characters, Matheo and Hippolito, couple some degree of individuation with purely functional roles in relation to her, and it is inappropriate to worry about whether in the second part they are consistent with the persons bearing the same names in the first part. (In fact, there are no grave contradictions, and over the ten acts two actors could contrive perfectly rational and convincing readings.) But it is in the second part that Matheo's language and gesture come most remarkably alive, as when he strips off Bellafront's gown in order to sell it (iii.ii). This elaborated vitality spills over from Dekker's appetite for rendering the surface of life. It is the documentary and prose equivalent for those poetic beauties which lured nineteenth-century verse dramatists away from the business of the play. Dekker's indulgence in it enforces a

---

7. *Endeavors of Art* (Madison, 1954), p. 366.

local belief in Matheo's rakehelly existence which is not strictly necessary to, and may actually distract from, his function in relation to Bellafront. Matheo is, as we shall see, not the only character in *The Honest Whore, Part II*, who contributes to an imbalance between realism and convention in which it is the 'principes naturalistes' that weight the scales.

In the second play it is Bellafront who takes over responsibility for the contributions originally made by Candido and Hippolito to the themes common to both plays. She is the chief characterological vehicle of such thematic continuity as obtains between the two parts. Consider what happens in the temptation scene, iv.i, the counterpart of Act ii in *The Honest Whore, Part I*. This scene has just enough from Hippolito to justify the title-page: 'The Honest Whore, perswaded by strong Arguments to turne Curtizan againe.' But Dekker is plainly nervous about those strong arguments. Some think that Milton had the same difficulty with *his* Devil; it is the old recurrent problem that comes from literature's entanglement with rhetoric. Either Dekker feared offending his audience's sense of propriety or (in Hardin Craig's terms) corrupting it with his own oratory; or perhaps he thought it would have been untrue to 'psychological theory' (and therefore artistically unconvincing?) to show any woman, even a strong-minded one like Bellafront, as unpersuaded by a really powerful speech. Hippolito, at any rate, has only one speech; it is thirty lines long and obviously sophistical (one can hear the audience's groans of derision). It is set against nearly a hundred lines of Bellafront's 'brave refuting'. She has changed places, thematically, with the old Hippolito. Nothing illustrates more clearly the purely functional character of his role than the inability of *her* rhetoric to convert *him*. He must continue to be wicked so that her story may flourish. (Yet even here a detail or two may show Dekker's lingering wish to reconcile the functional with the naturalistic, for he makes Infelice and the Duke speculate on Hippolito's motives for conduct which they do feel to be extraordinary; by so doing, they sketch an explanation of it in terms of psychological pressures rather than theatrical, narrative necessity [iv.ii.41–56].)

More importantly, in view of the collapse of Candido, Bellafront has taken over his role, too. By keeping alive the theme of Patience she partially saves the unity of the double play. The

passionate convertite of the first part becomes the patient sufferer of the second. The eventual consignment of this chaste
woman to Bridewell (specially associated with the punishment
of whores) amounts to an ironic comment on the society that
puts her there in the same way that it puts the patient man in the
madhouse. Or it would amount to this, if we could feel perfectly confident that Dekker was interested in developing
Middleton's joke. There are, unfortunately, signs throughout
the second part that he isn't. In the first part Candido, within
his own story, was handled in such a way that all the emphasis
was thrown upon him; his allies help to make him likeable, his
persecutors are carefully subordinated to their functional roles
(though at one time, in *Part I*, 1.ii, it looks as though Fustigo
might be going to steal too much interest for himself); consequently, we have a good example of the 'impure art', a parable of patience which leaves us with a memorably individuated
comic personage. But in the patient woman the balance has gone
wrong.

One reason may be that Dekker is doing something new in
presenting the struggles of the converted courtesan in a social
situation where most things seem to go against her. A brilliant
stroke is the haunting assumption made by so many of the bystanders that 'once a whore always a whore'. Even her reputation as a paradoxical miracle of nature is a handicap (see, for
example, *Part II*, 1.i.81 ff.). Working under different conditions
Dekker might have developed this side of the matter into something combining the perceptions of *Moll Flanders* with those of
Amelia. It would at least not have been impossible for Bellafront's context, so far as it is constructed out of the behaviour of
other persons, to have nourished her as Candido's in the first
part nourishes him. Instead, Bellafront's struggle with the easy
assumptions of her society is soon swamped by the portrayal of
the vigorous life of that society itself. Matheo, as we have seen, is
one element in this process. He derives from the special Dek-
kerian gift for showing contemporary social types, with their
knotty rhythms and savoury locutions. More important than
Matheo is Friscobaldo, the father in disguise. In himself one of
the best of Dekker's inventions in the Simon Eyre vein and
rightly singled out for admiration by Hazlitt,[8] he conducts an

8. *Lectures on the Dramatic Literature of the Age of Elizabeth* (London, 1821 ed.), p. 119.

experiment, not always an openly benevolent one, on Bellafront and Matheo, much like the Duke's in *Measure for Measure*.
But whereas, in the eyes of some critics at least, the Duke's
behaviour may be justified partly by his own symbolic nature
and partly by its being a means for exploring the central moral
problems of the characters, Friscobaldo's stratagems actually
distract us from Bellafront's dilemma. Her problem is of course
not one which resembles those in the Shakespearian problem
comedies in that it arouses uncertain or divided responses in the
minds of the audience (Dr Schanzer's criterion), although the
implicit challenge of the title may indicate that the play itself
might have been a challenging experience for those who (if they
existed outside as well as inside the play) has assumed that 'onc
a whore always a whore'. Primarily, though, Bellafront's pro
blem is like those which are found in the other kind of problem
play, the ones written by Ibsen or Shaw. It is social and personal:
how to stay honest in face of the combined pressures of a wastrel
husband and an amorous courtier. Nothing at all is made of the
fact that once she loved the latter. That is a sufficient indication
that if *The Honest Whore, Part II*, were to be deepened, it would
move in the direction of the profoundly felt sociology of *Women
Beware Women* and not of the poetic and religious antinomies of
Measure for Measure. The objection is not that Bellafront's
dilemma is too simple and stale but that Friscobaldo, both by
the vitality of his surface and the irrelevance of his devices, draws
attention away from an honest study of it. On the one hand, his
fairy-godfather presence softens the edges of the problem with
promises and reassurances; on the other, it augments the
documentary content for its own, and not her, sake. It echoes
the bustle of the London (or Milanese) streets and delineates the
manners of cities. From Friscobaldo through Hazlitt there is a
direct route to Dickens. The irony is that the agent who thrusts
Bellafront towards a folk-tale solution of her story clearly testi-
fies to an art capable of embodying, in Hazlitt's phrase, 'the
inmost movements of the mind in everyday actions and familiar speech'.

The two parts of *The Honest Whore* exhibit many artistic compromises and withdrawals; they sketch a system of thematic
correspondences which might easily tempt criticism to mistake
the draught for the accomplishment. There are many passages

which are strictly beneath criticism—too brittle and opportunistic to sustain it; there are many others in which the 'familiar speech' appears both splendidly exact and abundantly theatrical. The plays have something of the power of a long novel—of the 'baggy monster' variety—in which for the time being we gratefully live. But their balance is often upset, sometimes by the passion for documenting the 'emotions of cities', sometimes perhaps by the necessity of entertaining those whose behaviour they mirror. For to the various paradoxes this last one may be added: Bellafront and her servant Roger would probably have preferred to spend the afternoon watching something romantic and high-toned like the Infelice episode rather than something as exact and naturalistic as their own scenes together. If the literary and theatrical conditions of 1604-5, disrupted by the new interest in city comedy, are responsible for some of the compromises, others may be attributable to dual authorship. The Candido scenes of the first part, the one completely unflawed portion of the work, may derive from the presence of a talent more radically witty than Dekker's ever was. The coupling of his name with Middleton's is the last oxymoron, and perhaps the most fascinating.

APPENDIX

If characters such as Candido and Chamlet and their wives are mockeries of the honest citizen, then—so, according to some authorities, the history goes—they are part of a large theatrical movement which brought about a strong counter-movement. Towards the end of 1604 Dekker, now hopelessly infected by the new modes, joined with Webster to produce *Westward Ho* for the Paul's Boys. This is a play which (Felix Schelling thought) descended to 'the depths of gross and vicious realism'. As a result, Jonson, Marston, and Chapman arose, strong in the righteousness of bourgeois morality, and delivered at the Blackfriars, fairly early in 1605, a 'conscious protest' in the form of *Eastward Ho*. Dekker and Webster rejoined later in 1605 with *Northward Ho* for the Paul's Boys. (That Webster has a much larger share in *Westward Ho* and *Northward Ho* than has previously been supposed is argued from new evidence about colloquial contractions by Peter B. Murray in *Papers of the Bibliographical Society of America*, lvi, 1962, 482-7. He concludes that

Webster wrote about 40 per cent of each play. A review of earlier opinions is given by Mme Jones-Davies, vol. ii, pp. 371–3.) At about the same time Marston was also weighing in on the side of righteousness with *The Dutch Courtesan*. Parrott thought that the 'vigorously repulsive' portrait of Francischina the harlot in this play was intended to offset the 'sympathetic and delightful' and sentimentalized character of Bellafront in *The Honest Whore* and presumably her counterparts in other plays (such as the courtesans in *Blurt, Master Constable* and the Middleton plays). According to G. K. Hunter ('English folly and Italian vice' in *Jacobean Theatre*, ed. J. R. Brown and B. Harris, London, 1960, p. 109), *The Dutch Courtesan* offers a dose of real-life nastiness and is braced by a rigid morality framework which resembles that of *Eastward Ho*.

Parrott was writing in 1914 and Professor Hunter in 1960, so this version of the matter has persisted for a long time. They are not in entire agreement, since Hunter is rather sceptical about the view that *The Dutch Courtesan* is an attempt to offset *The Honest Whore*; but he agrees with the judgement, most fully expressed by C. H. Herford in 1925 in the Oxford *Jonson* (vol. ii, p. 40), that *Eastward Ho* strikes an unusually emphatic note of solid bourgeois morality.

There are difficulties about the whole theory of protest and counter-protest in so far as it embraces the *Ho* plays, Marston's play, and *The Honest Whore*. Two of them are literary and one of them is chronological.

(i) It is very doubtful indeed whether Parrott's, Herford's, Hunter's (and, incidentally, Louis B. Wright's) reading of *Eastward Ho* as a serious piece of citizen moralizing can be accepted. Much the best interpretation of this fine comedy is provided by Anthony Caputi in his *John Marston, Satirist* (Ithaca, New York 1961); he firmly concludes that it is 'practically devoid of literal seriousness'; it is comedy of a kind whose deft ambiguities quite forbid us to regard it as either a defence of middle-class morality or a protest against its detractors. Before Caputi, Miss Bradbrook (*The Growth and Structure of Elizabethan Comedy*, 1955, pp. 139–41) very justly maintained that *Eastward Ho* is parody and not protest; that it is satire or 'mischievous badinage', and caricatures the lawful ambitions of the Industrious Prentice. This view of the play removes the linchpin from the theory that the *Ho* playwrights were engaged in some kind of simple-minded argument about the propriety of 'questionable' scenes.

(ii) Another way of removing a linchpin is to insist that Schelling's reading ('gross and vicious realism' and so forth) of *Westward Ho*, the first of the *Ho* sequence, is just nonsense. There is a certain amount of obscene chatter; but the core and framework of the whole thing are as basically sound and 'wholesome' as the morality of *The Honest Whore* itself. The main characters all turn out to be extremely proper, and not just in a superficial way at the denouement. It is unlikely that there was ever anything that anybody except a Victorian editor could conceivably protest about; certainly the authors of *Eastward Ho* were not the men to do so and would hardly worry about its depiction of citizens as gulls. Rather, they helped on the good work, and in their play exploited title, popularity, and something of the structure and colour of the first *Ho* play.

(iii) In order to be able to determine the relationship between *The Dutch Courtesan* and *The Honest Whore, Parts I and II*, we would need to be certain about a few more dates. *The Dutch Courtesan* might be later than *The Honest Whore, Part I*; Caputi indeed argues that it is at least 'concurrent' with *Eastward Ho*; this would also make it concurrent with *The Honest Whore, Part II*. If this is right, Marston might be breaking angrily into the middle of the Dekker/Middleton success series. But there is no certainty on the point; Chambers dates *The Dutch Courtesan* in 1603–4 and so do Harbage and Schoenbaum (*Annals of English Drama*, London, 1964, p. 88). Incidentally, if Marston really intended his Francischina to be a portrait of a courtesan corrective to that offered in Bellafront he was, as I hope this paper has suggested, reacting to *The Honest Whore, Part I*, in as bad a way as possible; he would need to be classed with fools (depicted in *The Honest Whore, Part II*) who think complacently 'once a whore always a whore'.

12

A note on 'Opinion' in Daniel, Greville, and Chapman

The *OED* does not much illuminate the signification of the word 'Opinion' as that is found in certain seventeenth-century poets. A lexicographer of another age wrote: 'Among the *old Heathens* was a goddess that was worshipped under the notion of presiding over men's sentiments, which for the most part are purely conjectural; she was represented in the form of a young woman with a bold look, but a reeling or staggering gait.'[1] To some seventeenth-century writers, indeed, Opinion presented herself in the guise of a goddess of this kind. The most striking example is to be found in Ben Jonson's masque of *Hymenaei*, wherein Opinion is disguised as Truth and conducts a 'barriers' *débat* with Truth herself.[2] Extended passages on Opinion are also to be found in Guilpin's *Skialetheia* (satire vi), in Guilpin Opinion's opponent is Reason;[3] in Selden's *Table-Talk* (no. xcvi 'Opinion');[4] and in an essay by Cornwallis 'Of Opinion'.[5] The second stasimon of the chorus, seventy lines in length, in Daniel's *Cleopatra* provides perhaps the finest description of the havoc wrought by Opinion on Truth and Reason:

First published in *Modern Language Review*, xlvi, 1951, 331–8.

1. Dyche and Pardon, *A New General English Dictionary* (London, 1752), sv 'opinion'. *OED*, art. 'opinion', I.c., draws nearest to opinion as discussed in this note and cites, 'Opinion is a powerfull, bold and immeasurable party' from Florio's Montaigne. Johnson (4th ed. of his Dictionary, 1773, sv 'opinion') cites the passage from Jonson's *Discoveries* mentioned in n. 7 below.

2. *Ben Jonson*, vol. vii. On which see D. J. Gordon in *Journal of the Warburg and Courtauld Institutes*, v, 1945, who cites Charron and de la Primaudaye (*French Academie*, 1618, pp. 454–5) to explain Jonson's figure. See also A. H. Gilbert, *The Symbolic Persons in the Masques of Ben Jonson* (Durham, NC, 1949), sv 'opinion'.

3. *Skialetheia*, Shakespeare Association facsmile no. 2 (London, 1931).

4. *Table-Talk . . . of John Selden* (Temple Classics ed., London, 1898), pp. 93–94.

5. *Essayes* (ed. D. C. Allen, Baltimore, 1946).

> O malecontent seducing guest,
>   Contriver of our greatest woes:
>   Which borne of windes, and fed with showes,
>   Doost nurce thyself in thine unrest.
> Judging ungotten things the best,
>   Or what thou in conceit designst,
>   And all things in the world dost deeme,
>   Not as they are but as they seeme.[6]

All these writers define Opinion as untrustworthy, shifting and dissimulatory, that which 'gave [Man] all of the Trouble and made all the Confusion in the world' (Selden), 'the mother of Hipocrisie' (Cornwallis), 'the Proteus Robin-good-fellow of change' (Guilpin). They agree with Charron that Opinion is

un vain et leger, crud et imparfaict jugement des choses, tiré et puisé des sens exterieurs, et du bruict commun et vulgaire . . . elle est inconstante, incertaine, volage, trompeuse . . . qui faict teste à la raison, de laquelle elle est une ombre et image, mais vaine et faulse.[7]

Sir John Davies sees her as a form of Wit, one of the powers of the soul: 'When her assent [Wit] lightly doth incline / To either part she is Opinion light.'[8] Donne even enlists the idea in the campaign that he wages on behalf of Renaissance naturalism and 'libertinism' against 'custom': Bredvold has explained how Opinion, which is seen as arbitrarily prescribing laws and manners to nations, is one of the agents that overthrow the 'golden laws' of Nature:

> Our liberty's revers'd, our Charter's gone,
> And we're made servants to opinion,
> A monster in no certain shape attir'd.[9]
>   (*Elegy*, xvii)

---

6. *Tragedie of Cleopatra*, ll. 1071–8 (ed. Lederer, in *Materialien zur Kunde des älteren englischen Dramas*, xxxi, Louvain, 1911).

7. *De la Sagesse* (Paris, 1836), p. 80. Jonson is plainly indebted to Charron in his definition of Opinion in *Discoveries* (*Ben Jonson*, vol. viii, p. 564). Cf. his use of opinion in 'An Epistle answering to one that asked to be sealed of the tribe of Ben', ll. 1–4, ibid., p. 218.

8. *Nosce Teipsum*, in *Silver Poets of the Sixteenth Century* (London, 1947), p. 379.

9. See L. I. Bredvold, 'The naturalism of Donne in relation to some Renaissance traditions', *Journal of English and Germanic Philology*, xxii, 1923, 475, who, however, cites no other examples of the usage. Daniel's 'Syren' in 'Ulisses and the Syren' defends naturalism and scorns opinion exactly in Donne's manner.

Donne's use of the word in an argument in defence of naturalism appears to be exceptional. In the passages I have so far cited,
fragments of older philosophies are seen to be inhering. Opinion
(δόξα) was an important feature in the epistemologies of Plato,
Aristotle, the Stoics, and the neo-Platonists:[1]

Those who see the many beautiful, and who yet neither see absolute
beauty, nor can follow any guide who points the way thither; who see
the many just, and not absolute justice, and the like—such persons may
be said to have opinion (δοξάζειν) but not knowledge.[2]

Do you not know ... that all mere opinions are bad, and the best of
them blind?[3]

The well-known words of Plato provided the starting-point for
an epistemological concept that proved to have an extended life
in the elaboration of theories of knowledge and sensation developed by later philosophers. For our purpose, since it is particularly those poets who are influenced by the neo-Stoic revival
who use the Charronesque conception of Opinion to support
their view—so unlike that of Donne—that what man needs is
less libertinism and more inward discipline, it is worth noting
that Epictetus, who has been called 'the central inspiration of
European neo-Stoicism',[4] had discussed Opinion in an important
passage of the *Discourses*:

Behold the beginning of philosophy!—a recognition of the conflict
between the opinions of men, and a search for the origin of that conflict, and a condemnation of mere opinion (τὸ ψιλῶς δοκοῦν), coupled
with scepticism regarding it, and a kind of investigation to determine

---

1. Plato, *Republic*, v.476–8 (trans. Jowett, Oxford, 1892, pp. 175 f.), vi.508 (ibid.,
p. 209), vii.534 (ibid., p. 237); Aristotle, *Posterior Analytics*, i.33 (*Works*, trans. Ross,
Oxford, 1928, vol. i, 88b–89a); cf. Ross, *Aristotle* (London, 1923), p. 49. For the
epistemology of the Stoics and the part played by opinion, see R D. Hicks, *Stoic and
Epicurean* (London, 1911), especially p. 69; for the neo-Platonists, E. H. Gombrich,
'Icones Symbolicae', *Journal of the Warburg and Courtauld Institutes*, ix, 1948, 170,
provides a convenient summary statement. Aquinas (*Summa Theologica*, ii–ii, Q2,
art. 9) cites *Post. An.* i.33, agreeing that Opinion is weak and infirm in 'assent' (*Basic
Writings of St Thomas Aquinas*, New York, 1945, vol. ii, p. 1088).
2. *Republic*, v.479.   3. Ibid. vi.506.
4. By M. Higgins, *MLR*, xxxix, 1944, 184.

whether the opinion is rightly held, together with the invention of a kind of standard of judgement.[5]

We recognize here the familiar opposition between Opinion and Judgement, for, Epictetus declares, 'The opinion which each man holds is not a sufficient criterion for determining the truth.'

For Epictetus and his predecessors Opinion remains an abstraction, a philosophical formulation playing its part in epistemologies elaborated from the Platonic basis. But, like so many philosophical concepts when these were reformulated in the Renaissance, it bore within the potentiality for another kind of life. The hypostatization of Opinion which we find in *Hymenaei*, the allegorical figure the details of whose deportment Jonson owed to Lilius Giraldus,[6] is an example of that dominance of the visual image endowed with a symbolic significance which Gombrich has explained as the 'pivot of the exegetic method' of the neo-Platonists.[7] Jonson's 'adulterate Truth', 'her gaudy colours, pieced with many folds', is a small exemplification of the whole process whereby the neo-Platonic movement gave birth to the cult of emblem and hieroglyph, formularized for the use of poets in the works of a Conti or a Giraldus and seen by the philosophers as the means whereby, as Gombrich puts it, 'truth [was] condensed into a visual image'.[8] The culmination of such a process in the work of the poet divorces Opinion from any very precise connection with the epistemological systems of which it originally formed a part.

It is in the light of this material that we can examine the meaning of the word as it is found in the work of three writers— Daniel, Chapman, and Greville—who were not uninfluenced by the neo-Stoic revival and by the Renaissance habit of allegorization. As regards the first influence, it is a case of showing how the special pejorative meaning which the word Opinion had acquired since the time of Plato is sharpened by its association with a favourite Stoic and neo-Stoic emphasis—the idea that man's chief good is to be sought within himself, or, as St Augustine more precisely put it: 'Dicebat Stoicus mihi frui mea mente

5. *Discourses* (trans. Oldfather, London and New York, Loeb ed. 1926), II.xi.13.

6. Gilbert, sv 'opinion'.

7. Gombrich, p. 178. H. R. Patch in *The Goddess Fortune in Medieval Literature* (Cambridge, 1927) hints at a connection between Opinion and the other hypostatized figures of Fame and Fortune in the medieval period.

8. Gombrich. p. 173.

bonum est.'[9] The second influence, the neo-Platonic hypostatization of philosophical concepts, in this case operates in the realm of semantics rather than of moral philosophy. For, where it shows itself in the conscious and explicit allegorizations of Hymenaei, or, less striking but still plainly discernible, in Guilpin's satire and Daniel's Cleopatra chorus, the influence is not far to seek; but it also affects the force and meaning of the word 'opinion' when that concept, as is the case with Greville and Chapman, is not explicitly allegorized but merely used in conjunction with statements and analyses of a neo-Stoic complexion.

It is, of course, not uncommon to find these writers using the word with no pejorative signification attached, in one or other of the less unusual senses fully defined in the OED. Thus Daniel in Musophilus urges that the learned Academies should concern themselves with regaining 'that reverend hand of lost Opinion'.[1] Similarly, Wither in Abuses Stript and Whipt uses the word both pejoratively and otherwise without making any distinction except one implicit in the context.[2] But in the 'Epistle to the Ladie Lucie Countesse of Bedford', wherein Daniel seeks to persuade the Countess to fortify the citadel of herself 'Since

---

9. Sermo, clvi, quoted by N. Abercrombie, St Augustine and French Classical Thought (Oxford, 1938), p. 32; cf. City of God (Everyman ed.), i.292. One may not, of course, claim that this kind of emphasis is peculiar to the Stoics: St Augustine himself was the 'master of the inner life' (see M. H. Carré, Nominalists and Realists, Oxford, 1946, pp. 11–12) and Calvin—to name no other—followed him in this (see, for example, Institutes, trans. Beveridge, Edinburgh, 1845, vol. i, p. 434). But the difference between the Platonic–Stoic nosce teipsum and 'Christian Socratism' is succinctly stated by Gilson (Spirit of Medieval Philosophy, London, 1936, pp. 213–14). That there was a conflict between the two in a writer like Chapman may be suspected; and Greville's case against the Stoic virtue (as stated, for example in Of Religion, stanzas 36–37, and called attention to by U. M. Ellis-Fermor in her chapter on Greville in Jacobean Drama, London, 1936) may be the product of Calvinistic Socratism since it is certainly opposed to Stoic Socratism. For my purpose here it seems sufficient to emphasize the resemblance between the patterns of thought in Greville, Daniel, and Chapman rather than the distinction which tends to cut Greville off from the other two. The pattern is the Stoic contrast between the mens adepta and the outward fortune-dominated sphere of perturbations and corruption. This is most frequent in Chapman—see (one example among many) Eugenia, ll. 638–43.

1. Musophilus, 809–10 (Complete Works, ed. Grosart, np, 1885, vol. i, p. 251). Opinion is used by Daniel in the sense of 'popular favour', 'estimation bringing about harmful effects' in Civil Warres, vii, stanza 50 (Complete Works, vol. ii, p. 275), and cf. ibid. v.114 and vi.36.

2. See Abuses Stript and Whipt: 'Inconstancie' (Spenser Society ed. of Wither's Juvenilia, i.226) for the pejorative use, contrasted with the 'normal' use in ibid. 219, 240, 281.

all the good we have rests in the minde', Art and Opinion are the enemies of Nature and Conscience:

> How oft are we forc't on a cloudie hart
>   To set a shining face, and make it cleere,
>   Seeming content to put our selves apart,
> To beare a part of others weakenesses!
>   As if we onely were compos'd by Art,
>   Not Nature, and did all our deedes addresse
> T'opinion, not t'a conscience, what is right.[3]

This use of the word is clearly set out by Fulke Greville, as in the following examples:

> Opinion raignes without, and truth within.
> Who others please against themselves must sin.[4]

> Opinions, idols and not God express.
>   Without in pow'r, we see Him everywhere,
>   Within, we rest not till we find Him there.[5]

For Greville, Opinion is the agent which stirs up kings to war;[6] it is a 'Tyrant everywhere';[7] its natural ally, which helps to establish it—almost in Donne's sense—is worldly power;[8] its art helps to make the delusive goddess Pleasure acceptable.[9] The neo-Stoic and Calvinist in Greville saw Opinion in the light in which Charron described it and Ben Jonson figured it: to trust to outward opinion was to forsake the task of creating an inward discipline of virtue of the kind that Daniel urged upon the Countess of Bedford, and Greville himself wrote of in the *Letter to an Honourable Lady*, whom he advised to enrich herself 'upon your own stocke; not looking outwardly but inwardly for the fruit of true Peace whose roots are there'.[1]

The Stoic emphasis on the inward rather than the outward man, which Greville enriched and darkened with his Calvinism, and which is vital to his ethical thought and to that of Chapman (to a lesser degree to Daniel's ethic too),[2] is thus sharpened by

3. *Complete Works*, vol. i, p. 211.
4. *Alaham*, I.i.313–14 (*Poems and Dramas of Fulke Greville*, ed. Bullough, Edinburgh and London, 1939, vol. ii, p. 150).
5. *Of Religion*, stanza 8 (*Works of Fulke Greville*, ed. Grosart, np, 1870, vol. i, p. 241).
6. *A Treatie of Warres*, stanza xviii (*Poems and Dramas*, vol. i, p. 271).
7. *Alaham*, III.iii.12 (ibid., vol. ii, p. 182).
8. *Of Religion*, stanza 94 (*Works*, vol. i, p. 271).
9. *Caelica*, xcvi (*Poems and Dramas*, vol. i, p. 141). Cf. *Letter to an Honourable Lady* (*Works*, vol. iv, p. 239).
1. *Works*, vol. iv, p. 260.   2. But see n. 5 above.

Greville's feeling that it is a mistake to trust oneself to Opinion, which lies outward, and by his view that Opinion is one of the natural allies of outward destructive powers (kings and wars in *Alaham* and *A Treatie of Warres*). Chapman's use of the word Opinion reveals an aspect of his thought in which he draws close to the regions inhabited by Greville. In 'A Hymne to our Saviour' Chapman writes:

> we are tost out of our humane Throne
> By pied and protean Opinion.[3]

This, indeed, is almost the major theme of two of his tragedies, *Caesar and Pompey* and *The Conspiracy and Tragedy of Charles Duke of Byron*, although the word is not, so far as I can discover, used in them in the sense that I have been discussing. Rather, the contrast between a world of inward Peace and discipline and an outward world of 'opinion' is symbolized in the whole action of the plays. Thus Pompey's tragic error is to forsake his own judgement, his 'own god-inspir'd insight', as Brutus puts it, and to continue on his warlike course simply because he is afraid of displeasing his own rash and fickle followers:

> I cannot, sir, abide men's open mouths,
> Nor be ill spoken of . . .[4]

Fighting because the great world expects him to fight, Pompey disobeys his Stoic mentor Cato, and is ruined. In the sequel he repents and embraces again the full Stoic doctrine: he recognizes, that the 'tumour / And bile of rotten observation' swelled him, for

> Griefs for wants outward are without our cure,
> Greatness, not of itself, is never sure.[5]

Pompey's belief that greatness which is not the product of an inward discipline is doomed to fall is more fully stated in a speech later in the play. In that speech the hero expresses his resolve not to stand 'on others' legs, nor build one joy without me . . . I'll build all inward'.[6] Similarly, Byron is aware that if he trusts himself to the conspirators he may have to 'build himself outward',

> To trust [his] blood in others' veins, and hang
> 'Twixt heaven and earth in vapours of their breaths.[7]

---

3. 'A Hymne to our Saviour on the Crosse', 213–14 (*Poems of George Chapman*, ed. Bartlett, New York, 1941, p. 225).　　　4. *Caesar and Pompey*, IV.i.45–46.
5. Ibid. v.i.183–4.　　6. Ibid. v.i.203–6.　　7. *Conspiracy of Byron*, II.ii.140–1.

And later he confesses that 'In my late projects I have cast my-self / Into the arms of others.'[8] This, too, is one of the themes of Daniel's *Philotas*, another play about a 'great man' and con-spiracy, in many ways analogous to Chapman's Byron plays. It is the theme of Cato's final declaration before his righteous suicide in Chapman's Roman play:

> ... as if I could
> Be rack'd out of my veins to live in others,
> As so I must, if others rule my life,
> And public power keeps all the right of death;
> As if men needs must serve the place of justice,
> The form and idol, and renounce itself,
> Ourselves, and all our rights in God and goodness,
> Our whole contents and freedoms, to dispose
> All in the joys and ways of arrant rogues![9]

If in the dramas Chapman, without naming it, makes Opinion a factor influencing and distorting the heroic nature of the Stoic, in some of the poems he is more precise. In *Eugenia* there is the familiar opposition of Truth and Opinion:

> Even Artists (borne with the traditionall streame)
> Others of their coate trust, as others them:
> Not knowledge, but opinion, being their Guide;
> Not truth, nor love of Truth: but lust and pride.[1]

This reminds us of *Hymenaei* and is given explicit form in *Euthymiae Raptus*: Peace explains that merely 'intellective men', those whom she condemns as mere clocks or walking diction-aries, cannot know the reality of either εὐθυμία or Truth:

> They have some shadowes of [Truth] . . .
>   . . . but never see
> Her true and heauenly face. Yet those shades serue . . .
> To make them thinke, *Truths* substance in their armes:
> Which that they haue not, but her shadowes charmes,
> See if my proofes, be like their Arguments
> That leaue *Opinion* still, her free dissents.[2]

---

8. *Conspiracy of Byron*, III.iii.33–34.

9. *Caesar and Pompey*, v.ii.10–19. Cf. Daniel's remarks about those who cast them-selves into 'other men's uncertainties' in 'A Funerall Poeme upon the Earle of Devonshire', 307 ff. (*Complete Works*, vol. i, p. 183); and cf. Greville on Hypocrisy (*Of Religion*, stanza 32) and on 'popular vaine pride' (*Fame and Honour*, stanzas 65–68).

1. *Eugenia*, 284–7 (*Poems*, p. 278).   2. *Euthymiae Raptus*, 453–62 (ibid., p. 183).

Inward Peace is declaring that the proofs of her real presence in an individual have no resemblance to the foolish arguments (the word is here used pejoratively) of merely intellective men, which allow free scope for 'raw and imperfect' Opinion; the *eroici furori*, as Bruno did not fail to make clear, have no more to do with the pedant than with the artisan. 'Such hypocrites, opinions only have,' adds Chapman in his poem 'Of learned men';[3] and he characterizes 'A sleight man' as one who has climbed to 'learn'd opinion' and stands there:

> Starke as a statue; stirres nor foote nor hand.
> Nor any truth knowes.[4]

Enough has perhaps been said to indicate the special pejorative meaning which these writers attach to Opinion and how it is bound up with their Stoic and Calvinist emphasis on inward discipline and virtue, to which Opinion is an exterior ill. There are examples of less elaborate and integral uses of this complex of ideas by other writers of the period. Drayton speaks of Humour becoming 'Opinion's wife' in *The Owle*, in a passage describing the corruption of the court.[5] From *Pericles* we may cite one Shakespearian use: when the Lords express surprise at the appearance in the emblematic show of Knights of a figure clad in rusty armour who presents nothing but 'A wither'd branch that's only green at top', Simonides warns them:

> Opinion's but a fool, that makes us scan
> The outward habit by the inward man.[6]

Of more interest than further citations of this kind is the fact that Opinion in this pejorative sense is often closely associated with those whom Chapman calls 'arrant rogues'. It is no accident that the stasimon on Opinion in Daniel's *Cleopatra* is spoken by the Chorus of Egyptian people. Opinion has been associated with the multitude (οἱ πολλοί) by Plato, and it

3. Ibid., p. 250.   4. Ibid., p. 230.
5. *The Owle*, 458 (*The Works of Michael Drayton*, ed. Hebel, Oxford, 1932, vol. ii, p. 492). Cf. *Barons Warres*, I, stanza 59; iv, stanza 54.
6. *Pericles*, ii.ii. Of other dramatists, the neo-Stoic Marston uses 'Opinion' with force, ironically, or in the sense of corrupt, popular, sycophantic, or womanish estimation: eg in *What You Will* (*Plays*, ed. H. Harvey Wood, vol. ii, pp. 232, 237, 253, 269), *The Fawne* (ibid., p. 148) and *Antonio and Mellida* (ibid., vol. i, pp. 5, 44).

remained the special prerogative of the People, who were in-
constant and empty like their deity. Cornwallis, in whose essay
appears the characteristic opposition between Opinion and inward virtue, speaks of Opinion as 'living upon the breath of the
vulgar'.[7] This conception is significantly present in Daniel's
handling of the relationships between 'great men' and popular
opinion throughout the *Civil Warres*, as well as in *Philotas* and
Cleopatra: in the sixth book of the *Civil Warres* Nemesis commands Pandora to

> Opinion Arme against Opinion growne:
> Make new-born contradiction still to rise;
> As if Thebes-founder, *Cadmus*, tongues had sowne,
> Instead of teeth, for greater mutinies.[8]

Guilpin writes:

> Shall graue *Lycurgus* straite repeale his lawes,
> Because some Cobler finds fault with this clawse,
> Some Ale-Konner with that? or shall the state
> Be subiect to each base-groomes arbitrate?
> No, let's esteeme Opinion as she is, . . .
> It's but the hisse of Geese, the peoples noyse.[9]

The whole conception is activated in the *Coriolanus* mob,

7. Cornwallis, p. 54. Cf. Charron, 'C'est le guide des fols, des sots, du vulgaire'.
8. *Civil Warres*, vi, stanza 36 (*Complete Works*, vol. ii, p. 229).
9. *Skialetheia*, satire vi. Opinion in these passages becomes assimilated to 'public
esteem' (see p. 216, n. 8 above) and thus has relation to the Renaissance attitude to
Fame seen by some writers as the gift of the people. The hypostatized Fame of
Chapman's *Eugenia* sifts the bad from the good herself and is a goddess of a higher
sphere; but Greville in *Fame and Honour* is closer to political realities. Although he
agrees that Fame is worthless in so far as it is the 'breath of the vulgar', he yet
admits its value as an 'echo' 'both of wrong and right' (stanza 26). A long chain of
writers gives evidence of a permanent ambivalence in the Renaissance attitude to
popular Fame: St Augustine (*City of God*, v.xix, Everyman ed., London, 1945,
pp. 168–70), Boethius (*The Consolation of Philosophy*, ii, pr. vii.62, London and Cambridge, Mass., 1936), Montaigne (*Essayes*, trans. Florio, ii.xvi, Everyman ed., London,
1910, vol. ii, p. 353: 'If this false-fond opinion doe notwithstanding serve and stead a
commonwealth to hold men in their dutie') agree that Fame and 'opinion' are
follies but have their uses in the 'earthly city', and the argument is clinched by
Machiavelli (*Prince*, chap. xix) and Bacon ('Of Vain-Glory', *Philosophical Works*, ed.
Ellis and Spedding, London, 1905, p. 800). Daniel's attitude to Opinion shares in this
ambivalence, which is aggravated by the fact that some writers, such as Chapman,
are talking about a hypostatized goddess Fame in the context of a moralized religion; while others, such as Greville and Machiavelli, are trying to see Fame as a
factor in the *regimen principum*.

'rubbing the poor itch of your opinion', as Coriolanus puts it to them, 'to make yourselves scabs'. The mob in this play exactly reflects the behaviour of Opinion, as personified by Daniel, Guilpin, and Jonson—marked as Truth, grasping after impossibilities, a blind guide 'turned towards the twilight'.

We have observed the connection between 'opinion' and the current *moralia*. It is equally important to note, in the confidence with which Chapman and Greville handle the word itself, what may best be termed a latent hypostatization of the abstract idea for which it stands. Jonson, in *Hymenaei*, and to a lesser degree Guilpin and Daniel, did not hestitate to personify and allegorize what had originally been part of an abstract epistemology. In Greville and Chapman the term has become an abstraction again, but draws part of its meaning and vigour from its potential ability to be allegorized, and made to 'stand on its own feet'. Chapman, at least, after the fashion of Giordano Bruno and the makers of masques, did not hesitate to turn many other abstractions into *icones symbolicae* for the purposes of poetry and the propagation of a moralized 'Religion'; Greville shares something of Bacon's attitude,[1] but he also fashioned the visual image, though not so frequently or boldly as Chapman. The visual image is certainly not far from his treatment of Pleasure in *Caelica*, xcvi, or from the Time and Eternity chorus in *Mustapha*.[2] One wonders how many other words, besides 'Opinion', drew life and meaning from such latent powers in the period before Bacon attempted to end a phase by his famous

---

1. See, for example, his implicit *refusal to allegorize* throughout *An Inquisition upon Fame and Honour*.

2. In *Caelica*, xcvi, the 'concealed' visual image in the first two stanzas is that of the Renaissance 'perspective picture' or, as in Chapman's *Ovid's Banquet of Sense*, stanza 3, 'statue'. (On these pictures cf. *Eugenia*, 173 ff. and Bartlett's note on this passage, *Poems*, p. 456.) In *Mustapha* Greville's hypostatization of Time and Eternity in the third chorus is like the personification of αἰών and χρόνος effected by the neo-Platonists (on which see Proclus, *Elements of Theology*, ed. E. R. Dodds, Oxford, 1933, p. 51, and Dodds's note on this passage). Greville's conception of Time and Eternity is partly Boethian (*The Consolation of Philosophy*, v, par. vi) and hence not unrelated to the *Timaeus* (see A. E. Taylor, *A Commentary on the Timaeus*, Oxford, 1927, appendix on the concept of time), although at the same time influenced by the medieval habit of assimilating time with Fortune (on which see Patch) and perhaps also by Machiavelli's view of Fortune (*Prince*, xxv.3, p. 92). That this mixture of elements produces Greville's finest poetry suggests that the combination of hypostatization with 'refusal to allegorize' as well as the survival of what Cassirer calls 'mythical thinking' was nothing if not beneficial to Greville.

attack on the εἴδωλα imposed by words on the understanding—
those 'names of things which do not exist . . . fictions which owe
their origin to false and idle theories'.[3]

3. *Novum Organum*, lx, *Philosophical Works*, p. 269. The goddess certainly survived
Bacon: 'Opinion' has a later history in the Puritan distinction between Opinion
(regarded as a disorder in the faculty process—the imagination forming a hasty and
false impression of facts) and Science (understanding rightly achieved): see Perry
Miller, *The New England Mind: The Seventeenth Century* (New York, 1939), p. 259.
'Opinion' also appears without apparently having lost any of its emblematic force
in Peacham's *The World is Ruled and Governed by Opinion* (?1640), a broadside with an
engraving by W. Hollar of 'Opinion, a blindfolded goddess with the world in her
lap and a chameleon on her wrist', reproduced in William Haller's *Tracts on Liberty
in the Puritan Revolution* (New York, 1934) vol. i [frontispiece]; cf. Haller's *The Rise
of Puritanism* (New York, 1938), p. 365.

13

The Widow of Ephesus:
some reflections on
an international comic theme

The story of the Widow of Ephesus is one of those tales which men—especially men—never seem to tire of. The Widow is as old as the Roman Empire, remarked a seventeenth-century writer, but 'she is yet youthfull, sprightly and gamesome and hath not a wrinckle in her face'. The folklorists recognize her story as one of the types of the folk-tale, and I quote Aarne and Thompson's convenient summary of it in their catalogue of these:

No. 1510. The Matron of Ephesus (Vidua). A woman mourns day and night by her husband's grave. A knight guarding a hanged man is about to lose his life because the corpse has been stolen from the gallows. The matron offers him her love and substitutes her husband's corpse on the gallows so that the knight can escape.[1]

By far the most famous version of the tale thus baldly presented by the folklorists is the one in Petronius' *Satyricon*. To this first-century version nearly all the writers who use the tale after the Renaissance are fairly directly indebted. One of the characters in Petronius' novel, Eumolpus, relates the affair as being one which 'happened in his lifetime' and which, according to him, demonstrates that no woman can be so chaste as not to be led away into utter madness by passion for a stranger. As he tells it, it is an elegant, ironic, and sophisticated little comedy. The widow is famous for her virtue and for her extraordinary resolution to starve herself to death in her husband's tomb; she is accompanied by a devoted maid. They have been mourning in the

First published in *Durham University Journal*, NS, xviii, 1956-7, 1–9.

1. A. Aarne, *The Types of the Folk Tale* (trans. and enlarged by S. Thompson, Helsinki, 1928); see also A. H. Krappe, *The Science of Folklore* (London, 1930), pp. 48–49.

tomb five days when the soldier—a young man, handsome and elegant—sees their light, enters the tomb, and offers to share his supper with them. The maid yields soon to the temptation of food and drink; next soldier and maid combine to persuade the mistress, first to eat, and then to love. On the third night of stolen pleasure, the body of one of the crucified robbers which the soldier has been guarding is secretly removed by his friends. The soldier, anticipating death as the punishment for his neglect of duty, decides on suicide, but the widow saves him: the husband's body is taken out of its coffin and fixed up on the empty cross (see Plate I).[2] There, in Petronius, the story ends; we hear nothing more of the fortunes of widow, soldier, or maid. Those who have listened to the story react in different ways—the sailors roar with laughter, the women blush, and one man exclaims savagely that it was the widow herself who should have been crucified in place of the missing thief. This is the nearest Petronius gets to the drawing of a moral that is to weigh down some later treatments of the theme.

Scholars have argued furiously together about where Petronius got this tale, and whether his version is earlier or later than that attributed to the contemporary fabulist Phaedrus. Is Petronius simply reporting an affair that did occur in his own time? Is he, perhaps, parodying portions of the fourth book of the *Aeneid*?[3] Does his story derive from an international folk-tale with analogues in India and China? In this connection, attention has been focused on a Chinese Buddhist novella which presents a general parallel and which, when it became known in modern Europe, was to be used by several writers, including Goldsmith and Voltaire. To this Chinese version I shall come back later on. There are no versions of the story in extant Greek literature, but a Greek origin for the Petronian version—in the lost Milesian tales of Aristides of Miletus—seems to be the most orthodox hypothesis about the Widow's provenance amongst English Petronians.

The story spread—one of the sweetest and most oft repeated cupfuls at the fount of fiction, to adapt Henry James's words about Hop o' my Thumb. Petronius had actualized the tale, but

2. *Satyricon*, 111–12.
3. A. Collignon, *Étude sur Pétrone* (Paris, 1892), pp. 124 ff; cf. with Petronius, *Aeneid*, iv.25 ff.

somehow he succeeded in leaving it flexible enough for writers of marked individuality or different ages to see it and rewrite it in terms of their own preconceptions. Petronius' touch is light and ironic, but when the tale is concluded, he hints at a sterner moral attitude—one which already, or shortly afterwards, Phaedrus makes more explicit when he tells us that the Widow, previously respected, was now shamed throughout her city.[4] This above all is the aspect which the medieval redactors seized upon. The great name here is that of John of Salisbury in the twelfth century, who was familiar with the then known parts of the *Satyricon*. He gives a full version of Petronius' story in the eighth book of the *Polycraticus*, but adds, on the authority of a certain Flavianus: 'Mulierem tradit impietatis suae, et sceleris parricidalis, et adulterii poenas luisse.'[5] John of Salisbury was a learned writer, but it is particularly in the numerous popular medieval versions that elements of the macabre and disgusting, always latent even in the graceful Petronian version, are fully brought out. In proportion as these elements are insisted upon, so does the note of moral reprobation of the Widow's conduct strengthen. Whether it is stated in Italian, French, or English, the naïve moral is, as Cesari says,[6] always emphasized: 'non fidarsi delle donne, mai'. One of the most widely dispersed vehicles of the story is the collection of fifteen tales known in its Middle and Early Modern English versions as *The Seven Sages of Rome* or *The Seven Wise Masters*. There are versions of this collection in nearly every European language, and in India.[7] The Emperor Diocletian is being urged by his son's stepmother to condemn the boy to death for treason; to persuade him, she tells him seven alarming tales about the treachery of sons and subjects. Each of her stories is countered by one of the Seven Sages with a tale about the treachery and double-dealing of women. Of these, the 'Vidua' story, suitably medievalized, is one. The story is also widespread in fables and *novelle* in Latin and Italian.

The twist that has been given to it is seen in two non-Petronian

4. Phaedrus (Oxford Classical Texts ed.), Appendix Perottina, no. xiii ('mulier vidua et miles').

5. Migne, *Patrologia Latina*, cxcix.755.

6. A. Cesari, 'La Novella della Matrona d'Efeso', *Amabile di Continentia, Romanzo Morale del Secolo XV* (Bologna, 1896), p. clxv.

7. See J. E. Wells, *Manual of Writings in Middle English*, sv 'Seven Sages'.

features. First, there is the added detail of the mutilation of the husband's corpse, which increases the horror and brutal logic of the Widow's act. For instance, in the English southern version of *The Seven Sages* the missing robber's corpse lacked some fingers in one hand, and the widow smites off three of her husband's fingers to make the bodies match and conceal the substitution.[8] In the version in *Il Novellino*, the collection of a hundred moral tales of mid-thirteenth-century date,[9] as in Giovanni Sercambi's fourteenth-century version, it is her husband's teeth which she strikes out. All these versions show a second non-Petronian feature: at the least, the Widow is publicly shamed, and usually as well the soldier deserts her, disgusted at her behaviour: 'Lady, since you showed so little regard for one towards whom you professed such love, so would you have even less regard for me.'[1]

> Fare well, y parte fro the,
> The fleand deuyll wyth the bee.[2]

> Tal donna la lasció di simil sorta
> Per mai vederla piú viva ne morta.[3]

It is not the Widow's wantonness but her maltreatment of the dead body that upsets him.

In the Renaissance, the latent cruelties recede, and some writers who use the theme wholly recapture the Petronian tolerance. The change is seen in the differences between two notable prose versions in French, for it is the French who now take the story to their hearts. Brantôme, in his version, still retains the medieval device and temper; it is the corpse's ear which the Widow strikes off, a 'shameful and exceedingly villainous act', says Brantôme.[4] Saint-Évremond, on the other hand, in the next century, is fully conscious of what he calls the

8. *The Seven Sages of Rome* (ed. K. Brunner, Early English Texts Society, os, 191, 1933), p. 203.

9. For *Il Novellino*, see *The Hundred Old Tales* (trans. E. Storer, Broadway Classics, London, nd), tale no. lix; for Sercambi, *Novelle di G. Sercambi* (ed. A. D'Ancona, Bologna, 1871), pp. 138–44.

1. *The Hundred Old Tales*, no. lix.   2. *The Seven Sages of Rome*, p. 204.

3. 'Opera Nuova Bellissima da intendere di una donna chiamata Angeletta', in Cesari, appendix.

4. 'Par ainsy sauua son galant par ung acte oprobre et fort villain à son mary.' Brantôme's version is given in the appendix to H. Regnier's edition of La Fontaine (Paris, 1890), vi.363–5.

'politesse', the 'graces inimitables', the 'natural and easy air' of Petronius, and tries to render them in an elaborate and courtly version. When he comes to describe the reception of Eumolpus' story in Petronius, he gratuitously adds his own comment on the words of the man who cried that the Widow ought to have been crucified: 'This opinion was found so inopportune and in such bad taste that nobody made any pretence of listening to it, and everyone started laughing again more loudly than before.'[5] Peals of fashionable laughter drown the cries of the moralist, and the moralist pure and simple has never succeeded in taking over the story again. But he has, as we shall see, managed to creep in by the back door.

In the seventeenth century, perhaps, the main interest is in seeing what individual authors do with a theme that every reader could identify. La Fontaine, indeed, in his delightful version, apologizes for using so common and well-worn a tale, but undertakes to rejuvenate it; his treatment is predominantly gay and cynical: 'La femme est toujours femme', and his moral: 'Mieux vaut goujat debout qu'empereur enterré'[6]—'A live lout's better than a dead emperor.' This is fully in the Petronian/Saint-Évremond tradition. In England, there is greater originality and eccentricity in the treatment of the theme, and the English seventeenth century begins exploring the Widow's psychological as distinct from her moral condition. Jeremy Taylor, who has John of Salisbury's gift for baptizing those pagan classics which might seem least amenable to the rite, sees the story as a warning against immoderate grief: if the Widow had not weakened the powers of her soul by unreasonably lamenting her dead husband, she would not have fallen so easy a prey to the soldier.[7] A somewhat similar psychological analysis is undertaken by Walter Charleton in his novel *The Ephesian Matron* (1659). This curious and little-known work, never reprinted since the seventeenth century, deserves more attention than it has had from the literary historian.

Charleton was a physician, a friend of Dryden and of Dr John Wilkins (a founder and Secretary of the Royal Society), and a

5. Saint-Évremond's version is also given by H. Regnier, edition of La Fontaine, vi.365–71.

6. Conte vi, *Contes*, Cinquième Partie (ed. Regnier, Paris, 1890, p. 86).

7. Taylor, *Holy Dying*, chap. v, sect. viii (*Works*, ed. Heber and Eden, London, 1847, vol. iii, pp. 447–9).

disciple of Hobbes. He wrote his novel in an odd Euphuistic style, as though he thought that Lyly's was still the manner in which a novel should be written—food is called 'corporall refection' and love-making 'Cytherean rites'—but every now and then Hobbesian forthrightness keeps breaking in. Charleton takes 124 duodecimo pages to tell the tiny story; under cover of telling it, he is really defining love and making an attack on the current fashionable cult of 'Platonic' love. His doctrine is the one that Dryden satirized twenty years later when he put it into the mouth of his false Achitophel:

> Nor let his love enchant your generous mind;
> 'Tis Nature's trick to propagate her kind.

Physical beauty, says Charleton, is simply a mark of the perfection of the 'power generative' in its possessor; love and lust may both be denominated as 'an appetite to procreation'; there is no real distinction between them, so the Widow is not to be blamed, though Charleton feels free to indulge in much sardonic humour at her expense.[8] This book must have been somewhat of a scandal in its time, a minor ripple on the great whirlpool of scandal that *Leviathan* stirred up; it remains a curious example of the explosion that may occur when a sceptical and materialistic mind encounters an ancient literary theme. Dacier, the French eighteenth-century academician who was perhaps the first person to make an independent study of the Widow of Ephesus story, was deeply shocked by Charleton, which he read in its Latin version; he calls the book 'half-philosophical, half-obscene',[9] and rightly, for Charleton spends many pages describing, with materialistic fervour, his Widow's charms.

8. Cf. Hobbes, *Human Nature*, chap. viii (*English Works*, ed. W. Molesworth, London, 1839–45, vol. iv, p. 38). Charleton girds against the current fashion of 'Platonic' love in his preface and against the Epicureans elsewhere. A full account of the anti-'Platonic' aspect of his novel is given by G. Williamson in *RES*, xii, 1936, 445–9. The novel appears to have been well known abroad in its Latin version. The English was reprinted as the first story in *The Ephesian and Cimmerian Matrons, Two Notable Examples of the Power of Love and Wit* (London, 1668), but in this edition sardonically illustrative quotations from Chaucer have been inserted into the tale, presumably by P. M., Gent., the author of the second story in the volume, 'The Cimmerian Matron'.

9. M. Dacier, 'Examen de l'histoire de la Matrone d' Éphèse', *Mémoires de littérature, tirés des Registres de l'Académie Royale des Inscriptions* . . . (Paris, 1780), vol. xli, pp. 523–45.

But the chief seventeenth-century English version preceded Charleton's by about fifty years. Chapman's comedy *The Widow's Tears* is the first known dramatization of the subject, and was by far the most ambitious treatment yet attempted. It is a dark comedy, in which Chapman has not neglected the macabre and sombre aspects of Petronius' story. The original tale, which must have seemed to him grotesquely thin for a five-act Elizabethan comedy, Chapman has boldly adapted: the husband does not really die, but only pretends to; his object is to test out a wife who seems suspiciously fond of proclaiming her unshakeable constancy; he returns to his supposed tomb disguised as the soldier. As he pleads with her, Petronius' ironic verve vanishes before the advance of Jacobean melancholia.

The soldier [narrates Petronius] began to urge the mourner not to persist in useless grief . . . for all men made the same end and found the same resting-place, and so on with the other platitudes which restore wounded spirits to health.

In Chapman, this becomes:

> Dear ghost, be wise, and pity your fair self . . .
> This is the inn where all Deucalion's race,
> Sooner or later, must take up their lodging;
> No privilege can free us from this prison.[1]

The wife is led dangerously astray by the false soldier, but a third party reveals to her just in time who he really is, and she contrives to turn the tables on him. In this way Petronius' anecdote is naturalized as a full-dress Elizabethan comedy of manners with disguise, resurrection, male jealousy, and female wit, and a quite fresh narrative pattern. It is an astonishing result.

A certain chauvinism compels me to add that the behaviour of the half-dozen or so French, German, and Italian scholars who have studied the diffusion of the Widow's story is even more astonishing. Several of them have never heard of Chapman's play and even those who have heard of it seem not to have read it. Its originality might have upset them, for this is the special characteristic of the seventeenth-century English adaptations; Taylor, Charleton, and Chapman knock Petronius' story about

---

1. IV.ii.64 ff. (*Comedies of George Chapman*, ed. T. M. Parrott, London, 1914, p. 410).

in their own interests in lordly fashion. French versions—in both the seventeenth and eighteenth centuries—still stand close in spirit to the 'politesse' of Petronius. The eighteenth century, especially in France—for Italy is only thinly represented[2]—is the great age of the tale so far as frequency of occurrence goes. During the eighteenth century two developments affect the history of the tale's diffusion in France and England. The first is the introduction into Europe of the Chinese novel on a similar theme, which I have already mentioned. This was translated into French;[3] soon afterwards Bishop Percy, of Percy's *Reliques* fame, rendered it into English, and it was used almost simultaneously by Goldsmith in letter xviii of *The Citizen of the World*. The only English translation direct from the Chinese which I have seen is that of the nineteenth-century sinologist Samuel Birch (1872).

Chwang-sung, a philosopher, tells his wife Tien-shi about the horrid infidelity of a certain widow, whose dying husband had made her promise that she would not marry again until the mound of earth upon his grave was dry; after the funeral, still dressed in her white mourning robes, she is found vigorously fanning the mound to hasten the process. Tien-shi declares that never, never could she behave like that. Soon Chwang-sung the philosopher dies, and seven days after his death a young prince, accompanied by an ancient servant, appears at the house. The lady uses the servant as a go-between, and depreciates the character of the dead philosopher; a marriage is arranged, but just before it is consummated, the new husband has a fit which can only be cured by drinking a decoction of human brains boiled in wine. A dead man's brains will do, provided he hasn't been dead too long. The bride breaks open the philosopher's coffin with an axe, intending to use Chwang-sung's brains for the medicine, and finds him alive within. He asks her searching

2. Chiefly by the version of the story in Forteguerri's *Ricciardetto*, the last of the Italian comic epics (canto xiii, stanzas 90–107: see the Collezione Salani edition, Firenze, 1931); this follows the *Il Novellino* type. The spread of the story in Italy is studied by A. Rini, *Petronius in Italy* (New York, 1937); in France by A. Collignon, *Pétrone en France* (Paris, 1905). Both are indebted to the works by Dacier, Regnier, and Cesari already cited, and to the pioneer study of E. Grisebach, *Die Wanderung der Novelle von der treulosen Witwe durch die Weltliteratur* (Berlin, 1886); see also L. Herrmann, 'La Matrone d'Éphèse dans Pétrone et dans Phèdre', *Bulletin de l'Association Guillaume Budé*, no. 14, January 1927.

3. For the French translations see Herrmann, p. 43, n. 1.

questions: 'Why are you wearing embroidered clothes?' 'Why
has my coffin been shoved out of the way into this old barn?'
Meanwhile prince and servant have disappeared. It is revealed
that, through his knowledge of magic, Chwang-sung has been
able to employ 'the law of dividing himself into shadow [the
old servant] and substance [the prince]'. The disgraced wife
hangs herself; the philosopher pops her in the coffin, sings a
sardonic elegy, sets fire to the house, and goes roaming off:
'Some say', the novel concludes, 'that he met Lao-tsze.'[4]

Goldsmith offers a compressed and rationalized version of
this; he leaves out the magic element, so that the philosopher's
resurrection is grotesquely unexplained, and turns the human
brains into a human heart. In Voltaire's version, in the second
chapter of *Zadig*, the curative member is the nose. P. R. Lemon-
nier in 1764, still more discreetly, makes it a magic ring. Lemon-
nier wrote an elaborate comedy-ballet in two acts, based on the
Chinese novel.[5] He softens the character of the Widow, for the
strange reason, which he explains in his preface, that no man believes that women will ever cease to be *cocottes* because they are
exposed as such in comedies, and that therefore it is both un-
pleasant and useless to have to contemplate them on the stage.
In this piece the husband's valet and the wife's maid play as
large a part as the principals and a happy ending is contrived for
all.

Bishop Percy's version of the Chinese novel occurs in a little
volume which he edited for the Dodsleys in 1762, *The Matrons:
Six Short Histories* (see Plate II). This is second only to Charleton
as a curiosity of the subject. Besides the Chinese story it contains translations of the Petronian and the *Seven Sages* versions,
the stories of two other false matrons, British and Turkish, who
are unconnected with the Widow's tale,[6] and, freshest of all, the
'French Matron', from one of Sir George Etherege's letters.

4. S. Birch, *The Chinese Widow* (London, 1872), p. 23.

5. *La Matrone chinoise ou l'Épreuve ridicule*, comédie-ballet en deux actes, en vers
libres (Paris, 1764).

6. Except in so far as both stories deal with the unfaithfulness of a widow,
'The British Matron' from 'a Narrative, intitled The Widow of the World.
1775' is the longest of the six tales in this volume. It is the story of a
'Machiavel in petticoats' (p. 156), and her lover John Rover Esquire, her second
husband Sir William Worthy, and her fellow-conspirator the Reverend Mr
Coupler. I have not identified the author; the tale has the air of being based on
actual events.

Here, in the smart prose of the Restoration dramatist, is a neat adaptation of the Petronian story, rewritten for modern manners, about a distressful widow whose husband is drowned. A 'grave Lutheran minister' plays the part of the maid in Petronius and warns her that excessive grieving may harm her soul. Etherege seconds him, by telling her that it may damage her complexion, and presses her to eat and drink. She finds this argument more cogent, but Etherege himself does not become her second husband, a portion reserved for 'a smooth-chin'd ensign of count Trautmandorf's regiment, that had not a farthing in the world but his pay . . .'[7]

The Chinese novel gratified the period's eager appetite for Oriental fiction. Another element which affects eighteenth-century treatments is a half-ironic nervousness about the anti-feminist implications of the story. Here, in the world of *politesse*, we are at the furthest remove from the brutality of the medieval versions. Bishop Percy, no doubt, is only keeping his pot boiling, but he feels distinctly anxious about its anti-feminist ingredients, and assures the 'Fair Reader' that his book 'comes from a sincere admirer of your elegant sex', not 'from the accumulated spleen of some surly old bachelor'. Isaac Bickerstaffe in his comic serenata of 1769, for which Charles Dibdin wrote the music, tries to cancel out the effect with a closing air and chorus:

> Thus, old wits, in wicked satires
> Formerly the fair malign'd;
> Call'd them light, vain, false, affected,
> And unsteady as the wind.
> If they copy'd after nature,
> Bless'd are English dames I trow,
> So much alter'd from what ladies
> Were two thousand years ago.[8]

Steele and Restif de la Bretonne both produced upside-down

---

7. This letter, which is addressed to the Duke of Buckingham, is reprinted only in part in *The Matrons*; it is given in full by S. Rosenfeld in *The Letterbook of Sir George Etherege* (London, 1928), pp. 416–21.

8. I. Bickerstaffe, *The Ephesian Matron: A Comic Serenata after the Manner of the Italian. As it is performed at Ranelagh House* (London, 1769). Bickerstaffe introduces a Widow's Father; he helps, like the Maid, to persuade her to choose life instead of death.

versions in which the faithless one is the man.[9] We can see from all this how greatly the macabre as well as the moralistic elements in the original are now being played down, and it was during the eighteenth century that the story had its gayest commercial success as opera, farce, and vaudeville. It is a technical exercise, though perhaps one of small value, to watch the different authors managing as best they may with the tiny cast, which they sometimes enlarge even to the number of seven, one writer adding an old father, a comic cook, and so on.[1]

Soon, in the next century, all this is changed, and we encounter the most dramatic of the alterations in the story's fortune. In England, the curtain drops for a time, and in France and Italy the post-romantics use the tale very much for their own purposes. The Widow of Ephesus appears in some surprising and terrific disguises and her appeal is to the over-serious rather than to the elegant and gay. Lionel Trilling has suggested that the prison-breaker is the true symbolic hero of the century that opened with the Fall of the Bastille; all the nineteenth-century versions which I shall discuss are about the attempt to escape from the prison of the self and from the conditions imposed by society, morality, and law.

There is, for example, Alfred de Musset's verse drama, *La Coupe et les Lèvres* (1832), where we enter upon the waste land of the romantic agony. Frank, the young Tyrolean mountaineer who has risen to be emperor without being able to slake the ineffable desires of his own soul, is believed by his mistress to be dead. In disguise, he watches her approach the empty tomb; she is a figure directly evolved out of the state of mind that linked

---

9. Steele, *Spectator*, no 11 (13 March 1711); Restif de la Bretonne, *Les Contemporaines* . . . in *Œuvres* (Paris, 1930), vol. iv, pp. 78–79.

1. See, for example, the elaborate version by A. Houdart de la Motte, *La Matrone d'Éphèse* (1702). This piece has seven characters: the Father and his valet, the Widow and her maid, and a comic cook. The moral sentiments are put into the mouth of the betrayed Father (who is not the Widow's Father, but the Soldier's and his rival for her favours): 'Quoi, perfide Euphemie! ne vous seriez-vous renfermée dans le tombeau de vôtre mary, que pour le faire servir de rendez-vous à un amant qui le deshonore? . . . je ne veux plus vivre après ce que j'ai vû! toutes les femmes sont desormais pour moi autant de monstres que j'abhorre! ce n'est que legereté, qu'inconstance, que dissimulation, que perfidie, & tous les vices du monde ensemble!' (pp. 40–41). In Jean-Baptiste Radet's 'comédie . . . mêlée de vaudevilles' (1792), the Maid is paired off with a second Soldier. The provision of a second amorous intrigue of a low comedy variety seems to have been thought a necessity in eighteenth-century France.

pain and pleasure, beauty and death after the fashion so brilliantly analysed by Mario Praz:

> Quelle atmosphère étrange on respire autour d'elle!
> Elle épuise, elle tue, et n'en est que plus belle.
> Deux anges destructeurs marchent à son côté;
> Doux et cruels tous deux—la mort,—la volupté.
> —Je me souviens encor de ces spasmes terribles,
> De ces baisers muets, de ces muscles ardents,
> De cet être absorbé, blême et serrant les dents.
> S'ils ne sont pas divins, ces moments sont horribles.[2]

Frank spreads gold on his own coffin, but when his mistress yields to the temptation it represents, he reveals himself and chases her out of the palace. This incident leads eventually to the tragic catastrophe of the play.

Then again, there are two stories of the 1880s by Paul Alexis and by D'Annunzio, which are admirable justifications of the view that Freud was not the inventor of a system, but the artist who saw and described a landscape. Paul Alexis's contribution to the famous collection of realist writing *Les Soirées de Médan*, in which Zola, Huysmans, and others participated, was a tale of the Franco-Prussian War, 'Après la Bataille'. A wounded soldier, formerly a pious young abbé, stops a carriage which contains the Marquise of Plémovan, who is bearing back to his ancestral lands the dead body of her husband, killed in the fighting. We can see how the story ends: the yielding of the couple to each other, in the presence of the passive dead, is explained as the sudden breaking of the web of sexual frustration which had tormented them both since their youth. D'Annunzio, six years later, in a melancholy and voluptuous study in sexual realism, copied from Paul Alexis but chose a different setting: the young widow of the dead mayor, and his brother, a novitiate priest, watch by the coffin during a long summer night, and buried memories of a suppressed youthful episode rise up to overwhelm them.[3] Both these stories are studies in sexual repression and in desire asserting itself in the immediate presence of death. This

2. *Poésies, 1828–1833* (*Œuvres*, Paris, 1876, p. 285).

3. 'L'Idillio della Vedova' in *San Pantaleone* (Firenze, 1886), pp. 96–109. D'Annunzio, as several correspondences show, knew Alexis's story well.

PLATE I. For description see p. 235

Ecce . . . . . sine luce facem !

Ergo assume novas . . . . . flammas.

Ovid.

PLATE II. For description see p. 236

theme is unquestionably latent in Petronius, but his manner of proceeding largely negatives our awareness of it.

Alphonse Daudet, in the same decade, restated the theme in terms not of sexual but of social unease. His novel *L'Immortel* (1888) is a bitter tragi-comedy of academic and social place-seeking. One long episode deals with the love affair of a widowed duchess and an ambitious young architect. Like Queen Victoria, the faithful widow preserves all her husband's things in their accustomed places, even his cane in the entrance hall and his place at the table, and writes letters to the dead man somewhat pawkily addressed 'To Herbert, in heaven' ('A Herbert, au ciel'). The architect has been commissioned by her to design an enormous mausoleum for the dead man in Père Lachaise cemetery; it is within the half-built structure itself that he completes his conquest. 'Why,' someone exclaims later in the book, 'it's the matron of Ephesus you're describing...!'[4]

As some of these examples show, it is forms such as the novella, fable, and short story, closest to the form which Petronius imposed upon it, which best rejuvenate the tale. Twentieth-century versions have used a large range of forms, but I must neglect most of these in order to say something about the play with which Christopher Fry made his reputation in 1946. In *A Phoenix Too Frequent* the humorous ingenuity of the language fails to conceal the thinness of the action; it is thin because, like most dramatizers of the subject, Fry was obliged, for reasons of theatrical decorum, to keep the macabre elements, the crucified men and the substitution of the bodies, as much in the background as possible. The extreme faintness of the iconographical tradition connected with the tale may be due to a similar cause. I thought at first that there might be a good deal of pictorial material, since the tale seemed to provide an obvious temptation to Renaissance artists to draw such favourite subjects as classical tombs, funerals, and marriage ceremonies. But, although I have consulted the best South Kensington authorities, I have largely drawn a blank.[5] Perhaps the predominant association of crucifixion has kept the artists away from what might

4. *L'Immortel* (Paris, 1888), p. 232. The moral of this accomplished novel seems to be: 'de tous les mensonges de société, il n'y en a pas de plus effronté, de plus comique que l'engouement pour les choses d'art' (p. 98).

5. I am particularly grateful for the learned and sympathetic assistance of Mr J. B. Trapp, Librarian at the Warburg Institute.

seem a dangerous analogue. Some Petronian scholars, indeed—though, one gathers, of a rather cranky kind—have seen in the story a parody of Christian belief.

Because they were obliged to keep the indecorous elements in the action subordinated, some dramatists had to provide extra characters and additional intrigues to fill up the business of the stage; but often they only muddle the main story and rob it of its individuality by doing this. Fry produces a simple sentimental version with a single action, but the chief interest of his play from our point of view is the curious, though by no means unique, inversion of the traditional moral 'Non fidarsi delle donne, mai.' Formerly it was wrong for the Widow to save the soldier by dishonouring her husband's corpse; now it is wrong for her not to. She has become an instrument of a twentieth-century life-force. 'Hang your husband?' exclaims Fry's soldier, in the shocked accents of the medieval fabulist, 'It's terrible, horrible.' She replies:

> How little you can understand. I loved
> His life not his death. And we can give his death
> The power of life. Not horrible: wonderful!

This theme, too, is latent in Petronius, and it is quite clearly brought out by the Loeb translator when he renders the widow's 'Malo mortuum impendere quam vivum occidere' as 'I would rather make a dead man useful, than send a live man to death'.

The various versions, so far as I have surveyed them, correspond in general to our predominant notions of what the ages to which they belong were like. It is no surprise to find the Middle Ages insisting on the anti-feminist moral, the English seventeenth century original and even eccentric in its treatment, the eighteenth century rational, gay, and disengaged, and the nineteenth century uneasy, imaginative, and oppressed. These, of course, are rather superficial categories. No one would claim that Petronius' story is a great work of art: it is plainly the minor, not the major, achievement in this kind that will more easily provide a mould for the more obvious tendencies of different periods.

Another way of looking at it is less historical. There are those who see the joke and those who don't. Seeing the joke here depends upon appreciating the perfect articulation of the original and its suspended ending—'the people wondered the next day by what means the dead man had ascended the cross.' The man who spoils a joke when he tells it is the man who muddles the articulation of its parts and destroys their proportions. The man who can't see the joke is the man who never will—who always asks, 'What happened next?' when the story is really finished. Such men are amply represented amongst those who have handled the tale: they have turned to moralistic rigidity in interpretation and tidied up the end of the story so that the widow gets her deserts—the joke is a joke no longer; or they have turned to psychological explanations of the whole affair, as in the nineteenth century, discontented with the self-consistent pattern of the funny story. Paradoxically enough, both these methods lead to an over-insistence on those horrific elements which are themselves, to the moralist, an initial cause of shock, and as a result bring the tale into that uneasy no-man's-land where the comic and the horrible jostle one another. Just as the high art of the tragedian is to keep us unaware of the comedy always latent in tragedy, so the high art of such a comic writer as Petronius is to keep us unaware of the elements of horror latent in his comedy. The man who doesn't see the joke does not know this. Petronius allowed for him, too, as he allowed for everything. The man who didn't see the joke was the man who said that the widow ought to have been hung on the cross by the just governor. There he is for ever in Petronius' pages, turned to stone by the Gorgon-eye of his own moral indignation, his mouth perpetually open in hurt astonishment, while the sailors roar with laughter.

A NOTE ON THE PLATES

Pictorial versions of the story are found mainly in the numerous illustrated editions of La Fontaine, such as those by Fragonard and Jean-Baptiste Oudry. The two illustrations reproduced here are outside this tradition. Plate I, with its characters in classical costume, is from an edition of Petronius published at London in 1707 (Warburg Institute Library). It is the only one I have come across which attempts to depict the placing of the husband's corpse on the cross. The engraving may be by H. Hulsbergh (d. 1729), a Dutch engraver on copper who worked in London from about 1700. Plate II, in unabashed eighteenth-century dress, is from Percy's *The Matrons: Six Short Histories*, 1762 (British Museum). The lines beneath it are harshly wrested from two different places in Ovid: *Amores*, III.ix.8–9 ('ecce, puer Veneris fert eversamque pharetram / et fractos arcus et sine luce facem') and *Remedia Amoris*, 485–6 ('ergo adsume novas, auctore Agamemnone, flammas / ut tuus in bivio distineatur amor').

14

The poetry of Sir Walter Ralegh

When Sir Walter Ralegh paid a visit to Edmund Spenser in the autumn of 1589, a few months after Spenser had acquired his castle and estate near Cork, he was a man who had already created his own legend. He was perhaps the most brilliant figure at the brilliant court, hated and courted for his pride and power, already a sea captain, an empire-builder, and an Irish landowner. Spenser has left us an idealized account of their poetical intercourse in *Colin Clouts Come Home Againe*. They read each other's poems. Spenser reports that the poem which Ralegh had to offer was

> a lamentable lay,
> Of great unkindnesse, and of usage hard,
> Of *Cynthia* the Ladie of the sea,
> Which from her presence faultlesse him debard.
>
> (163–6)

The poem of Ralegh's that Spenser refers to in these lines, and elsewhere, is the long work, perhaps originally there were twenty or more books of it, which Ralegh wrote in praise of Queen Elizabeth, and of which only one unfinished book is now extant. Unfinished as it is, it is still Ralegh's most considerable poetical relic. At Kilcolman Castle another poem, which is also unfinished, was read in the autumn of 1589; this, of course, was Spenser's own offering, the first three books of *The Faerie Queene*, which were to appear in print the following year, and were to carry in the printed version a commendatory sonnet by Ralegh himself. We can now follow to the end the episode of Kilcolman Castle. We have Spenser's word for it that when Ralegh's time came to leave and he had to go back from the Irish peat-beds to the dangerous and glittering court in London, he persuaded Spenser to accompany him and try *his* luck in court once again:

First published in *A Review of English Literature*, i. 3, 1960, 19–29. See also Preface.

He gan to cast great lyking to my lore,
And great dislyking to my lucklesse lot:
That banisht had my selfe, like wight forlore,
Into that waste, where I was quite forgot.
The which to leave, thenceforth he counseld mee,
And wend with him, his *Cynthia* to see.

The two poets travelled back to England together across Ralegh's domain, the wide wilderness of waters that was the Shepherd of Ocean's element. But in little over a year Spenser was
back at Kilcolman, having lost many illusions about his aptitude
for court favour; and Ralegh's career, in the many years that
remained to him, was to take on an increasingly ghastly aspect
until the shameful moment, twenty-eight years later, when
King James cut off his head to please the Spanish ambassador.

The episode at Spenser's Irish castle and its poetical interludes
are perhaps the pleasantest glimpses we have of Ralegh, although the scarlet thread of his political ambition runs through
even that. It would be easy to draw false inferences from the
episode. Both men were old acquaintances, both were conscious proponents of the English Protestant Renaissance; both
were engaged on ambitious poems dedicated to and in large
measure about their sovereign, and both were hoping by such
means to advance their fortunes in the state. Yet, if we set their
poetry side by side, what strikes us is not the likeness but the
difference. Ralegh must have been as fully aware as anybody else
alive in his time that he was living in the Age of Spenser. But he
was not a Spenserian. It is not simply that *The Faerie Queene* demands a lifetime's study, while you can, if you wish, read
through all Ralegh's poems in an afternoon—there are not
more than forty in the canon, and all of them, except for
the five hundred lines of *Cynthia* (his poem to the Queen, or,
rather, what survives of it), are quite short. The differences go
deeper than that.

Writing poems to and about the court and the Queen is often
the compositional centre in the work of both men. But Spenser,
although he touched the fringes of preferment and hoped to enjoy
more of it, writes essentially as an outsider. Because of this, he
was able to see the brilliant and perilous working of power as a
whole. In *The Faerie Queene* he was able to convey a sense of the
court as only a part of the nation, a sense of the existence of the

nation itself. When he addresses the Queen, the tone is distant, humble, and yet proud. He is the inspired Bard of England speaking to England's Sovereign, and both are servants of something greater than themselves. 'Queen of Love', 'Prince of Peace', he calls her, 'Great lady of the greatest isle':

> Dread Soverayne Goddesse, that doest highest sit
> In seate of judgement, in th'Almightie's stead,
> And with magnificke might and wondrous wit
> Doest to thy people righteous doome aread,
> That furthest Nations filles with awfull dread ...
>
> (*Faerie Queene*, v, Prologue 11)

But the court is Ralegh's own ground, and, when it proves to be a quicksand, the poems that reject it have a note of personal feeling which is not present when Spenser writes of his retirement from it. Ralegh's note can be one of savage disassociation— his own world has betrayed him and that is hard to bear—as in the obsessive rhythms and brutal anaphora of 'The Lie':

> Say to the Court it glowes
>   and shines like rotten wood,
> Say to the Church it showes
>   whats good, and doth no good.
> If Church and Court reply,
>   then give them both the lie.
>
>   . . .
>
> Tell men of high condition,
>   that mannage the estate,
> Their purpose is ambition,
>   their practise onely hate:
> And if they once reply,
>   then give them all the lie.

This theme of the rejection of the court is a traditional one. It is used by Sidney in his 'Disprayse of the Courtly Life', and many poems on the subject will be found in *Tottel's Miscellany* and the other anthologies that preceded the work of the major Elizabethan poets. But in the 'The Lie' it has a personal force that is a long way from a merely theoretical contempt of the world epitomized by the court. And what is savagery in this poem can be transformed in Ralegh's other poems into a throbbing clamour of personal regret and sadness of spirit, as though Ralegh could not see further than his own disappointments. We know from his prose writings that in actuality he could see much further. As a man, he had as keen a sense of the nation and of the world beyond it as Spenser; but he keeps all that out of his poems. Therefore his great poem of disappointment, the five hundred lines of *Cynthia*, Ralegh's counterpart to *The Faerie Queene*, is a very private poem. When Ralegh addresses his sovereign, the convention which he adopts is quite different from the one employed by Spenser. Spenser plays the role of the vassal-bard, Ralegh that of the rejected lover. The analogy between the courtier out of favour and the dismissed lover is pressed home until it becomes a sharp lament over a waste land and a wasted life:

> From fruitfull trees I gather withred leaves
> And glean the broken eares with misers hands,
> Who sometyme did injoy the waighty sheaves
> I seeke faire floures amidd the brinish sand.

The praise of Elizabeth with which the poem is charged has this personal note too. Of the two ways in which Elizabethan poets were most accustomed to celebrate the Queen, as a sovereign divinity or as a virtuous mistress, Ralegh naturally chose the latter. It is what we would expect of an insider. Spenser himself made the point in the induction to the third book of *The Faerie Queene*. There he tells the Queen that, with his humble quill, he is only writing at a distance from her living colours; if she wishes to see herself rightly pictured in her true beauty, let her turn to Ralegh.

Ralegh's own compliment to Spenser is also interesting. It occurs in the form of a sonnet printed in 1590 in commendation of the first three books of *The Faerie Queene*. But it is interesting not so much because it conveys Ralegh's opinion of that great work as because of its own magnificence. It is one of the best of Ralegh's poems, and one of the greatest of Elizabethan sonnets:

> Methought I saw the grave, where *Laura* lay,
> Within that Temple, where the vestall flame
> Was wont to burne, and passing by that way,
> To see that buried dust of living fame,
> Whose tombe faire love, and fairer vertue kept,
> All suddeinly I saw the Faery Queene:

At whose approch the soule of *Petrarke* wept,
And from thenceforth those graces were not seene.
For they this Queene attended, in whose steed
Oblivion laid him downe on *Lauras* herse:
Hereat the hardest stones were seene to bleed,
And grones of buried ghostes the hevens did perse.
   Where *Homers* spright did tremble all for griefe,
   And curst th' accesse of that celestiall theife.

In some ways, this sonnet might be by a contemporary of Wyatt and Surrey; in others, it belongs very much to the era of Sidney and Shakespeare. Ralegh has taken the ancient *topos* of the great new poet outdistancing and outshining the classical giants. For its time, his diction is a little old-fashioned—the *groaning ghosts* and *bleeding stones* take us back to *Tottel's Miscellany*. But, on the other hand, the ordering of the sentences, the wonderful planning of the sonnet as a whole (a feature on which Sir Edmund Chambers remarked) are signs of the new flowering of poetry in the 1580s and 1590s. Yet, magnificent though the sonnet is, it is also puzzling. It celebrates the appearance of a great new work of art, yet it has a tragic rather than a joyous air. Jonson, who used the same *topos* when he praised Shakespeare in the first Folio, was able to impart an air of jollity, of bell-ringing, fireworks, and water music to the occasion. That is much nearer the note we expect when a theme of this kind is handled. Ralegh's welcome to Spenser is, by contrast, very dark. He seems more moved to pity by the fate of the displaced poets than pleased because a new one has outclassed them. His sonnet is constructed so that all the force of feeling gathers into the sestet, on Petrarch's weeping soul, and on 'Oblivion laid him down on *Lauras* herse': a magnificent conceit, but too grim and ghastly for the occasion, as though Michelangelo's 'Night' had suddenly been glimpsed at the heart of the revel. And by the two concluding lines we are irresistibly reminded of that grand thief Satan climbing up into God's fold in the third book of *Paradise Lost*. Indeed, it has long seemed likely that Milton did borrow from this sonnet when he wrote his own sonnet 'Methought I saw my late espoused saint'; but Milton's sonnet is concerned with his vision of his dead wife, and the tragic tone is fitting.

   There is, therefore, a faint air of miscalculation about Ralegh's poem, of emotion in excess of its object, of a man being more serious than he really intends to be. It is probably foolish to suggest that there was something in the commonplace of the displaced poet that went too near to Ralegh's heart. For displaced poet did he too easily read displaced courtier? However this may be, it is true that the tragic note, the note of fear and betrayal, which seems to make such an indecorous intrusion on this gay occasion, is recurrent in Ralegh's extant verse. We can observe this tone—one might almost call it an obsession—at work in such a poem as 'Nature that washt her hands in milke'. In this poem it has the effect of producing a new, sombre, and fearful poem out of the old shell of what was originally a gay and pretty one. The poetic toy suddenly turns into a weeping funeral verse, and we see the skull beneath the skin. Ralegh describes in the first stanzas how nature took snow and silk at love's behest and made from them a fair but heartless girl. With that pretty fancy, such as it is, the poem might well have seemed complete. But then Time comes on the scene:

> But Time which nature doth despise,
>   And rudely gives her love the lye,
> Makes hope a foole, and sorrow wise,
>   His hands doth neither wash, nor dry,
> But being made of steele and rust,
> Turnes snow, and silke, and milke to dust.
>
> The Light, the Belly, lipps and breath,
>   He dimms, discolours, and destroyes,
> With those he feedes, but fills not death,
>   Which sometimes were the foode of Joyes;
> Yea Time doth dull each lively witt,
> And dryes all wantonnes with it.
>
> Oh cruell Time which takes in trust
>   Our youth, our Joyes and all we have,
> And payes us but with age and dust,
>   Who in the darke and silent grave
> When we have wondred all our wayes
> Shutts up the story of our dayes.

There is no question here of emotion in excess of the object, or inappropriate to it, and we have come a long way from Spenser. Spenser was often plangent about the ruins of Time, but he had none of this shrinking horror, and for him, in the end, Time itself was only an aspect of revolving change.

It is tempting, indeed, to take these stanzas as an index of Ralegh's modernity as compared with Spenser's antiquity. Was Spenser unable to sound this note because of his share in the large-eyed innocence of an earlier, golden world; because he was a man who died before the Elizabethan adventure ran aground in the shallows of Jacobean disappointment and anti-climax? In these three stanzas, it might be argued, there is reflected the true voice of Jacobean feeling, of Hamlet by the graveside, of Vindice and the poisoned skull in *The Revenger's Tragedy*, all that melancholy and malcontentism which is supposed to have invaded literature at the turn of the century. 'Nature that washt her hands in milke' could be used as a handy symbol of the transition from Elizabethan to Jacobean, the delicate art of its first portion and the disgusted disrelish of the second straddling the two worlds of *The Faerie Queene* and *Hamlet*. Other evidence for Ralegh's transitional status could be brought into court in the form of his most celebrated poem, the 'Nymph's Reply to the Shepherd' (if it is indeed by Ralegh—we have only Izaak Walton's word for it). Christopher Marlowe's song, to which Ralegh's poem is an answer, 'Come live with me and be my love', is the perfection of pastoral innocence, of uncorrupted and uncourtly pleasure. The reply said to have been devised by Ralegh is another of his savage reminders of mutability, an utter refusal to dream:

> Thy gownes, thy shoes, thy beds of Roses,
> Thy cap, thy kirtle, and thy posies,
> Soone breake, soone wither, soone forgotten:
> In follie ripe, in reason rotten.

Here, perhaps, Jacobean disillusion deliberately flouts the Elizabethan hope.

Yet the argument would be a very weak one. What we are listening to, in the last three stanzas of 'Nature that washt her hands in milke' or in the 'Nymph's Reply', is not Jacobean disaccord. It is an altogether older note: an echo of the sententious mournfulness of the 1570s. The anthologies of that period, which are the chief repositories of such verse as has survived from the earlier years of Elizabeth Tudor, are full of poems which contemplate the ghastliness of the grave, the swiftness of time's passage, or the vanity of youthful love. 'My youthfull partes be played', they never tire of saying, 'And I must learne to die':[1]

> To earth the stout, the prowd, the ritch shall yeeld,
> The weake, the meeke, the poore, shall shrowded lye
> In dampish mould, the stout with Speare and Sheeld
> Cannot defend himselfe when hee shall dye.[2]

Or:

> Hope for no immortalitie, for welth will weare away,
> As we may learne by every yeare, yea howres of every day ...
> Then rage of stormes done make all colde which somer had made so
> Wherefore let no man put his trust in that that will decay,   [warm
> For slipper welth will not continue, pleasure will weare away.
> For when that we have lost our lyfe, & lye under a stone,
> What are we then, we are but earth, then is our pleasure gon.[3]

Spenser, too, can write like this, but it is not what we chiefly remember about him. He moved away from gazing at the ruins of Time, finding the Heavenly Jerusalem more interesting. Another glance at the contrast between Ralegh and Spenser will strengthen the argument that Ralegh is more affected by post-medieval melancholy than by Jacobean disillusion. It is a true generalization about Spenser to say that he is one of the great pioneers of the rich, splendid, and decorated style, despite his many qualities of sageness and sobriety. Ralegh, although he, too, has touches of gold, mainly practises the plainer style, the sententiousness and lack of adornment characteristic of Spenser's predecessors. The contrasting ways in which each poet mourned in verse the death of their mutual friend, the great Sir Philip Sidney, illustrate this. Spenser adopts the creamy elegance of the pastoral guise; Sidney becomes Astrophel the shepherd boy:

> For he could pipe and daunce and caroll sweet,
> Emongst the shepheards in their shearing feast:
> As Somers larke that with her song doth greet
> The dawning day forth comming from the East.
> And layes of love he also could compose,
> Thrise happie she, whom he to praise did chose.
>   *Astrophel*, ll. 31–36

1. *A Gorgeous Gallery of Gallant Inventions* (1578) (ed. H. E. Rollins, Cambridge, Mass., 1926), p. 44.   2. Ibid., p. 99.
3. *Tottel's Miscellany* (1557–87) (ed. H. E. Rollins, Cambridge, Mass., 1928), vol. i, p. 153.

Untimely slain while hunting the boar, like Adonis, Astrophel too is transformed into a flower. Spenser marries Ovidian legend with Christian fancy, for in another part of the poem the dead soldier's soul lies in paradise on beds of lilies, roses, and violets, 'like a newborne babe'. This is Spenser's way.

Ralegh's is very different. Critics have noticed how each stanza of his sixty-line poem on the death of Sidney reads like something carved on stone. The lines are plain, stern, lapidary. They use their big, uncompromising words without conceal-ment or reservation, words such as 'virtue' or 'honour', names such as 'England' or 'Flanders'; it is not Astrophel who is being laid to rest but 'the right Honorable Sir Philip Sidney, Knight, Lord Governor of Flushing':

> Backe to the campe, by thee that day was brought,
> First thine owne death, and after thy long fame;
> Teares to the soldiers, the proud Castilians shame;
> Vertue exprest, and honor truly taught.

> What hath he lost, that such great grace hath woon,
> Yong yeeres, for endles yeeres, and hope unsure
> Of fortunes gifts, for wealth that still shall dure,
> Oh happie race with so great praises run.

> England doth hold thy lims that bred the same,
> Flaunders thy valure where it last was tried,
> The Campe thy sorrow where thy bodie died,
> Thy friends, thy want; the world, thy vertues fame.

This note of marble gravity is common enough in Ralegh's extant poetry for it to be safely regarded as characteristic of him. We meet it again, for example, in 'The Advice', a strange poem, ostensibly a warning to a virgin to beware of those who would betray her. But it resembles the sonnet to Spenser in its excess of strength and tragic sound. It is almost as though half the poet's mind was on power, not love; on the betrayed statesman as much as on the betrayed girl. This ambiguity is characteristic of Ralegh, and ambiguities of one kind or another must tor-ment every judgement of Ralegh's poetry as of his personality.

The ambiguities indeed, deserve the final emphasis. Ralegh's greatest poem is 'The Passionate Man's Pilgrimage supposed to be written by one at the point of death'. It is his greatest poem, but his least characteristic. So uncharacteristic is it that his authorship of it has often been questioned, although it has as good authority for being admitted to the canon as many others. Much of what has been said here about Ralegh is denied by this poem. 'The Passionate Man's Pilgrimage' is a vision of death and judgement, but it is not one of a stern or mournful kind. The heaven that the poet imagines is a florid and baroque place of nectar fountains and milky hills, diamond ceilings and bowers of pearl. As well as its wealth of golden imagery, it is charged with a combination of humble joy and metaphysical wit which is found nowhere else in Ralegh. Its vision of the judgement of the soul marvellously combines the continued witty image with the heart-felt prayer. It speaks of

> heavens bribeless hall
> Where no corrupted voices brall,
> No Conscience molten into gold,
> Nor forg'd accusers bought and sold,
> No cause deferd, nor vaine spent Journey,
> For there Christ is the Kings Atturney:
> Who pleades for all without degrees,
> And he hath Angells, but no fees.

> When the grand twelve million Jury
> Of our sinnes and sinfull fury,
> Gainst our soules blacke verdicts give,
> Christ pleads his death, and then we live,
> Be thou my speaker taintless pleader,
> Unblotted Lawer, true proceeder,
> Thou movest salvation even for almes:
> Not with a bribed Lawyers palmes.

If this is Ralegh, it is a Ralegh whom Spenser never knew. And by a strange irony, it is a Spenserian Ralegh, which turns upside down the usual contrast between the two poets. In this poem Ralegh draws close to Spenser in his vision of heaven (which resembles the Red Cross Knight's vision of the Heavenly Jerusalem in the first book of *The Faerie Queene*) and in the *allegoria* of the soul-as-pilgrim, which is emblematized in the Spenserian manner.

To consider Ralegh's poetry, therefore, is to conclude upon an enigma. He was thoroughly enigmatic to his contemporaries, and since his death he has had a dozen incompatible reputations. The Shepherd of Ocean who piped so pleasantly to Spenser in his dark little Irish tower was to Sir Edward Coke a damnable atheist, a traitor with a Spanish heart.

> Ralegh doth time bestride,
> He sits 'twixt wind and tide,
> Yet up hill he cannot ride
> For all his bloody pride.
> He seeks taxes in the tin,
> He polls the poor to the skin,
> Yet he swears 'tis no sin.
> Lord, for thy pity![4]

The mischievous Machiavel of the anonymous rhymester[5] was the same man as the liberal historian and champion of liberty devoutly admired by the seventeenth-century parliamentarians. The grotesque lover whom Shakespeare may have caricatured in the person of Don Armado in *Love's Labour's Lost* is the paragon of Elizabethan gallantry who used to figure in the school history books. But one reputation is increasingly firm: he ranks ever better amongst the minor poets of his time and was lucky in his muse, if in nothing else.

NOTE

Punctuation and spelling have been slightly modernized in some of the quotations. The standard edition of Ralegh's *Poems* is edited by A. M. C. Latham (London, 1951). There is an introductory study by Philip Edwards (London, 1954), and a study of his thought by E. Strathman (New York, 1951). The standard biography of Ralegh is by William Stebbing (Oxford, 1899).

4. Quoted in E. Thompson, *Sir Walter Ralegh* (London, 1955), p. 151.
5. *Poetical Miscellanies* (ed. Halliwell, Percy Society, 1845), pp. 13–14.

ERRATA

The publishers regret that errors have occurred in the text and index and accept responsibility for them

p. 85, last line: *for* Tragedy *read* Revenge
p. 135, n. 2: *for* Bullough *read* Bartlett

INDEX

Alexander: *for* 64 *read* 64n
Alexis: *for* Apres *read* Après
Allen: *for* Dryden *read* Marston
Annunzio: *delete*
Antonio and Mellida: *delete* Antonio's Tragedy
Before Appius and Virginia *add* Apius and Virginia, 64
Atheist's Tragedy: *for* Greville *read* Tourneur
Baldwin: *for* Shakespeare's *read* Shakspere's
Bradley: *for* A. G. *read* A. C.; *for* Shakespearian *read* Shakespearean
Bullen: *for* 188n *read* 189n
Carré: *for* M. E. *read* M. H.
Cartwright: *for* 95 *read* 95n
Cassirer: *for* R. *read* E.
classicism: *for* 111; *read* 111
Conti: *for* Augusto *read* Natale
Croll: *delete* ed.,
Daniel: *delete* 'Opinion', 111
Before Daudet *add* D'Annunzio, Gabriele, San Pantaleone, 232
Davenant: *for* 96 *read* 96n
Doran: *for* Endeavours *read* Endeavors
Ekleblad: *read* Ekeblad
Ford, Lady's Trial: *for* 159n *read* 158n; Perkin Warbeck: *for* viii *read* vi
Gascoigne: *for* Government *read* Governement
Gent: *delete* entry
Greville: *delete* Atheist's Tragedy, 120; Of Religion: *for* 216 *read* 216n
Guipin . . . Skialethia: *read* Guilpin . . . Skialetheia
Isocrates: *for* Nicodem *read* Nicoclem
Jonson, The Case is Altered: *for* 82 . . . 210n *read* 77; Hymenael: *read* Hymenaei
Kant: *delete* entry

Knights: *delete* 189; *for* 188 *read* 189; *for* Shakespearian *read* Shakespearean
Before MacCallum *add* M., P., Gent., 'The Cimmerian Matron', 226n
Machiavelli, Prince: *for* 218, 219 *read* 218n, 219n
Marston: *delete* 197; Antonio's Revenge: before 86 *add* 85; *delete* Antonio's Tragedy
Maxwell: *for* 'Shakespeare: the middle plays', 226 *read* J. Q. Adams Memorial Studies, 190
Before May *add* Maxwell, J. C., 'Shakespeare: the middle plays', 226
May: *for* 85n *read* 85n
Montaigne: *delete* 183
'Opinion': *delete* Daniel
Orsini: *for* 188 *read* 118
Parrott: *for* 169 *read* 168
Praz: *add* 232; before 'Machiavelli . . .' and delete 232 at end of entry
Richards: *for* Nathaniel *read* Nathanael
Rollins: *for* 224n *read* 244n
Rosenfeld: *for* Etherage *read* Etherege
Schanzer: *for* Dr *read* Ernest
Schelling: *for* Felix, *read* Felix
Shakespeare: *for* Anthony *read* Antony; Hamlet: *delete* 69; Henry V: *delete* entry; Macbeth: *for* viii *read* vi
Sherman: *delete* Tragic Muse of John Ford, 160
Spenser: *delete* 84 (both occurrences)
Swaen: *for* Materialien . . . Dramas *read* How a Man May Choose a Good Wife from a Bad
Before Swinburne *add* Swinburne, A. C., George Chapman: A Critical Essay, 123;
Swinburne: *delete* George . . . 123;
Tourneur: *add* Atheist's Tragedy, 120
Ure: *for* vii, viii *read* v, vi
Virgil: *delete* 62
Webster: *delete* 64
Whitaker: *for* K. *read* Virgil K.
Wilson, H. S.: *for* Tragedies *read* Tragedy
Zola: *for* Emil *read* Émile

Index